BEYOND BABY TALK

BEYOND

KENN APEL, PH.D., CCC-SLP
JULIE J. MASTERSON, PH.D., CCC-SLP

*Sponsored by the American
Speech-Language-Hearing Association*

THREE RIVERS PRESS · NEW YORK

BABY TALK

FROM SPEAKING TO SPELLING

A GUIDE TO LANGUAGE AND LITERACY
DEVELOPMENT FOR PARENTS
AND CAREGIVERS

Published in the United States by
Three Rivers Press, an imprint of the
Crown Publishing Group, a division of
Random House, Inc., New York.

www.threeriverspress.com
www.crownpublishing.com

THREE RIVERS PRESS and the Tugboat
design are registered trademarks of Random
House, Inc.

This revised edition, minus its photographs,
was originally published in paperback in the
United States by Prima Publishing, a division
of Random House, Inc., Roseville, California, in
2001, and subsequently reprinted that same year
in paperback by Three Rivers Press, an imprint
of the Crown Publishing Group, a division of
Random House, Inc., New York.

Library of Congress Cataloging-in-Publication
Data is available upon request

ISBN 978-0-307-95228-8
eISBN 978-0-307-95229-5

Printed in the United States of America

BOOK DESIGN BY ELINA D. NUDELMAN
COVER DESIGN BY JIM MASSEY

10 9 8 7 6 5 4 3 2 1

Revised Edition

*To Lynda and Jerry, for their love and support,
and to our children and grandchildren, for bringing
joy and wonder to our life's work*

CONTENTS

How Does Your Child Hear and Talk?   *viii*

Acknowledgments   *xv*

Introduction   *1*

ONE *Getting Started: How You and Your Infant Create Language Together*   *11*

TWO *Earliest Words: Discovering Your Baby's Style*   *33*

THREE *Building First Sentences: Natural Ways to Encourage Your Toddler*   *53*

FOUR *Preparing for Written Language: Setting Your Preschooler on the Right Path*   *76*

FIVE *Reading, Writing, and Spelling: Helping Your Child Achieve in School*   *102*

SIX *The Influence of Gender and Birth Order on Language Development*   *122*

SEVEN *The Influence of Culture on Language*   *140*

EIGHT *The Influence of Media on Language Development*   *161*

NINE *Language Development and Child Care*   *193*

TEN *Fads, Scams, and Myths: Knowing What to Look For*   *215*

ELEVEN *When You Suspect a Language Delay: Getting Help*   *235*

Bibliography   *263*

Index   *275*

Children develop at their own pace. This checklist shows the average ages when most children have developed these skills. Your child might not have all skills until the end of the age range.

Take this checklist with you to doctor checkups and day care or school meetings. Use it to talk about your child's understanding and talking skills.

HEARING AND UNDERSTANDING

BIRTH–3 MONTHS

Startles to loud sounds.

Quiets or smiles when you talk.

Seems to recognize your voice and quiets if crying.

4–6 MONTHS

Moves eyes in direction of sounds.

Notices toys that make sounds.

Pays attention to music.

Responds to changes in tone of your voice.

7 MONTHS–1 YEAR

Turns and looks in direction of sounds.

Looks when you point.

Turns to own name when you call.

Recognizes words for familiar objects and people, like *cup, truck, juice*, and *daddy*.

Begins to respond to simple words and phrases, like "No," "Come here," and "Want more?"

Plays games with you, like peekaboo and pat-a-cake.

Listens to songs and stories for a short time.

1–2 YEARS

Points to a few body parts when you ask.

Follows 1-part directions, like "Roll the ball" or "Kiss the baby."

Understands simple questions, like "Who's that?" and "Where's your shoe?"

HEAR AND TALK?

1–2 YEARS

    Listens to stories, songs, and rhymes for a longer time.

    Points to pictures in books when you name them.

2–3 YEARS

    Understands opposite words, like *go–stop*, *big–little*, and *up–down*.

    Follows 2-part directions, like "Get the spoon and put it on the table."

    Understands new words quickly.

3–4 YEARS

    Responds when you call from another room.

    Understands words for some colors, like *red*, *blue*, and *green*.

    Understands words for some shapes, like *circle* and *square*.

    Understands words for family, like *brother*, *grandmother*, and *aunt*.

4–5 YEARS

    Understands words for order, like *first*, *next*, and *last*.

    Understands words for time, like *yesterday*, *today*, and *tomorrow*.

    Follows longer directions, like "Put your pajamas on, brush your teeth, and then pick out a book."

    Follows classroom directions, like "Draw a circle on your paper around something you eat."

    Understands most of what is said at home and at school.

TALKING

BIRTH–3 MONTHS

    Makes cooing sounds.

    Has different cries for different needs.

    Smiles at people.

4–6 MONTHS

    Coos and babbles when playing alone or with you.

    Makes speech-like babbling sounds, like *pa*, *ba*, and *mi*.

4–6 Months

Giggles and laughs.

Makes sounds when happy or upset.

7 Months–1 Year

Babbles longer strings of sounds, like *mimi upup bababab*.

Uses sounds and gestures to get and keep attention.

Points to objects and shows them to others.

Uses gestures like waving bye-bye, reaching to be picked up, or shaking head no.

Imitates different speech sounds.

Says 1 or 2 words, like *hi, dog, dada, mama*, or *uh-oh*, around first birthday. All words may not be clear.

1–2 Years

Uses a lot of new words.

Uses *p, b, m, h*, and *w* in words.

Starts to name pictures in books.

Asks *what, who*, and *where* questions, like "What's that?" "Who's that?" and "Where's kitty?"

Puts 2 words together, like "More apple," "No bedtime," and "Mommy book."

2–3 Years

Has a word for familiar people, places, things, and actions.

Talks about things that are not in the room.

Talks during pretend play, like saying "beep-beep" when moving cars.

Uses *k, g, f, t, d*, and *n* in words.

Uses words like *in, on,* and *under*.

Asks *why*?

Familiar people understand your child's speech.

Puts 3 words together to talk about and ask for things. May repeat some words and sounds.

HEAR AND TALK?

3–4 YEARS

Answers simple *who*, *what*, and *where* questions.

Says rhyming words, like *hat-cat* and *silly-billy*.

Uses pronouns, like *I*, *you*, *me*, *we*, and *they*.

Uses some plural words, like *toys*, *birds*, and *buses*.

Most people understand your child's speech.

Asks *when* and *how* questions.

Puts 4 words together. May make some mistakes, like "I goed to school."

Talks about what happened during the day. Uses about 4 sentences at a time.

4–5 YEARS

Says all speech sounds in words. May make mistakes on sounds that are harder to say, like *l*, *s*, *r*, *v*, *z*, *j*, *ch*, *sh*, and *th*.

Responds to "What did you say?"

Talks without repeating words or sounds most of the time.

Names letters and numbers.

Uses sentences that have more than 1 action word, like *jump*, *play*, and *get*. May make some mistakes, like "Zach gots 2 video games, but I got 1."

Tells a short story.

Keeps a conversation going.

Talks in different ways depending on the listener and place. May use short sentences with younger children or talk louder outside than inside.

SPEECH-LANGUAGE PATHOLOGISTS AND AUDIOLOGISTS CAN HELP!

A speech-language pathologist or audiologist can help if you are concerned. Don't wait. It's better to get help early.

GET HELP FROM AN AUDIOLOGIST WHEN

- You checked *no* to most of the "hearing and understanding" items for your child's age.
- Your child does not seem to hear or respond to you.
- Your child needs the TV or radio volume to be much louder than others.

Talk to your child's doctor if your child pulls or tugs at his or her ear, cries more than usual, and doesn't respond to sounds. Your doctor can check to see if your child has an ear infection.

GET HELP FROM A SPEECH-LANGUAGE PATHOLOGIST WHEN

- You checked *no* to most of the "talking" items for your child's age.
- Your child stops talking or playing with you.
- You have concerns or questions about stuttering. Your child gets upset about sounds or words not coming out.

HELP YOUR CHILD HEAR AND TALK

- Talk about what you are doing, what your child is doing, and what your child sees. Use longer sentences as your child grows older.
- Communicate with your child in the language that you are most comfortable using.
- Use a lot of different words with your child. Don't worry about using "big" words. Children enjoy new and unusual words.
- Listen and respond to your child.
- Help your child listen. Give directions for your child to follow.
- Have your child's hearing tested if you have to repeat a lot or use a loud voice.
- Tell stories and read to your child a lot. Ask questions and talk about what happened. Read to your child in each language he or she is learning.

- Don't interrupt to correct speech sounds. It's okay if your child makes some mistakes with sounds. Say the sounds correctly when you talk.

- Set limits for TV and computer time. Make time for talking, reading, and playing together.

- Ask questions that need more than a *yes* or *no* answer. Encourage your child to ask you questions.

Don't wait to get help for your child if you are concerned. You know your child best. Getting help early can stop later problems with behavior, learning, reading, and social relationships.

How Can I Find an Audiologist or Speech-Language Pathologist?

Look for an audiologist or speech-language pathologist who has the Certificate of Clinical Competence (CCC) from the American Speech-Language-Hearing Association (ASHA). ASHA-certified audiologists have "CCC-A" after their name. ASHA-certified speech-language pathologists have "CCC-SLP" after their name.

A Qualified Speech-Language Pathologist or Audiologist Has:

- A master's or doctoral degree
- The Certificate of Clinical Competence (CCC) from ASHA
- A state license, where required
- Participated in continuing education activities

To find an ASHA-certified speech-language pathologist or audiologist near you, go to www.asha.org/findpro or call your local public school.

For more information, contact:

American Speech-Language Hearing Association
2200 Research Boulevard
Rockville, MD 20850
800-638-8255 or (TTY) 301-296-5650
actioncenter@asha.org
www.asha.org

ACKNOWLEDGMENTS

We wish to acknowledge all of the researchers in child language and literacy, especially Margaret Lahey, whose work has been particularly influential on us.

YOUR BEST TOOL: KNOWING ABOUT LANGUAGE

*D*ID *Y*OU *K*NOW?

- Parents are the primary "language role models" for their children.

- Language involves more than just a child's vocabulary. It involves the sounds we use, the sentences we make, the words we read and write, and the way we use language to get what we want.

Kurt and Emily were talking with their child's pediatrician. She had just finished her six-month evaluation of their son, Luc. Everything seemed to be fine. Luc, to quote the doctor, was "right on schedule." The pediatrician asked them to wait a moment while she got some information for them about language development. Kurt and Emily were confused. Why would the doctor be giving them information about language development? Was the doctor talking about learning to speak another language? Why would they want Luc to do that? This was rather bizarre. He wasn't even talking in any language now.

How Do Children Develop Language?

Most infants come into the world eager, ready, and able to learn language. Their innate capabilities are amazing. They

> ## *The main tool your child will need to acquire language will be you.*

have an inner desire to communicate and the ability to pick up at least the basics with minimal amounts of exposure to language. Of course, as a loving and informed parent, you will want to provide your child with lots of exposure to language so that she can reach her potential as a communicator. But you may be surprised that your child won't need flashcards, computer programs, lessons, incentives, correction, or bribes to learn language. In fact, such things almost always backfire, boring a child or turning her off to language. Rather, the main tool your child will need to acquire language will be *you.*

In language learning, consider your child's early years as windows of opportunity. Even before she starts kindergarten, her brain is "wired" to learn a tremendous amount about language and communication. While researchers still debate exactly what that wiring involves—wiring specifically for language learning or a more general wiring for learning a variety of complex systems, including language—you will find your child learns language best when the "wiring" she brought with her into the world encounters your models of language use.

Throughout this book, you will hear us repeatedly say that you should *model* language for your child, not quiz her or make her repeat or imitate you. When we talk about modeling language for your child, we mean that you talk *with* your child, using words and sentences that are related to what she is focused on. It also means that if she says something "incorrectly," you should say what she said, or something similar, the correct way, without asking her to imitate you. Asking your child to imitate you does not allow her to learn *why* she might be saying that particular sound, word, or sentence, or when she should say it. Keep this in mind: *Language is developed, not taught.*

You might be surprised to hear us talk about reading, writing, and even spelling in this book. If this book is on language, why are we talking about literacy skills? Well, that's because literacy (reading, writing, and spelling) *is* language. It's language in written form. Literacy, or written language, is in many ways like spoken language; it is used to produce or comprehend thoughts and messages. You will read, then, that just as you are the main model for helping your child learn spoken language, you also will be your child's model, and first teacher, for written language.

Rich language skills, both spoken and written, will come out of the ordinary things you and your child do. You don't need lesson plans and she doesn't require elaborate activities and toys. Let her safely explore her environment and the familiar items around her. Encourage imaginative games and symbolic play, and follow up on her natural curiosity. Read to her and show her how and why we write. In simple and attentive ways, you can raise an enthusiastic communicator with an interest in the world and lots of interesting things to share with others verbally and in writing.

Do Children Develop Language Similarly?

Most children follow a similar path of language development. As language development specialists, we have certain milestones for language skills during certain periods or stages (see the chart that follows the table of contents). However, we also know there is some give and take as far as when certain skills should appear. For example, if your niece uses short sentences at 16 months and your son is still using single words at 20 months, you may be concerned. Yet we would consider both children to be within the expected range of typical language development. The variability can be affected by children's styles, temperaments, and personalities as they acquire language. Thus, while there is a similar path of language development that most children take, we must acknowledge the flexibility necessary in this area of human development.

As we discuss how children acquire language over the first eight years, we also are aware of other factors independent of the child that may affect development. One factor that may affect what a child learns and when she learns it is the family's own cultural and language background. Different cultural groups have different language rules that need to be learned. Some cultural groups may vary in their expectations of what's usual and acceptable for children and parents. One family may expect a three-year-old to be an active participant in conversations and show a strong interest in books, whereas another family may feel that children should be listeners more than talkers. In chapter 7, we will provide some information on cultural styles and differences that may influence language development.

For our review on language development (chapters 1 to 5), we will discuss spoken and written language acquisition, in a general sense, for children who come from families who speak English as their primary language, knowing that modifications in language development owing to different cultural or language backgrounds are equally valid. In other words, children from these cultures learn language in a different way, not a wrong way.

Getting Started

During your child's first eight years, you have a great opportunity to help him acquire the most important skill he'll ever learn—the ability to use language to speak, read, and write. Language is the main way your child will communicate. It involves the sounds and meanings of the words your child uses, how he orders those words into understandable sentences, and how he selects what he says depending on his purpose for communicating. It also includes knowing how we use letters to represent sounds on paper (or a computer screen!) and the rules for how combinations of those letters help convey the correct meaning. Language is so vital because it's his primary connection to you and others, his path into family and culture, his way of expressing himself, his main tool for succeeding in school, and his means of getting his needs met.

Developing language is a complex, fascinating process, one in which you and your child each have essential, intertwining roles. As your child grows, you'll marvel at the ease with which he learns to communicate—so much seems to come naturally. Yet you'll also discover that he will benefit in reaching his potential through your active partnership. The whole process is challenging, enjoyable, and rewarding—and one of your best chances to have a positive and lasting effect on your child's life.

As language specialists and parents (and grandparents!) ourselves, we're intrigued by the process of learning language; we know the joys firsthand, and we also know the uncertainties involved. In the course of our work, we've talked to thousands of parents about their issues and questions. "Why isn't my daughter talking yet?" "I'm so exhausted at night I can't read aloud as much as I think I should." "Is a bilingual sitter okay?" "My older son learned colors and letters a lot faster than my younger one." "Can computers teach my daughter to read?"

We've written this book to give you the information you need, share exciting discoveries in our field, reassure you, and help you succeed with this most important job. You're exposed to a lot of advice from the media and other sources, and we'll help you understand and evaluate what you hear. Throughout this book, we will show you what to expect during your child's first eight years and offer practical suggestions for everything from choosing books to maximizing household chores for learning.

How Should I Use This Book?

There are several points we hope you keep in mind as you read this book. Some of these points have to do with how you compare your child to the information you read. Other points deal with how we have chosen to write this book.

Your Child's Language Development

Remember, the main purpose of this book is to help you become a knowledgeable parent on the topic of child spoken and written language development. This knowledge will serve you well in several situations. First, with your new knowledge in hand, you should be able to resist other individuals or the media who encourage you to push your child and his language skills ahead by sending him to an "academic" preschool or by using flashcards, workbooks, computer programs, or language-oriented videos to *teach* him language. Media sources and businesses promote the notion that children who talk early know the greatest number of concepts and those who read first are the only ones headed for success. These messages help create the pressure many parents feel to give their child some sort of language boost or preschool competitive edge. This advice may be well intentioned, and some of the products may not be "bad" when used as extra experiences for your child. However, such products often treat language as a subject to be taught or drilled rather than something to be acquired through rich, everyday experiences. The real boosts and edges to enriching your child's language development come from common, everyday, personal interactions between a child and the people who care about him.

A second reason for arming yourself with an understanding of child language development is that you will know how to resist feelings of guilt and shame when you hear well-meaning others report how their child is using a certain language skill way before your child is ("My Johnny can recite the alphabet and count to 100!"). In other words, you will know the range of typical development and feel comfortable whether your child is advanced or just where he should be in development.

Finally, knowing how language typically develops will help you ignore potentially misleading reassurances that come from people who seem to take an overly casual approach to language development and downplay the possibility of problems ("Don't worry, she'll outgrow this. After all, Albert Einstein didn't talk until he was three!"). Should you read the first 10 chapters of this book and question your child's language skills, we provide information in chapter 11 that will help you decide what to do, whom to see, and what to say. Be assured that your actions do make a difference to your child's language acquisition and that it's good to look for help when you suspect a problem. Early intervention can make a world of positive difference to your child.

The real boosts and edges to enriching your child's
language development come from common, everyday,
personal interactions between a child and
the people who care about him.

The Style of This Book

Although we are child language specialists, as parents we wanted to write this book in an understandable, illustrative way. We believe you should know as much about spoken and written language development as possible. We also feel that your learning should be easy, fun, and engaging. Thus, we have written this book with a few points in mind.

First, because each of us has one son and one daughter, we wanted to give equal time to both genders. So, as you read, you will notice that we alternate between male and female pronouns. In this way, we demonstrate that language development is similar for both boys and girls. Plus, this approach helps us to deal with one of the tricky aspects of English grammar: There is no gender-neutral, singular pronoun! We can say "they" to refer to both boys and girls; however, it means more than one. What do you do when you want to refer to only one person in a general sense? English makes us commit to either a girl (she/her) or a boy (he/him)! We tell you this partly to explain our use of pronouns in this book and also to begin to give you an appreciation for just how complicated our language system can be! Yet most children will master the fundamentals somewhat effortlessly. We can almost guarantee that after reading this book and finding out what language acquisition involves, you will truly be amazed and quite impressed with your child!

Second, child language specialists and researchers often break language development into a number of small stages or phases; however, we broke the process down into five main stages, represented by the first five chapters. In each of these stages, we will use a different term for your child, to distinguish that stage of life from the other ones. In chapter 1, we will cover your *infant*'s first year and the skills she is developing to prepare her for her first words. In chapter 2, we will discuss your *baby*'s first words, which occur during the second year of her life. It might seem odd to have a whole chapter about babies who are using only one word at a time. However, this is a critical period of development for children and one that depicts the complex skill of language in many ways.

Our goal in chapter 3 is to provide you with a wealth of information about your *toddler*'s movement from one-word to multiword sentences. This covers your toddler['s] fourth years of life, roughly ending on his fourt[h ...] In chapter 4, we will discuss the fifth and sixth ye[ars of] *preschooler*'s life, when he is not only completing developmental portion of learning about spoken but is also learning the foundation skills for written language (reading and writing). Finally, in chapter 5, we will discuss your *student*'s first two to three years in elementary school and the types of sophisticated (and complicated!) information he is learning to help him read, write, and spell.

We also hope that our abundant use of examples, often taken from our own children, will shed additional light and understanding on what we discuss. Our children are adults now; two of them have their own children. However, through their examples over the years, they have helped us better understand and explain to others how children develop language.

Our children are our delights, and we think you will laugh and enjoy them along with us as we provide examples of what they have said or done over the years. Caleb and Caitlin, currently 27 and 23 years old, respectively, are the son and daughter of Julie. Nick and Genevieve, 28 and 25 years old, respectively, are Kenn's children. Gage and Reid are Kenn and Julie's grandchildren, respectively. To help cut down on unnecessary words, we introduce you to them now. We think you will become quite well acquainted with them as you read through the next five chapters.

Summary

Language is a rich, complex, adaptable system—it's the way we combine sounds, words, signs, letters, and sentences to communicate our thoughts and understand others. Language is how we, as humans, socialize and learn. If, as a parent, you also take this broad and more complete understanding of language, you'll be more likely to look appreciatively and realistically at *all* the dimensions of your child's language development: what he has to say and write, how he says or writes it, what he understands and reads, and how he uses language to interact with you and others.

The first eight years are indeed exciting. During your child's first eight years, she'll acquire the foundation for a lifetime of communication. As she grows, language will continue to be central to most things she does. The stronger her language skills, the better she will be able to express her feelings and explain her ideas and thoughts; connect with family, friends, caregivers, and teachers; pursue her interests and talents; learn both in and outside of school; speak up for herself and watch out for her interests; help and encourage others; gather information so she can make good decisions and evaluate what she hears and reads; and understand new technologies and the changing world. As you can see, language is the bridge to almost any aspect of your child's life. That's why we think it is so important for you to understand how language develops.

We hope you will enjoy this review on how language develops across your child's first eight years of life as much as we like talking about it. Language development has become a lifetime study for us not only because it is our job but also because we are parents. Like you, we were overjoyed with our children's first *goo*, ecstatic with their first words, mesmerized by their first stories, thrilled with their initial attempts at reading, and surprised with their first written spellings of their names. Join us in this fascinating journey of language development.

1

GETTING STARTED: HOW YOU AND YOUR INFANT CREATE LANGUAGE TOGETHER

DID YOU KNOW?

- At birth, infants prefer their mothers' voices to other women's voices.

- To an infant, the human face is a fascinating object.

- Infants can express many desires and wants before they can talk.

As young, first-time parents, Jim and Karen were relatively calm and self-assured in their parenting skills for their infant daughter. Three weeks after their daughter's birth, Karen and the baby had a nursing schedule set, and Jim was fast becoming an expert diapering service. They marveled over how beautiful their daughter was and wondered what her voice would be like when she began to talk. They knew children did not talk until about age one, and they were anxious to begin communicating with their little one. However, during that third week, something interesting happened. As Jim was changing her diapers, she smiled. He also noticed that her eyes seemed to brighten when Karen spoke from the other room. Suddenly he realized that his little girl was actually communicating already!

Believe it or not, this first year of life will contain one of the greatest accomplishments of your infant's life. It is during this first year that she will catch on to the notion of communicating. She will learn to take control of her mouth, forming the sounds of language that will serve her well as she begins to talk. She will learn to relate her needs in more predictable ways that can be easily understood by you. She will develop, in essence, the foundation for all future language learning. And your part in this learning is vital. As you will see, your actions and interactions with her will help her catch on to this incredible communication tool: language.

What Is Language?

The quality of your child's life is dependent, to a great extent, on her ability to communicate. Language permeates all aspects of her experience; it's an essential part of her being, how she connects with others, expresses herself, and gets the care she needs. Language is also important because it's your window into your child's personality—her words let you in on her thoughts and feelings. Through language, you are able to guide and influence your child and pass your values on to her.

So what *is* language? Language is composed of six systems or aspects of communication, all equally important, all different from one another. These systems include sound, meaning, word order, grammar, letters and letter patterns, and the social uses of language. Taken as a whole, they represent the rules we must follow when we communicate so that others will understand us and make sense of what we are saying.

The Sound System: Phonology

The first language system deals with the speech sounds that we all use when we speak. This aspect of language is formally called phonology. When we speak, we use certain sounds that are accepted by our listeners as valid sounds for communicating. So, for example, we use speech sounds such as *p*, *d*, *k*, *s*, *sh*, and *n*. These speech sounds are the building blocks for exchanging information among individuals. There are other sounds we could make, but if they are not part of the meaningful words that we use to convey meaning, then they are not speech sounds.

The quality of your child's life is dependent, to a great extent, on her ability to communicate.

Some speech sounds we make are not speech sounds in other languages, and some other languages use sounds that are not speech sounds in our language. For example, Spanish has a trilled *r* sound, whereas English does not. Further, differences that are important in one language may not be important in another. For instance, the difference between the vowel sounds in *seat* and *sit* is important in English. Changing from one to another can result in different words (*beat/bit*; *seen/sin*; *leap/lip*). However, this difference is not important in Spanish, which is one of the reasons why native Spanish speakers struggle with those sounds in English and pronounce some of the *i* words with an *ee* sound (*feet* for *fit*). Children acquiring the sound system of their language must learn which sound differences are important (and worthy of attention) and which ones are not (and can be ignored).

It's important here that you understand that we are talking about sounds, not letters (we will talk about those later). For adults, this is sometimes confusing, because we are so used to thinking about words as made up of letters. The danger to thinking of speech sounds as letters is that sometimes speech sounds are represented by two letters. We write the word *bath* using four letters, but when we say bath, we hear only three speech sounds—*b, a, th*. On the other hand, the letter *x* is just one letter, but when it is said in a word, it represents two sounds—*k* and *s*, as in *box* (*b-o-k-s*).

Thus, when we are talking about children's developing language skills, we are including in that discussion how they learn to articulate or pronounce the sounds that make up their language. As you will see, children must come to understand that certain rules must be followed when speaking. These rules involve including all speech sounds that should be in a word and using them in the right places of the word, and not adding or using speech sounds that should not be in a word.

Of course, not everyone will use speech sounds when communicating or using language. Some individuals will use sign language to convey their thoughts and ideas. In this case, then, the aspect of language that involves speech sounds is replaced by the system of hand gestures, movements, and placement around the body. This gestural system is equivalent and as important to communicating through sign language as sounds are for spoken language. The speech sound system is the only component of language that is not shared between spoken language and sign language. The remaining systems are found in both types of language.

In the first four to five years, children will be learning how to produce correctly the speech sounds of their language(s). They won't be conscious that they are learning their sounds, though; it will happen somewhat subconsciously. However, as you will learn in chapter 4, there will come a point, usually around the age of four or five, when they will start thinking about speech sounds. This actually is great because being able to think about speech sounds is highly important in the process of learning to read and spell words. So, as you will see, speech sounds are important for both spoken *and* written language development.

The Meaning System: Semantics

Children learn very early in development that they can use words to express lots of different ideas and concepts that they have to offer. As you will see in chapter 2, when your child first learns to talk, he will use several types of words. These words will allow him to discuss actions, request help, comment on passing objects or people, and greet you as you come in the door. He will do this with a set of words that, although limited at first, expands dramatically over the first five years. Thus, semantics involves both general *types* of words and the *meanings* of individual words.

Many people, including some educators, pediatricians, and caregivers, seem to think of early language as though it were synonymous with semantics, the meaning system of language. Often, it seems people talk about language as lists of concepts like colors and numbers; the more concepts a child knows, the better and more advanced his language is. However, as you are learning in this chapter, language involves a whole lot more in addition to vocabulary and concepts. In addition, semantics is more than just the words and concepts children use when they speak. As children learn to read and spell, they also will learn that meaning affects spelling (and vice versa). For example, if a child wants to write about a large animal in the words, she will need to develop an understanding that she must write *bear*, not *bare*, to get across her correct message to her readers. What's the bottom line message for semantics? It is an important language skill that, along with other language skills, allows children to communicate their message in a meaningful way.

The Systems for Word Order and Grammar: Syntax and Morphology

Some of you may recall learning Spanish, remembering how confusing it was at first that the order of words was different for English than it was for Spanish. We might say, "I see a red car" in English, but in Spanish, we would say, "Yo veo un coche rojo" (I see a car red).

Word order is different for each language. Within each language, we need to follow the rules for which words go where in spoken, and written, sentences. It would not do to talk to others in English using Spanish word order. Imagine the confused looks on others' faces if we didn't include the subject pronoun and put the adjective after the verb in declarative sentences! The system that provides the rules for word order, syntax, is highly structured and rigid. As your child develops language, she will need to learn the rules for how to order her words and what word orderings are allowable. It is quite the task considering no one actually will sit down and tell her which words to put where in a sentence. In addition, once she starts to read, she will learn more complicated and less familiar rules of word order that only seem to appear in books.

Besides word order, we also need to think about the endings and beginnings we attach to basic words and the "filler" words that help us link thoughts across sentences. The term *grammar*, or *morphology*, as we call it, is often used when describing the aspect of the language system that dictates how we let others know about the number of objects we are discussing (two cats), whether we are talking about events in the past, present, or future (I jump*ed* over the fence), the direction of a moving object (The dog ran *around* the house), and how to make the subject of the sentence "agree" with the action of the sentence (She *sings*; they *sing*). The grammar of a language is complex, containing many dos and don'ts. It is not uncommon to hear someone refer to "proper grammar" or comment that an individual's sentence was "grammatically incorrect." While as an adult you may take grammar for granted, we think you will be amazed when you read how children learn this rule system for both spoken and written language with remarkable ease and speed.

The Letter System: Orthography

We use spoken words to communicate our thoughts verbally; we use written words to communicate our thoughts in print. Written words are made up of combinations of letters, which follow very specific rules and patterns. This is a good thing because learning written language would be extremely difficult, if not impossible, without a rule-governed system to guide us. We use the term *orthography*, which literally means to "write correctly," to talk about this rule system that determines how and why we write words the way we do.

One aspect of orthography is simply knowing what letter or letters represent the sounds we use in our spoken language. We call this knowledge of letter–sound correspondence, or alphabetic knowledge. For example, we know when we hear the speech sound *b*, we can write the letter *b*, or sometimes *bb*, like in bubble. Some speech sounds only have one or two letters that represent them, and others have many possible letter(s) (e.g., the speech sound *k* can be spelled with the letters *c*, *k*, *ck*, *ch*, and so on). Alphabetic knowledge also includes the opposite: knowing what speech sounds letters can make. For example, when we see the letters *ch*, we know they can make the *k* sound or the *ch* sound. Having this alphabetic knowledge is highly important to reading and spelling words we don't know automatically from memory.

Orthographic knowledge goes beyond just knowing letter–sound correspondence. It also includes other rules for how we put our speech down into print. For example, children must learn that certain letters can never occur in specific places within a word (the *tch* letter combination can be used in the middle and end of words, but it can never be in the beginning of a word). Children also learn that some letter combinations can never occur *any* place in a word, such as writing the *kr* letter combination to represent the *kr* sounds, unless it is in a person's name, such as Kristen (or a certain donut company!). Finally, children also learn that there are rules for when one uses certain letters because of the other sounds in words. As a case in point, children need to learn that we use a single consonant in the middle of a word that has a long vowel (*later*) but a double consonant in the middle of a word that has a short vowel (*latter*).

As you can see, orthography is a pretty complex system that children must learn, and it is not surprising that that learning occurs once they have acquired a fair amount of their spoken language skills. Figuring out these rules is not an easy task, and even though a lot of that learning will occur between the ages of four and eight, children continue to learn them well beyond their first eight years. We will talk much more about orthography in chapters 4 and 5.

The System of Social Language: Pragmatics

Language does not exist in a vacuum. It would make no sense for an individual to have perfect knowledge of the sound, meaning, word order, letter patterns, and grammar systems of a language if that person never used that knowledge to communicate with other human beings. Thus, a very important system of language—pragmatics, or how we use language to socialize—must be learned as well.

In the first eight years of his life, your child will learn the many different reasons that humans talk, such as to inform, to question, to warn, and so on. He will learn that he needs to follow specific social rules when talking with others, such as taking turns in conversations, making eye contact with the other person, and revising what he has said when his listener is confused. He also will develop the ability to change the way he talks, depending on who he's talking to. He will talk "politely" to his grandparents and talk "babyish" to his younger sister. Further, he will learn how to ensure his readers understand why he has written what he has on paper or the computer screen. When children demonstrate these skills, plus many more, it attests to the fact that they have learned the rules for how we socialize and interact with others using language.

Your infant has been learning about language since before he was born.

In this chapter, we will cover the language and communication skills your infant is learning during the first 12 months of life. We also will cover the types of interactions parents should use with their infants to help them develop their ability to communicate with others. We find this first year to be completely fascinating. Your infant is starting to crack the code to a skill that is the most important skill he will learn. Let's begin!

The First Six Months of Life

In the first few weeks of life, your infant will cry, fuss, cough, hiccup, stare, and sleep. It may seem like he is not learning anything about you or his surroundings. However, he is way ahead of you. He actually has been learning since before he was born.

Listening Skills

Your infant may have already learned to recognize your voice while in the womb. Researchers have found that infants as young as three days old can recognize their mothers' voices compared to other women's voices. While infants have heard their mothers' voices since birth, it seems equally likely that they have been listening to their mothers' voices while still in the womb. Infants also prefer to hear human voices over nonhuman sounds, although one of our children sure liked the sound of a vacuum cleaner when he was an infant. A parent's voice most often soothes an infant when other devices, such as mobiles and music boxes, just won't do the trick. This is probably not new information to recent parents, who realize that often the only way to soothe their infant is by talking to him with a gentle voice.

An infant's ability to recognize a parent's voice is not the only hearing skill he has at birth. Your infant has come into the world ready to hear differences between the sounds we use for speech. Researchers have studied infants' abilities to hear slight differences between simple speech sounds, such as sounds like *ba* and *pa*. Pairs of speech sounds like *pa* and *ba* were chosen because they are highly similar in the way they sound. They vary only by minor differences in the sound spectrum. To study infants' early listening skills, researchers use specially designed pacifiers and noisemakers that create a sound, such as *pa*. As an infant sucks on the pacifier, the speech sound noises start. Initially, the infant sucks the pacifier repeatedly, enjoying the ongoing sounds of repeated *pa . . . pa . . . pa*. Soon, however, the infant stops sucking because the repetition of the sounds becomes boring or no longer novel. The researchers then switch to a new sound, in this case, *ba*, and the infant starts vigorously sucking again, suggesting that the infant has recognized a difference between the sounds. Infants do not do this when researchers use speech sounds that represent different "variations" of the way one particular speech sound can be said (*pa . . . paaaa . . . PA*).

Now keep in mind that when infants hear differences between sounds, it does not mean they understand that the sounds are meaningful or even part of their parents' language. For example, English-speaking infants will notice differences in speech sounds that are not part of the English language. They also do not hear differences between every pair of sounds, especially if the sounds are similar. In addition, infants are not the only little ones that have these skills. Research has shown us that some other mammals have similar listening skills. These studies tell us that your infant is ready to listen to some of the fine differences in your speech from the moment he is born. As he grows and develops, these listening skills will become stronger, at least for the speech sounds of the language his parents and those around him use. If nothing else, this helps prepare him to be ready to take in all the wonderful language you use when you cuddle him.

So what do these listening skills and preferences tell us about what parents should do with their newborns? Talk with your infant from his first day of life. He is listening to the fine details of your voice, a voice he prefers over other sounds. And he is learning!

Vocal Skills

Initially your infant's vocal skills will consist primarily of cries and burps, and maybe some *oooooo*-type sounds. The sounds she makes will not contain "real" consonants or vowels, at least not like the ones we use. However, soon she will start making noises that seem *almost* like the sounds you make. Within three to four months after birth, your infant will start making vowel sounds and then those *coos* and *goos* that every parent awaits. At first, these *coos* may be almost accidental. When infants are on their back, their tongue naturally lies back against the soft part of the roof of their mouth. This is exactly where we, as adults, make our *ka* and *ga* sounds. As infants begin to make sounds, suddenly a *k* or *g* sound emerges and the result is a sound that is highly similar to *coo* or *goo*. Soon the infant learns that he can do this willfully, and to the joy of every parent, the infant is *coo*ing and *goo*ing at all times of the day and night, especially in reaction to delightful sights, such as her parents.

Toward the end of the first six months, your infant will broaden her repertoire of sounds. Infants between four and six months often begin to experiment more with their mouth, tongue, and throat. They make raspberry sounds or screeches that sound like the cat out in the alley. These wild sounds and cries are your infant's way of testing her abilities. She is playing with her vocal system and seeing what it can do. Along the way, she also begins to say other new consonant sounds. She may begin to use a *t* or *p* along with a vowel. With practice and better control of her mouth, the number of different sounds she makes and the frequency with which she makes them should increase.

One thing you can do as a parent is react to these sounds your infant is making. When she makes these sounds, go ahead and make them back. In fact, you will probably find yourself interpreting her vocal play as real words (more on that in chapter 2). "Listen" to this particular interchange between Genevieve and her dad when she was nine months old and he was changing her diapers:

GENEVIEVE: "Ahhhhh . . ."

DAD: "Ahhhh. You like that infant powder, don't you? Ooohh, ahhhh."

GENEVIEVE: "Eeeeahhh!"

DAD: "Eeeeahhh? Oh? You are excited about this bath coming up. You love bath time, don't you?"

GENEVIEVE: "Ooooo, Ooooo."

DAD: "Ooooo, oooohhh. That's nice, isn't it?"

This small interchange between parent and child seems almost like a true conversation is occurring. To some extent, this is exactly what is happening, even though the infant is not aware. This is great! "Conversations" such as these will show your infant that you are interested in her and what she has to say. At times, it likely will increase the amount she vocalizes. Pretty soon, the two of you may be having a whole "vocal" conversation!

Interaction Skills

Is your infant ready to interact with you during his first few months of life? Yes, although like his *coo*ing and *goo*-ing, it may be somewhat accidental at first. Infants are born with certain abilities and preferences that indirectly lead to wonderful interactions between them and their caregivers. For example, during the first few months after birth, infants prefer to look at objects that are varied in their shapes and lighting. Infants like to see something that has angles and curves, as well as differences or contrasts in lightness and darkness. Perhaps you have seen toy mobiles on the market that are made up of different white and black shapes. These have been developed precisely for this reason. The idea is that infants love to look up at these devices. The exciting thing about this is that you have all the makings for an equally fascinating toy, and it's as clear as the nose on your face. In fact, it *is* the nose on your face . . . and your cheeks, your chin, and your ears. When you hold your infant and he is looking into your face, he is seeing different angles and shadows because of the way the light hits your face. And you didn't pay a thing for this tool!

Speaking of holding your infant so that he is looking at your face, this is an excellent position for him, given his visual skills at this time. At first, infants can best focus on objects that are within about eight inches of their face. Think about it. Most parents hold their infant close to their face. Parents want to see their infant and almost intuitively understand their infant wants to see his parent's face, even if at the time it is because of the angle of a chin or the shadowing by a nose. When parents hold their infant this way, they are positioning the infant to take full advantage of his visual range.

Infants also start smiling soon after birth. At first, it may be a nonsocial smile. In other words, your infant may be reacting to internal functions, if you get our drift. However, by about three weeks or so, infants begin to smile in reaction to sights that intrigue them. Again, it might be that a parent's face is particularly interesting because of the angles and shadows. It also might be that the infant is happy to hear a voice that he recognizes. Whatever the reason, the infant smiles and the parents light up.

So why are we talking about an infant's preference for your face and your voice, and how do these fit under interaction skills? It is because of the *effect* these preferences have on a parent. When you see your infant smile at you, or become seemingly entrenched in staring at your face, or turn when she hears your voice, you will become excited because it seems your infant is interested in *you*. And then you will enter the "dance" that occurs between parent and infant, that interplay of actions and reactions that will show your infant the importance of what she just did. You will try to get her to listen and look more. You will increase the amount you talk with her. You will be showing her the importance of face-to-face interactions and the exchange of smiles, sounds, and looks. These lessons will serve her well as she begins to learn about language and communicating.

Another significant skill your infant is developing, one that will help prepare her for language learning, is called joint attention. Joint attention is when two or more individuals are focused on, or observing, the same object, person, or event. This skill is important for your infant because when the two of you are looking at the same object, your comments about that object have more meaning for her. In other words, she will benefit more from your language models because the language you are using is directly tied to the object of her focus.

Your baby's joint attention skills develop in a systematic way over the first year. During the first few months, she will move through a series of steps in developing this skill. First, she will have the ability to focus on objects placed in front of her face. Next, she will be able to follow objects moved by you, quickly followed by reacting to the language you use that is directed to her. By about four to six months, your baby will be able to follow the direction your eyes take when looking from her to an object. She also will be responding to your directive to "look."

The Second Six Months of Life

Your infant is getting older now, and the foundational skills for speech and language are increasing. During this next six months, he will become purposeful in his interactions with you. By the end of this period, and maybe just before, he will say his first word.

By the end of this period, and maybe just before, he will say his first word.

Vocal Skills

Your infant has been *coo*ing and *goo*ing for some time. He has been using some other sounds, such as squealing and growling. Now he is ready to start babbling.

For most of us, when we think about babbling, we think of an infant saying *goo-goo-gaa-gaa*. In reality, your infant may already have been doing this when he was in that *coo* and *goo* stage mentioned earlier. However, around six months, your infant will begin saying a series of consonants and vowels, or strings of sounds, that reflect the ever growing maturity (control) of his vocal system (his mouth, tongue, throat, and so on). These babbles will contain replications of sounds that typically contain the same series of consonants and vowels. Chances are, the consonant sounds you hear will be such sounds as *p, b, t, d, m, n,* or *w,* because these sounds appear easiest to make in infants' little mouths. Thus, you may hear your infant say such profound statements as *awawawawawawa, ininininininini,* or *dadadada-dada.* Of course, when Dad hears the latter string of sounds, he will become very excited because his infant is saying his name. Unfortunately, at this point, there is a slim chance this is actually happening. Again, the infant is experimenting with his newly developing skills. Through these experimentations, he is learning how to make certain sounds and how to sequence sounds together. These are definitely skills that will aid him when he begins to use sounds for real words.

Toward the latter part of these six months, your infant will become even more sophisticated with her babbling. By about eight or nine months, she may start adding variety to her babbles. Now she will have long strings of sounds that contain several consonants and vowels, such as *badutigah* or *mameba*. Along with these, your infant may try to imitate a word that you say, even though she has no clue what it means. She also may imitate the up-and-down contours of speech, just like those you use when you ask questions or make comments. For example, you infant may produce a whole string of sounds that resemble a long question: *abadu-datadutah?* Researchers call this jargon, because it sounds adultlike in the way it is said, yet it has no meaning. Even if your infant has no idea why she is making these sounds in this way, she is still learning the various ways we use our speech when we talk.

Across these many months, your infant has learned a great deal about his vocal system and its potentials. All of this accidental and purposeful practice has led him to develop a whole repertoire of sounds and combinations of sounds. As he nears his first birthday, you will find that the sounds he uses are much like the sounds you use for real words. You also may find that he seems to have certain sounds or sound combinations he likes because these fill many of his babbling moments. He may even have a sound or series of sounds that seem to act like a word. These "pretend words" are not really words at all. Your infant is not trying to say a word that you always say. Instead, he has made up this particular sound or sound string to stand for a reason to communicate. For example, when Genevieve was about 11 months, she often would say *ga* when she wanted something: her doll, her blanket, her mom, her bottle. This "pretend word" then was her own creation that stood for "I want." Remember, encourage these and any type of babbling and jargon by babbling back and talking to your infant. Pretend you are holding a conversation with him. You are showing him the importance of human interaction.

Interaction Skills

Even though your infant has been crying and *coo*ing and making other noises, she hasn't been purposefully trying to communicate with you up until now. Rather, she has been reacting to the way her body feels or to her environment. When her stomach felt hungry or her bottom was wet, she cried. When she saw an interesting face or pleasing object, she smiled and *coo*ed. However, she was not trying to express her feelings or comment on her environment on her own. Researchers who study infants say that at about eight or nine months, infants begin to intentionally communicate with others to reach a particular goal or objective. In fact, infants will start communicating with their parents, and others, for two main reasons: to comment on what is in their environment and to request an object, action, or person.

At nine months of age, infants do not have words yet, so they try to communicate using other interesting and creative ways, by using gestures and the sounds with which they have been playing. For example, an infant may point at the cow outside her car window and let out an *eeeeeee*, as if to say, "There's a cow out there!" Another time, the infant may reach up with her arms toward her father and let out a grunt, as if to say, "Pick me up, Daddy!" With both of these purposeful actions, the infant's intent to communicate is clear. She wants to let her mother know she sees a cow or to convey that her father should pick her up. When an infant begins to show intentional communication, she has tackled a very important and crucial aspect of language: She is using some recognizable skill to let you know she wants you to listen to her and understand what she is thinking. This skill represents the very reason for communicating: sharing your thoughts and feelings with others.

During the second six months, your baby is taking on more responsibility for establishing and maintaining joint attention. Around six or seven months, she is reaching for objects, which often causes you to focus on that same object. Invariably, you will find that you start talking about that object. Finally, at around eight months of age, your baby will be reaching for toys or other objects, while also looking at you. Often this type of joint attention is saying, "Look, will you help me get this?" As your baby matures, she increases her ability to shift her eye gaze from you to the object and back. This type of "eye signaling" encourages a "dialogue" between the two of you. She looks at you, then the object, and then back to you. You begin talking about the object, following the lead she has set. She is actually telling you, without words, what the topic of conversation should be. What a powerful skill your baby has developed!

Helping Your Infant Create Language

Your infant has started an incredible journey during this first year of life, one that develops a skill that will affect his whole life. Without language, your child will not be able to express his feelings to others, participate in school or social events with his friends, get into college, or interview for a job. That sounds somewhat daunting, doesn't it? Relax, though, because both you and your child bring a lot of tools to help the process as it develops. Your biggest role during this year will be to be a caring, loving parent who recognizes the subtle changes in your child's abilities and reacts and encourages them. This can be done in any situation in which you and your child interact. Below we have listed three common situations—changing time, bath time, and eating time—because we know that these situations occur frequently throughout the day with infants. The suggestions we provide are not unique to any one of these particular situations. Rather, you can use these strategies within any situation.

Changing Time

As a parent of an infant, you undoubtedly are finding yourself changing your little one *multiple* times a day. Let's focus on changing clothes, even though you likely are changing his diapers more often! Are there specific things you can do and say during this time that will facilitate your infant's developing communication skills? Of course!

Not unlike your own clothes-changing routine (first the right leg, then the left leg), you probably have already established certain routines as you change your infant's clothes (first the right arm, then the left arm). Along with these specific, routine acts, you may find yourself saying the same thing: "Okay, first we take out this arm. Then we take out that arm. Ooooh. Naked baby! Naked baby!" At first, your infant hears a long string of sounds, without any specific awareness of where words stop and start. Perhaps it sounds like this: "Okfirstwetakeoutthis arm. Thenwetakeoutthatarm. Ooooh. Nakedbaby! Nakedbaby!" However, as he hears the same types of language (not identical, but similar) accompanying the same actions, he will begin to identify which word or words go with which objects or actions. Thus, unlike other situations where routine leads to quick boredom on your part, routines such as these are actually excellent learning experiences for your infant. Don't hesitate, then, to use routines for valuable language-learning experiences. During these everyday happenings, talk to your infant using similar types of words and sentences.

As you change your infant's clothes, you most likely will be in close proximity to him (well, except for those really nasty diapers). Remember, this is exactly where you want to be. You are providing your child with the "scenery" he truly enjoys. As your child enjoys the shapes and shadows of your face, he may very well start to *oooh* and *ahhh*. Take advantage of these vocalizations by *oooh*ing and *ahhh*ing back to

As you change your infant's clothes, he may very well start to ooooh and ahhh. Take advantage of these vocalizations by ooohing and ahhhing back.

him. Give meaning to his *ooohs* and *ahhhs*, so that he begins to see what he "says" is valuable and meaningful to you.

Bath Time

Just as with changing time, you most likely will fall into certain routines or actions that repeat across bathing times. Talk about what you are doing each time, just like you did during changing time. Remember, you are helping your child begin to identify the words that belong to the objects and actions for that routine. This is true for your infant whether he is 4 months old or 11 months old.

You also can encourage your infant's joint attention skills during bath time. Most infants beyond two months of age enjoy watching you repeatedly pour water out of the cup into the bath or bob the little yellow ducky under the water and back out. You can use these actions to help develop your baby's ability to change focus from you to the object (falling water or bobbing ducky) and back again, encouraging and establishing joint attention with your little one.

Mealtime

Early on, whether your baby is breast-fed or bottle-fed, you will be holding your child within the physical proximity that best matches her visual range. Thus, during these times, you can focus on your child's face, talking to her as she eats. This models for her good eye contact and encourages face-to-face interactions.

During mealtime, you can focus on your
child's face, talking to her as she eats.

When your baby moves beyond these types of feeding to other kinds of food, you then can take advantage of her growing joint attention skills to talk about what you are doing and the objects involved. The point here is not to try to teach your child by simply labeling the objects and actions, such as, "This is a spoon. These are peaches. I'm feeding you." Not only would that sound silly, it would not be a particularly helpful language-learning experience. Rather, you can simply talk about what is happening as it happens: "Okay, let's get the spoon. Here are some peaches. Scoop some up. Yummy, yummy peaches." In this way, you are providing names or labels for the actions in which you are involved, providing lots of opportunities for your infant to start recognizing what objects and actions are called in her world.

Chapter Summary

Many people would not assume that infants are developing language in their first year of life. When there are no words, how can you say children have language? As you have read in this chapter, children are learning a lot, and proving it, in their first year of life.

Throughout this first year of life, your child will learn a great deal about this system we call language. You are probably the most important variable in that learning process. Between you and your child, all the raw materials needed for language learning are available. Enjoy these first 12 months, and recognize all the important skills he is learning. And be prepared. He's about to say his first word!

2

EARLIEST WORDS: DISCOVERING YOUR BABY'S STYLE

- Babies often rely on the sounds in a word when deciding whether to say the word.

- Some babies practice talking just for the sake of it.

- Reading to your baby now is a valuable learning experience for her.

Fernando had been assigned to watch a mother and her baby son play together as part of a college course on language development. He was to observe how the mother interacted with her son and how the son reacted. Over the course of a week, he noticed that the mother frequently repeated what her baby boy said. If the boy said, "Ball," then the mother said, "Ball? Oh, you want me to throw the ball?" It seemed to the college student that this mother always repeated or talked about what the boy was saying. That seemed strange! Why not tell the baby new things, like about her day or about the upcoming three-day weekend? Then the college student noticed something. When the young mother talked to her baby this way, the baby looked at her.

All those months of diapering and sleep deprivation seem to be worth it when that child looks at you and says "Mama" or "Dada."

He seemed to talk more. And in fact, just now, the baby actually used two words together. Hmm. Maybe there was something to this type of talking.

Many parents view the appearance of their baby's first word as one of the most exciting events in their child's development. What will the first word be? What will her voice sound like? All those months of diapering and sleep deprivation seem to be worth it when that child looks at you and says "Mama," "Papa," or "Dada." In this chapter we'll talk about the many factors that lead to and influence how and why your baby says a word. We will review how you can determine that what she says is a real word, why she chooses to say other words besides *mama* or *dada* and what communication strategies you can use to help the language-learning process to develop further.

This second year of life is a fascinating one. Your baby is entering into what child language researchers call the one-word stage. Your baby will start off this year with a first word. And as the year comes to a close, she likely will have more than 50 words and will begin combining them into two-word sentences. In between these times, she will be learning new words, words with different meanings and various functions. This is an awesome task for such a young person. You have a definite role in this task. Let's begin.

What Is a Word?

The answer to this question might seem obvious; however, identifying a child's first use of a "true" word is a little tricky. As you learned in the last chapter, babies are pretty noisy. They're babbling and making lots of different sounds and maybe some "pretend words" before they actually produce their first true word. To identify when a child produces his first word, researchers had to agree on the definition of *word*. They came up with four characteristics that we use to qualify a group of speech sounds as a word.

First, we consider the group of speech sounds, that is, the production itself. It should have a clear vowel that sounds close to the actual vowel one expects for that word. Second, it should be a single production followed by a brief period of silence. This is in contrast to babbling, which consists of long strings of consonants and vowels. Third, a true word is used under specific recurring conditions; that is, the word refers to a particular person, thing, or situation. Fourth (and this is our favorite), true words are used in conversations with people! The baby is revealing his budding appreciation of the communicative value of speech and language. Let's look at one example.

Identifying a child's first use of a "true" word is a little tricky.

Caleb's first word was his own version of our dog's name. His production for *Chi-Chi* sounded somewhat like he was clearing his throat—it had a consonant sound that sounded like a cross between an *h* and a *k*. However, the vowel sounded just like the "long *e*" sound in Chi-Chi's name. Further, his production was consistent, both in terms of the sounds he used and the conditions under which he used it. He produced his version of her name whenever Chi-Chi walked into the room. Finally, he would produce her name and then wait. Sometimes he seemed to be labeling her; other times he seemed to be calling her to come to him. It was a bittersweet moment. He definitely was using her name with purpose. It was just a little sad that his first word referred to the dog rather than his mom.

Most babies use their first true words between 9 and 12 months of age, although there is some variability among babies. The size of their vocabulary increases steadily for the next few months as they use their one-word "sentences."

What Words Will My Child Use?

Caleb's first word was his dog's name. Why was that the case? All words are not created equally for use by your little one. Your baby's choice of the specific words that will make up her first vocabulary, or set of words that she can say, is influenced by five factors. We consider each of these in the following sections.

Environment

All of our children included the word *computer* in their early vocabulary, but none of them used the word *tractor*. We know of other children whose early vocabulary was just the opposite; that is, they used *tractor* but not *computer*. As you might guess, the difference in word use is due to the differences in the children's environments, such as their home, their day care, and so on. To a certain extent, children are going to use the words that they hear. Babies who live on a farm are more likely to use words like *chicken* or *tractor* than children who live in the city. Our children heard their parents use the word *computer*, saw their parents using a computer, and even tried using a computer themselves a few times during this early stage of development. Knowing that a baby's first words are influenced by those that she hears may tempt the parent to repeat *mommy* or *daddy* several times during the day in order to increase the chances that she'll use one of those words. Trust us—it doesn't really work! There are other factors that also play a role in the words that make up your baby's first vocabulary.

Word Type

Have you ever considered that a baby might say words such as *run* or *eat* during this one-word stage but probably won't include words such as *think* or *watch*? This is because the latter words are more abstract, or complex, than the former. Many of the words in a baby's early vocabulary consist of nouns, which are names for people and objects. However, other kinds of words also are used. Simple verbs that refer to common actions, such as *drink* or *go*, are used. Babies also will use social and occurrence words, such as *bye-bye, all gone, another,* and *again* to describe current circumstances. Some children use descriptive words, such as *hot* or *pretty*. Sometimes, to the dismay of the parents, one of the most frequently occurring early words is *no*. It's rare indeed to find a child who isn't quite proficient at using the word *NO!*

These different types of nouns, verbs, and descriptive words form the meaning system of your child's language system. We call this meaning system semantics. Your baby's semantic development is the hallmark of this one-word stage.

Sounds in the Word

Do you remember how difficult it was to say some words when you were a child? Words such as *statistics, aluminum,* and *breakfasts* may come to mind. The word structure, in terms of its speech sounds and number of syllables, can influence whether a baby will attempt to say it during the early stages of language development. In general, words containing several syllables are harder for babies to say than one- or two-syllable words. This is why you're more likely to hear *choo-choo* or *train* than *locomotive*.

Babies' first words can be influenced by the actual sounds that a word contains. Most children produce sounds like *p*, *b*, *n*, and *w* before they produce sounds like *g*, *s*, *ch*, *r*, and *l*. This is because the latter are somewhat harder to articulate. Of course, there are individual differences, and some babies may actually produce some of the harder sounds before they do the easier ones. They also typically don't produce two consonant sounds, such as *bl* or *tr*, together in their first words.

There is one more interesting point about how speech sounds in words affect what your baby will say first. Many babies may have a preference for certain speech sounds or types of syllables. It is unclear why they seem to prefer certain sounds and sound combinations, but nevertheless, they may capitalize on these preferences when choosing words to add to their vocabulary. Thus, they may choose to say words that match closely their sound preferences and avoid, or choose not to say, words that contain speech sounds and syllables that are quite different than their preferences. The following example, which proved to be somewhat disappointing to the mother involved, illustrates this principle.

Many babies may have a preference for certain speech sounds or types of syllables.

When Caleb was a baby, he preferred sounds that were made in the middle or back portion of the mouth over sounds made in the front. When he was babbling, we heard a lot more syllables with *t*, *d*, *n*, or *k* sounds in them than with *m* or *b*. This unfortunate preference carried over into his selection of first words, and he produced the word *daddy* long before he produced the word *mama*. Years later, when Caitlin was born, her mother was delighted to notice a strong preference for front sounds present in her babbling. The sounds *p* and *b*, which are made on the lips like an *m*, were actually produced more frequently than *t* or *d*, although she said these other speech sounds occasionally. Tragically, however, Caitlin had a strong avoidance of nasal sounds (those sounds made through the nose, like *m* and *n*), and this carried over to her selection of meaningful words. Her poor mother had to once again hear her child saying *daddy* many times before she ever said *mama*.

Caitlin's first use of *mama* was striking, though. Her family had a "night-night" routine that was followed each evening. Her parents would say "night-night" and sing songs, say prayers, and so on. Caitlin would respond several times with "digh-digh," her version of "night-night." One evening she surprised us (and herself) by saying, "Nigh-nigh." Like one of those cartoons that has a lightbulb appearing over the head as a concept clears, Caitlin's face brightened up and she said, "Mama!" Of course, we knew better, but it almost seemed like she was thinking, "Nasal sounds! Now I know how to do nasal sounds! I can say *Mama!*"

Usefulness

We've been talking about how characteristics of the words themselves (word meaning or semantic complexity, speech sounds in the word) influence whether a word will appear in your baby's first vocabulary. In addition to these factors, a child's choice of words is also determined by how useful a particular word may be to her. One of the classic examples from past studies of children's language development is that babies typically produce *sock* and *shoe* before they produce *shirt* or *shorts*. This is because babies can manipulate their own socks and shoes before they can do much with their shirts or shorts. Moms and dads are likely to see discarded shoes and socks lying on the floor long before they will see discarded shirts or shorts (a blessed fact that all too soon will change). Thus, babies say the words *shoes* and *socks* early more often than other clothing terms. The degree of usefulness, then, is probably the major reason that the word *no* is used so frequently. It's quite powerful for the child because it can be used in many (all?) situations.

Style

Some people are born risk takers. You know the type. They're the ones who can be found bungee jumping, riding dirt bikes, snowboarding, or engaging in other types of extreme experiences. On the other end of the continuum, you find the analytical, cautious person. Once again, you know people like this. They read reviews in trade magazines and do price comparisons for weeks or even months before they actually make a purchase. These same "styles" often characterize babies who are learning language. On one end of the continuum, we have our little risk taker. Terms such as *expressive* and *noun leaver* have been used to describe this style. These babies are about actions and interaction. They have lots to say and they don't seem to feel the need to wait until they can speak clearly before jumping right in to talk! Although they use a lot of nouns, they are more likely to use other kinds of words (*bye-bye, more, again, no*) quite frequently. On the other end of the style continuum, we have the cautious calculator. Terms such as *referential* and *noun lover* have been used to describe this style of acquiring language. As these terms suggest, these babies tend to prefer to label people and objects in their environment. They have sound preferences or avoidances that influence the words they will attempt. Later, when they start combining words, their new sentences tend to consist primarily of real words and less "jargon."

Which style is better for developing language? Neither. Both are just fine. Although the noun-lover child might have a slightly larger vocabulary in the earliest stages of development, the differences disappear over time. Interestingly, studies indicate that similarities in style between parents and children can facilitate language. Researchers have found similar styles in mothers as they interact with their babies. When there is a match in style (referential parent–referential baby; expressive baby–expressive parent), language development seems to be slightly enhanced. Finally, it's important to keep in mind that most children fall somewhere in the middle of the style continuum's extreme ends, just as most of us adults fall somewhere between the person who wants to climb Mt. Everest and the person who could write a book on SUVs by the time the purchase is done. The point here is that parents should try to match their style of interaction and language to their baby's, *if* there seems to be a strong tendency to one type or the other.

One of the most powerful ways to influence your child's language use is to model appropriate word use.

Understanding the influences on the words a baby is likely to use during the single-word stage can be helpful for parents. For one thing, it may make you less anxious if your baby is not using some words even though he has heard them several times and many people in his life want him to use them. Let's face it, Aunt Mildred may be one of your son's favorite people, but he might not attempt to say her name because it contains some hard sounds.

Second, knowing what kinds of words may be reasonably

Researchers have documented babies who can be heard saying words over and over again in their cribs, seemingly just to practice how to pronounce the words.

expected can help you emphasize those words as you interact with your baby. One of the most powerful ways to influence your child's language use is to model appropriate word use. Modeling is most effective when the language examples are reasonable or feasible for the child. Regardless of how many times we might repeat the Preamble to the Constitution for our baby, chances are he's just not going to recite it back for us! When you really think about it, why would we want him to do that? More than ever, parents feel pressure to make their children into superstars, to get them started in dance, music, sports, foreign languages, reading, and everything else as soon as they are born (see chapter 10 on fads for more)! When it comes to facilitating language, the best rule is to model words that will be meaningful for your child, words that will help him fit into his environment, words that will help him communicate with the people that he loves! So think about the five factors that influence a baby's first words and make sure that your child's *environment* consists of multiple models of the right *type* of words that contain *simple sounds*, are maximally *useful*, and fit with her *style* preferences for communicating.

Social Language Skills

The one-word stage is characterized by so much more than just the use of one-word sentences. Babies are social beings and thus are interested in using language to socialize. Before they say their first words, babies are socializing in non-language ways, such as through gestures, grunts, and so forth. Their social language skills, called pragmatics, are beginning to broaden this year. Now babies quite cleverly are using their expanding language skills for a variety of purposes.

As you know, babies use words to label people (*Daddy*) or objects (*book*). However, they also use words to request action or information. For example, a baby might point and say, "Cookie," not because she's informing you that the little round thing should be called a cookie but because she wants you to give it to her! Imagine a young baby looking at a book with his dad. He points to a picture of an animal and says, "Lion?" In this instance, he is likely requesting information. Other babies have a one-word version of the question "What's that?" It may sound something like *sat* and is said in a questioning manner, often accompanied by pointing. These are two examples of the way in which babies may request information.

Every parent is aware that young children use the word *no* to protest, but protests are not necessarily limited to the word *no*. Children can protest with the word *mine* as someone tries to take a toy away. Babies also use single words to call or greet someone. Some of our fondest memories of our young children were those early mornings when we'd hear our baby calling us from the nursery or when we'd come home and see that excited face as one of our children said, "Mom" or "Dad." Just as we respond to another adult when called or greeted with "Here I am" or "Hi," so we should respond when our babies call or greet us.

Finally, babies sometimes use language simply for practice. The practice function is indeed useful in the early stages of language. Researchers have documented babies who can be heard saying words over and over again in their cribs, seemingly just to practice how to pronounce the words. Sometimes your child may not want or expect a response from you or anyone else in her environment. She may just want to experiment a little with these incredible new skills she is acquiring.

We've discussed the reasons that children use language at the single-word stage. What about topics? What are young babies talking about? Margaret Lahey, one of the pioneers in child language research, writes that early language refers to "what the child is doing, what the child is about to do, or what the child wants others to do." What a great way to capture the focus of a baby's language: Her language use is definitely focused on her world!

We've talked about how powerful modeling is as a tool for facilitating language development in your baby. Knowing that your baby should be using language to label, call, greet, and protest should encourage you to include all of these uses in the language that you model for him. We've seen many parents who are quite adept at modeling the labeling function. This is great, but we hope you'll also remember that calling, greeting, and protesting are also important. At first glance, it may seem a little odd to suggest to a parent that you should help your baby become good at protesting. Many veteran parents will tell you that babies don't need any help in this area! However, in the first stages of language, babies are still learning about the power of words. Given that probably all children are born with the desire to protest, you might as well capitalize on this desire as a way to show the usefulness of language.

Opportunities to model all of these different uses of language occur in everyday, natural activities. There's simply no need to contrive or set up unique "teaching experiences." It's actually best to comment about business as usual each day. Keep in mind, just as your baby's early one-word sentences will be mostly about his world, so should *your* language models be focused on the people, objects, or actions to which your child is attending at the moment. Your baby is focused on the "here and now" of the world. He is not able to talk about and probably not interested in what happened yesterday or what will happen tomorrow. Talk about what he is doing at that moment and you will have an attentive, active language learner.

Child-Directed Speech

You've probably noticed that you can usually tell when someone is speaking to a child. There's a special way that adults (and, by the way, older children) talk to young children. The interesting thing is that humans seem to do this quite naturally (typically, no one teaches another person to talk like this). Researchers refer to this style of talking (or "register") as child-directed speech (CDS). Initially, this language style was labeled "motherese." However, the term changed to CDS when the style was observed in fathers as well as individuals who weren't even related to the babies with whom they were interacting.

Characteristics of Child-Directed Speech

There are specific features that distinguish CDS from the typical style of speech and language. If you listen to a speaker of CDS, you'll notice a special rhythm and pitch. There is somewhat of a musical quality to CDS. Overall, the pitch is higher. Plus, the speaker's pitch goes up and down more often than during typical speech. CDS speakers also tend to use a slower rate. It is as though they have an unconscious appreciation for the notion that the baby may need a little more time to take in or understand the incoming information.

When using CDS, speakers tend to use simple words. You're likely to hear a word like *bey-bey* or *blanket* in a conversation with a baby, but you probably won't hear *quilt*. CDS speakers use shorter sentences. Not only do the sentences contain fewer words, but they also have simple grammar structures. For example, you are more likely to hear

"See the ball? Big ball. Roll ball" rather than "Look at the rather large ball. Will you roll it to me?" People using CDS will stress, or put more emphasis on, the important words in the sentence. They may simplify the way words are said. For example, some parents may use terms like *blankie* and *ba-ba* for blanket and bottle.

Finally, CDS is characterized by a high degree of responsiveness. Adults using CDS are likely to respond to babies' barely meaningful productions as though they were profound statements. Many years ago, there was a television ad for a long-distance company. Two young parents and their baby were sitting on a floor and a telephone was handed to the baby, who happily produced a string of babbled syllables. It sounded something like "babadigawawikuwu." One of the parents took the phone and said proudly, "Did you hear that, Mom? She said *Grandma!*" Well, perhaps this is a little bit of a stretch; however, it's a great example of being responsive. Your baby will want to repeat activities such as these that make her feel good, successful, and so on.

As a footnote, we should mention that many children and adults use CDS when they talk to animals. Caleb and Caitlin can always tell when their mother is talking to a dog or a cat. Now they do the very same thing. The style of speaking that many people use when talking to animals shares most of the characteristics of CDS.

Effects of Child-Directed Speech

So why do adults talk this way to babies? Researchers have explored the purpose and effects of CDS. They concluded that adults aren't using this register, or language style, in a conscious effort to teach language to babies. If this were the case, it would be very difficult to explain the use of this register with animals. Instead, adults seem to be using it to maximize the chances for optimal communication *and* to express affection. The latter purpose probably explains the use of "animalese" with our pets.

As for the effects, you should know that, in general, using CDS is a very good thing to do! Researchers have found benefits such as greater vocabulary and better grammatical accuracy in babies whose mothers use CDS. With the exception of word simplifications, CDS likely results in more appropriate models. Further, CDS gives the baby confidence to be an active participant in conversations. Features such as attributing meaning to the baby's comments that might not really be so meaningful encourage her to take part in the interaction.

Some people might think that CDS sounds "silly" or "condescending" and shouldn't be used. Nonsense! There is no evidence that CDS slows down language development. Enjoy your baby at this level of development. Believe us, it will be over before you know it. On the other hand, the use of CDS is not absolutely crucial for language development. Several studies have shown that children who are not exposed to CDS, or even those who may miss a lot of exposure to typical language models, go on to develop language with a minimal amount of normal linguistic input.

Helping Your Baby Learn to Use Words

Your baby is taking a giant step in language development this year. He is beginning to use the code that his family has been using around him for over a year. As he begins to express himself with words, you can help that learning along by optimizing your interactions with him. This can occur in all situations, including reading time and playtime.

Reading Time

It is hard to exist in today's world without hearing how important it is to read to your baby. We cannot emphasize enough how true this is. However, what you may not realize is that even at this age, your baby's second year of life, reading is an important activity. By establishing a book-reading routine with your child at this early age, you are helping your child realize early on how important reading is. You also are setting up a routine that will, it is hoped, last far beyond even when your child can read to himself, and you are actually teaching him crucial skills for later reading (but more about that in chapters 4 and 5).

By establishing a book-reading routine with your child at this early age, you are helping your child realize early on how important reading is.

In this second year of life, reading time with your child may only last five minutes, if that. Don't get frustrated, though. For some babies, this is all the time they choose to devote to this activity, and that's okay. As you hear so many other places, at this point in development, it's the quality, not the quantity, of the time you spend with your child.

The books you choose for your child should be relatively simple. You will find that books that allow you to label pictures of objects, people, and actions that are *familiar* to your child will likely be most interesting to him. As you read, talk about the pictures of the objects, pointing to them as you label them. After several readings, you might occasionally ask your child to point to the pictures ("Where's the ball?").

Why do we say to only occasionally ask your baby to point to pictures? First, as we mentioned in the introduction, children want their parents to be parents, not teachers. If you begin to turn parent–child interaction times into "quiz times," you may actually decrease your baby's willingness and desire to interact with you. Similarly, you want

Some babies really like to name pictures and objects while other babies don't have this preference.

to refrain from asking your baby to imitate your naming of pictures. Directed imitation won't help your child know when to use a word or why it is used. However, if you find that your child *chooses* to use a word after you have said it, that's great! Child-initiated imitations, or reproductions of what you have said, show you that your baby is starting to understand that particular word or reason for talking.

Research suggests that children of varying ages tend to choose to imitate another person's language when they are preparing to use that type or level of language themselves. So, when your baby chooses to imitate something you have said, echo back that word and expand on it, or add extra information to it. This might sound like the following:

> PARENT: "Look, a truck."
>
> BABY: "Truck."
>
> PARENT: "Yes, truck. A big truck."

When you respond to your baby this way, you are saying that you understood what he said, that it had meaning, and that he can even add more information later as he matures. Quite a bit for you to help him learn in such a small amount of time!

There is one other reason for why you don't want to ask your baby to label pictures after you have named them. As we said earlier, some babies really like to name pictures and objects while other babies don't have this preference. As we will continue to say, you want to match your language and activities to your baby's preferences the best you can, if he seems to have a fairly strong preference.

Playtime

This year, your baby will be doing plenty of exploring of her environment. As she moves around her little world, she is learning so many new ideas and concepts, such as how certain actions can cause other actions to occur (pushing a car to make it move) and how objects can disappear and then reappear (playing peek-a-boo). She is discovering ways to make some objects or toys represent real objects (holding a toy phone to her ear). As she is learning all this new information, she will likely be talking about it. It is all so new and exciting! However, because of her focus and interests, chances are she won't necessarily want to talk a whole lot about what *you* are doing. This means that playtime should be focused on *her* interests. If she wants to play with the dollhouse and its people, follow this interest and play along with her, commenting on what you, your baby, and the dolls are doing. This child-centered play/focus, rather than a parent-centered play/focus (introducing an activity or toy your baby is not focused on), will most likely result in an increase in her use of words.

Playtime also is the time to follow your baby's language style. As you and your baby play, you may find that she prefers to play games that involve naming, such as the "What's this?" or the "Where's your (body part)?" games. If you see a preference for this, chances are your baby is more of a referential or noun-lover word learner. This doesn't mean she won't learn other words, but it does mean that you can encourage learning by playing the games to which she seems to respond well. Likewise, if your baby seems to enjoy games such as "peek-a-boo" and "this little piggie," the types of games where your child is expected to contribute a whole series of "words" (*peek-a-boo*) or sounds (*wee-wee-wee*), there is a chance she leans more to the expressive or noun-leaver style.

Follow your baby's lead, then. As you play with the doll-house, encourage the noun-lover baby to use her words by modeling labeling of items as you play: "Look! A dog, a cat, a baby. Lots of things!" The noun-leaver baby can be encouraged to use her words by modeling phrases: "Bye-bye Daddy. Car goes vroom-vroom."

The point is that, as we mentioned, we don't want to force babies into styles they don't prefer. Perhaps the best example of this took place between Nick, definitely more of a noun leaver, and his dad, who really wanted Nick to say *juice* correctly. Nick used the word *dada* to say *juice*, regardless of who happened to have juice or where the juice was. In other words, it was a true word, even though it did not seem to be close at all to the actual adult pronunciation.

NICK (Pointing at juice): "Dada."

DAD: "Juice? Say juice."

NICK: "Dada."

DAD (Emphasizing the pronunciation more): "Juuuuice."

NICK: "Dada."

DAD (Becoming a little impatient and forceful): "Juuuuiiiccee!"

NICK: "Daaaa daaaaa."

This example demonstrates two very important points. First, Nick was not a noun lover. Even though he was trying to produce a noun, his interest was more in the action of getting it than saying it anywhere near correctly. Second, imitation and demands for accuracy by a parent typically result in an unsuccessful outcome. In this case, however, we can happily report that the dad gave up, never to bring up the issue again (until this book, of course!).

Chapter Summary

When you think about it, language is really complex! When we teach introductory classes on language development, we tell our students that they should leave the class feeling like a genius, that once they find out just how much there is to acquiring a language, they will want to pat themselves on the back for having done it so well! During this second year of your baby's life, he has taken a giant step forward. Using many different strategies and preferences, he has begun to use true words. He has developed the basis for all future language, the ability to communicate with others using the same language system others around him use. And even though you have provided wonderful language models and created meaningful learning situations, he has done a great deal of the learning on his own as well. He is now ready to move on to another major milestone, linking words together. The miracle of language development continues!

3

BUILDING FIRST SENTENCES: NATURAL WAYS TO ENCOURAGE YOUR TODDLER

DID **Y**OU **K**NOW?

- The word *no* can mean many different things.
- Toddlers are language inventors.
- Three-year-olds can talk about the past and the future.

Shaquille was driving his three-year-old son, J'mari, home from day care. As usual, Shaquille was quizzing his son about what had occurred during the day. In the past, Shaquille would ask a question about one of J'mari's favorite pastimes, like "Did you finger paint today?" J'mari's typical response would be "yeah," possibly followed by a statement like "big boat" or "paint car." Shaquille loved these conversations, especially because lately he was noticing that J'mari's language skills were improving. It seemed in the last few weeks or so, J'mari's responses were more like "Yeah, I paint green tree" or "I painted me!" Today Shaquille asked the familiar question again. However, he wasn't prepared for J'mari's response: "Well, actually...painted a yellow house." Shaquille was shocked. Where did that "actually" come from?

Your toddler has been producing single words for some time now. It's been amazing to watch her vocabulary steadily increase. Sometime around your toddler's second birthday, she'll surprise you by combining two of those words to form her first "sentence." About the same time, her vocabulary will explode, and it will seem like she is learning more new words than you can keep straight! It was certainly that way with our own children. Even as researchers interested in child language development who had plenty of tools available to record our children's every move, we had trouble keeping up with what was happening in our children's language at this stage of development.

By the end of this period, you'll be able to carry on a respectable conversation with your toddler!

In this chapter, we will organize our discussion around developments in the toddler's sound system, vocabulary, types of words, sentences, grammar, and social language skills. We will cover the period of language development that begins with the toddler's first two-word combination and ends around the time she is ready for early reading and writing activities (ages four and five). We must warn you—this period has probably received more attention from researchers than any other. That's because so many noticeable changes occur in the toddler's language skills during this time. By the end of this period, you'll be able to carry on a respectable conversation with your toddler! So fasten your seat belt for an exciting adventure into a toddler's budding use of impressive language structures.

What Kinds of Words Will My Toddler Use?

One of the most striking characteristics of this stage is a "vocabulary burst," or the sheer number of words being added to your toddler's vocabulary on a regular basis. When the first two-word sentence is used, most toddlers have a vocabulary ranging from 30 to 50 words. By the time the toddler reaches age three, she'll probably be using more than 1,000 words and understanding even more.

Not only are toddlers rapidly acquiring new words during this period, they also are expanding the *types* of words they use. In the last chapter, we discussed how most early words were labels, simple action verbs, description words, and specific words such as *no*, *bye-bye*, and *all gone*. During the third stage of development, toddlers will use more and more words that fall within these categories. For example, the descriptive category will increase from simple words such as *pretty* and *hot* to more sophisticated words like *nice*, *fast*, and *sick*. Additionally, several new *kinds* of words will emerge. Your toddler will use verbs that express an internal feeling or condition, such as *want* and *need*. Later, other verbs that refer to the five senses will be used, including *see*, *hear*, *touch*, *smell*, and *taste*. Even more sophisticated verbs, which represent mental processes, will appear at the end of this stage. Examples include *think*, *know*, *wonder*, and *dream*. Verbs aren't the only category that changes. We also see toddlers start using words that refer to number concepts, such as *many*, *some*, *two*, and *four*, and time concepts, such as *now* and *then*. In fact, there are so many new words and word types developing during these two years that we could probably fill up the rest of this book with them.

In addition to word type, the factors that we discussed as being influential in chapter 2 (i.e., environment, sound makeup, and usefulness) will continue to play a role. For example, Julie's nephew Cooper was diagnosed with a serious illness at age 16 months. Part of his treatment was a steroid regime, which markedly increased his appetite. He was taking the steroids about the time when his language underwent the vocabulary burst. His mom, Heather, reported that a large majority of Cooper's new vocabulary items referred to foods! He was much more likely to be heard saying the words *cheese, cracker, apple, pretzel, beans,* or *ice cream* than other new words. The word *hot* was first used to refer to the status of his lunch or dinner rather than as a warning for a heater or iron or something similar, as is often the case with young children. Both his mom, a speech-language pathologist, and his aunt thought that this was a wonderful example of a child's insight into the power of language and his ability to apply it to what's important to him. The steroid treatment was successful in treating Cooper's illness, and it also resulted in unique vocabulary depth in this meaningful category!

What Kinds of Sentences Will My Toddler Use?

As we said earlier, the combination of two words into one sentence marks the beginning of a new developmental stage. The ability to combine words helps the toddler gain even more "mileage" out of the words he knows. Instead of saying only "more," he can now be more specific: "more juice" or "more cookie." With word combinations, less confusion about the toddler's intent will occur.

Word Combinations

These early combinations consist of words that the toddler had been using as single-word sentences up to this point. This is an important factor for parents to keep in mind. As we said, your toddler's vocabulary is expanding both in number and type of words that he knows. However, his first sentences will likely consist of those words (and word *types*) that have been around awhile. You heard productions such as *mama, daddy, cracker, more, bye-bye, no, all gone, pretty,* and *go* in the last stage. Now you'll hear these same words in basic sentences, *more cracker, daddy bye-bye, no night-night,* and so on. Toddlers, like adults, can only handle so many new tasks at any one given time. You'll likely hear new words and new word types appearing as single-word sentences initially. Gradually, these new words and word types also will be used in word combinations.

Early Grammar

Not only is your toddler now producing little sentences by combining words, he also is beginning to use English grammar. Grammar means using word endings and smaller words like *is, are,* and *am.* For example, at the beginning of this stage, your toddler might observe the family pet and say, "Doggie bark." After a while, however, he'll say, "Doggie barking." This is so smart! He is showing his appreciation for the notion that the *-ing* ending form tells us something important about the timing of the action, that the action is occurring right then. Language researchers consider the inclusion of grammar forms such as the *-ing* or plural *-s* or past tense *-ed* to be as impressive as adding another whole word to the sentence. The first forms of grammar appear a short time after the toddler starts using word combinations. Gradually, other forms will be added.

As toddlers attempt to figure out the use of these forms, some interesting language productions result. For example, Caleb once had an action-figure toy that could be seen in the dark. After the first night with the toy, he proudly proclaimed, "My dinosaur glew all night!" He had never heard that form used at home—we promise! When you hear a toddler use a word like that, you recognize it as a mistake; the past tense form for *glow* is *glowed* rather than *glew*. On the other hand, like his mother, you probably can appreciate how clever and creative Caleb was to come up with that word. It makes perfect sense: Today I *blow*; yesterday I *blew*. Today I *grow*; yesterday I *grew*. Why not "Today I glow; yesterday I glew"? Errors such as this one illustrate that language acquisition isn't a "giant memory task." Toddlers aren't memorizing every form they hear for future use. Instead, they are trying to "solve the puzzle," "crack the code," so they will be equipped to create sentences that they haven't heard before. Such creative geniuses are bound to make some mistakes along the way!

Word Order in Sentences

You know that your toddler's first sentences will be somewhat incomplete ("more cookie" for "I want some more cookies"). Gradually, words and other aspects of grammar will fill in the missing gaps. However, the process may seem a little odd to the watchful parent because even though the right words are added to the sentence, they might not be used in the correct order at first. The development of questions and negative forms (*no, not, don't*) are great examples of this phenomenon.

The toddler's meaning is not contained in just the words themselves. He's showing an understanding that speakers use inflection, or pitch changes, to also signal meaning.

The earliest way that a toddler "asks a question" is to raise his pitch at the end of the word. For example, if a toddler says "Daddy gone" with a falling, rather emphatic tone, he's probably using that sentence to tell you that his dad is indeed not present. On the other hand, if a toddler says those same words with a rising tone at the end, he's probably asking whether his dad is gone or not. The key is that the toddler's meaning is not contained in just the words themselves. He's showing an understanding that speakers use inflection, or pitch changes, to also signal meaning. Toddlers don't jump from saying "Daddy gone?" to "Is Daddy gone?" instantly. They will first insert the word *is* in the middle and keep the rising inflection at the end to signal that the sentence is meant to be a question: "Daddy's gone?" Later, with development, they'll make that final necessary switch to move the word *is* to the beginning of the sentence: "Is Daddy gone?"

Negative forms also go through a metamorphosis from the time they emerge to the time they are used in an adult manner. Of course the earliest form is the ever popular *NO*! Toddlers initially use this word to refuse something—that is, to refuse a request to share a toy, to refuse a request to go to sleep, to refuse the request to eat some vegetables. During this stage of development, you'll hear your toddler use the word *no* and other negatives, such as *not*, in other ways. Imagine a toddler putting his hand into a toy box to find a toy cow, but instead he pulls out a toy horse. The path to the sophisticated sentence "This isn't a cow" begins with a simple indication of no (as the toddler shakes his head, throws the toy horse aside, and continues to reach into the box). He says "no" as if to say, "This is not what I expected!" Later he might say, "No cow" or "Not cow," and later still, he'll add the words *this* and *a*: "This not a cow." Finally, he'll insert the word *is* for the final version: "This isn't a cow."

Sentence Complexity

The complexity of a sentence is determined primarily by the verb(s) involved. During the stage of development when toddlers progress from simple verbs such as *go* or *run* to more complex verbs such as *think* or *promise* come changes in the complexity of the entire sentence. Just as single words turn into simple sentences, so do simple sentences turn into complex sentences that contain more than one verb. Initially, you'll hear sentences with the word *and* or *then* between the verbs, such as "I jump and run," "Sit down and play," "Pick this one, then get this one." These changes in sentence forms reflect not only the toddler's increasing language skills but also her increasing ability to talk about events in the past or future. Later she'll display her understanding of cause–effect relationships by using sentences such as "He's crying because he lost the toy." Toward the end of your toddler's third year of life, the verbs that represent advanced concepts also will be used in longer sentences, such as "I didn't see her do it," or "I think she's pretty," or "Mommy said to go."

Using Groups of Sentences

Just as your toddler is learning to link ideas within sentences, so too is he starting to link ideas *across* sentences. Around age three, toddlers begin talking about events using two or three sentences that are related to the same topic. For example, a toddler might talk about a snack time event by saying, "We eat popcorn. We watch TV. We drink juice." These sentences, although they might not be in the exact order the actions took place, demonstrate the toddler's understanding that those actions together represented a situation or event experienced. As your toddler matures and garners more experiences with familiar events, you will find that the actions discussed will be in the right time order as well. This ability to talk about situations in the correct time sequence will lay the groundwork for your toddler's ability to tell and understand stories in the next few years.

Your toddler should be moving from deleting sounds to substituting sounds to using correct sounds.

What About Speech Development?

During the babbling and first-word stages of development, your toddler likely used words with speech sounds that are relatively easier to produce, such as *p, b, n,* and *w.* As we said in chapters 1 and 2, most of his productions were probably one-syllable words, with some two-syllable words used occasionally. Now you'll see all of the other speech sounds appear in the words he uses. During this stage of language development, your toddler will make astounding progress in the area of speech. During the second year of life, you probably had to interpret at least half of what he said to those nice strangers in the grocery store or even the grand-parents. However, your toddler's speech will improve to be almost completely understandable by everyone. Researchers in toddler speech development have found that most three-year-olds are understandable about 75 percent of the time. By age four, this increases to 90 percent or even higher.

Typical "Errors"

You know that when toddlers begin talking, their production of phrases such as *little red wagon* will not be totally correct in terms of speech sound use; what they might actually say is "wittle wed wagon." Let's face it—some sounds and words are just harder to say than others. Yet toddlers will need some of those tricky words in order to communicate. In chapter 2, we talked about how some one-year-olds may actually avoid words that contain sounds that are harder to make. However, two- and three-year-olds can't "afford" to keep avoiding words—they just have too much to say!

So what's the toddler to do with this "mismatch" between her ability to articulate and the difficulty of words that she wants to use? Well, she does the best she can. The young two-year-old might leave off final sounds (*si* for *sit*) or syllables (*e-fant* for *elephant*). Later these word parts will be included, but she'll still leave off parts of consonant blends (two or more consonants said together), such as saying *tick* for *stick* and *bu* for *blue*. In addition to deleting speech sounds, toddlers also substitute easier sounds for harder ones. It is easier for most toddlers to make the *t, d, p, b, m, n,* and *w* speech sounds and harder to make the *k, g, s, z, sh, ch, j, r,* and *l* sounds. Consequently, you're likely to hear your toddler substituting sounds from the first group for speech sounds for those in the last group.

It's important to keep in mind that your toddler should be moving from deleting sounds to substituting sounds to using correct sounds. Although many of the two-year-old's "errors" will be deletions, by the time she is three most of her "errors" should be substitutions. Further, some substitutions are cause for more concern than others. For example, substituting a *th* sound for an *s* sound wouldn't necessarily be a cause for concern in a three-year-old. However, substituting a *w* sound for the *s* would. In chapter 11, we will discuss what you can do if you're worried about whether your toddler's speech sound errors might be signals of a potential problem.

Social Language Skills

You will see major changes in your toddler's ability to use language to interact with those around him during his toddler years. One of the main reasons for this increase is that the other areas of language (speech sounds, word and sentence use) become so much better. It's easier to carry on a conversation with someone you can understand! Your toddler can tell you what's on his mind more effectively because he knows more words and can use better grammar.

At the same time, there are specific changes that occur as a result of your toddler's increasing knowledge about communication interactions. We get a lot of "unspoken" clues from people during conversations. For example, in most Western cultures, we know that eye contact usually means that the person to whom we're talking is listening, and conversely, a lack of eye contact, or looking away, typically means that the person isn't interested in carrying the conversation further. We also know to wait until our partner stops talking before making our own comments. Your toddler will begin to pick up on these clues, too. A busy parent will often hear, "Mommy, look at me!" when she is trying to continue doing household chores while her toddler is telling her something! Such requests offer evidence for the toddler's appreciation of the role that eye contact plays in conversational exchanges. Keep in mind, though, for some cultures, direct eye contact may not be encouraged—and a toddler will learn that, too!

As we said in chapter 2, babies use words that refer to the here and now. They talk about people, things, and events that are occurring at that time, in that place. Toddlers, on the other hand, begin to use language to talk about past or future events and about things or people that aren't in their immediate environment.

Toddlers first use language referring to the past, or the there and then, by discussing familiar events that tend to be associated with common routines. We call these scripted events. For example, most toddlers become familiar with a certain routine for bedtime, bath time, and later, birthday parties and fast-food restaurants.

The ability to talk about situations in the correct time sequence will lay the groundwork for your toddler's ability to tell and understand stories in the next few years.

Having a script for an event allows your toddler to "concentrate" more on what happens during that time, making it easier to learn the new language involved in that situation. He can predict how actions occur and what objects should be used, and thus, he can attend to the details of the situation. However, these expectations for what *should* occur may sometimes cause this finer, detailed learning to not occur if those expectations are not met. For example, when Nick was young, he had a script for birthday parties that involved, besides cake and presents, breaking open a piñata. This occurred because the first few birthday parties he attended had this activity. When he attended his first "non-piñata" party, he was unsure what to think and spent a great deal of time wondering about the piñata rather than learning what he could from the party. This example is given not to encourage you to never have variations in the activities in which your toddler is involved; rather, it is used to explain why some toddlers may not seem to understand or learn as much from one experience as they might from others.

Toddlers also begin to make more and more comments that relate to what their conversational partner, the person to whom they are speaking, said beforehand. During the one-word stage, babies pretty much "run the show." If the baby's one-word sentence relates to his conversational partner's, it's because the partner is following the *baby's* lead, not vice versa. Toddlers, on the other hand, do follow their partner's lead at times and comment on what was said before they add new information to the conversation. Additionally, toddlers are able to contribute more to conversations, sometimes saying two or three sentences before their partner says something else.

One of our favorite developmental changes during the third and fourth years of life involves the way toddlers talk differently based on their conversational partner. Older children and adults have many different styles or ways of speaking, and they use the style that is most fitting for a

> *Toddlers often use a different register when speaking to babies or animals. They tend to use a higher pitch with a more singsong rhythm.*

given situation. For example, you might use one style of conversing with a potential business client or your boss (respectful, formal, polite, reserved) and a different style if conversing with a close friend (chatty, informal, slang). During the toddler years, we begin to see a glimpse of this style change across conversational situations. In chapter 2, we talked about a special language style or register called child-directed speech (CDS). Interestingly, toddlers often use a different register when speaking to babies or animals. They tend to use a higher pitch with a more singsong rhythm. In other words, they use aspects of CDS. At the end of the toddler period, many toddlers use a third register for speaking to adults. Their language may be a little more formal, polite, or complex when speaking to an adult than when speaking to a peer.

At times, when two or more individuals are talking, there is a need for one of the individuals to clarify, or restate, what he has just said because it was not clearly stated or simply there was too much background noise. Typically, restating what was said occurs when another individual asks him to clarify, using either gestures (a perplexed look) or language ("What?" "Where did he go?" "Who did that?"). Your toddler is starting to learn how to use both of these skills. On the one hand, she is learning to ask for clarification. She may do this by saying, "What? Huh?" or by scrunching up her face. On the flip side, she also is learning, during these third and fourth years of life, to clarify or revise what she has said when her conversational partner is confused. Initially, she will do this by saying the same word or words again but attempting to articulate them more precisely, such as the following:

CHILD: "A fit."

MOTHER: "A what?"

CHILD: "A fish."

Soon, however, she will develop an additional strategy for clarifying her language. In addition to saying the word more accurately, she will know how to substitute a word for the word in question, such as the following:

CHILD: "I got a Ranger."

FRIEND: "What did you get?"

CHILD: "A car. A Ranger."

There are two final developments that occur in the area of social language during the toddler years worth noting. Have you ever considered how tricky it would be to explain to another person when to use terms such as *I/you, mine/yours,* and *here/there*? There's a technical word for such terms, *deixis,* and it refers to words that change depending on the perspective of the speaker. For example, when a mother refers to her shoe, she says "my shoe"; yet everyone else who wants to talk to her about her shoe must say "your shoe." It's a clear case of different words being used to refer to exactly the same thing. However, they can't be interchanged. The mother can't refer to her shoe as "your shoe" and no one else can call it "my shoe." Yet when referring to some other specific shoe, Mom must say "your shoe" and someone else out there must say "my shoe." We warn you—thinking about such things can give you a headache if you do it too long! Our point here is that toddlers seem to rather effortlessly understand and employ this principle of changing words depending on the person or location. They rarely confuse such terms. Isn't that amazing and quite impressive?

The final example of your toddler's incredible ingenuity as a language learner is in the area of ellipsis, which refers to leaving unnecessary words out of your sentences. Consider the following scenario:

> **CUSTOMER:** "I'll have the steak with a baked potato and salad."
>
> **WAITER:** "How would you like that cooked?"
>
> **CUSTOMER:** "Medium rare."
>
> **WAITER:** "What kind of dressing would you like?"
>
> **CUSTOMER:** "Ranch."
>
> **WAITER:** "Do you want butter and sour cream?"
>
> **CUSTOMER:** "Only butter."

Both of these speakers are using ellipsis throughout this exchange. Each speaker chooses words to include or exclude based on what he expects the other person to know or what's already happened in the conversation. Here's how the same exchange might look without ellipsis:

> **CUSTOMER:** "For my meal, I would like you to ask the chef to prepare a steak, baked potato, and salad. When they're ready, I'd like you to bring them to my table so that I can eat them."
>
> **WAITER:** "I'll certainly take care of sharing your order with the chef and then transporting the food back to your table. However, first I have some questions for you. Your steak can be cooked to several levels of doneness—including well done, medium, medium rare, and rare. Which level would you prefer?"
>
> **CUSTOMER:** "I'd like my steak cooked to the medium-rare level of doneness."
>
> **WAITER:** "You're having a salad and salads are usually served with dressing, which is a liquid-like substance that is mixed in

with the salad. We have six kinds of dressing: French, Thousand Island, Italian, blue cheese, ranch, and honey mustard. What kind of dressing would you like with your salad?"

CUSTOMER: "I'd like ranch dressing to be mixed in with my salad."

WAITER: "Customers often like to put butter, sour cream, and even chives on their baked potatoes. Do you want any of these extras?"

CUSTOMER: "I only want butter for my baked potato. I don't want sour cream or chives."

Obviously, this second exchange would be ridiculous. Frankly, it would waste time and waste words. Toddlers pick up on this quite early in their lives. In fact, perhaps the *only* time a toddler violates this use of ellipsis is when a well-meaning but misguided adult asks a toddler to "say the whole thing" when the child has been asked, for example, "Where will you go?" and he responds appropriately with an elliptical answer, "To the store." There is one obvious point to be made here, then: Don't expect toddlers, or anyone for that matter, to answer questions like this with anything but an appropriate, shortened version of the answer.

Helping Your Toddler Build Language

During this period of language development, perhaps more than in any period of his life thus far, you will see leaps and bounds in what your toddler is learning to say. If you are like us, you will be constantly amazed at what your toddler can express on his own. He seems to be a sponge, soaking up everything that people are saying and then using similar ideas, sentence structures, and vocabulary words in new and creative ways. You are a major source of knowledge and learning for your toddler. Almost anywhere and anytime, you will be providing the fertilizer for his blossoming skills.

Let's talk about some specific ideas to show you the effect you can have on your toddler's development.

Reading Time

We know you've been reading to your toddler for some time. As you undoubtedly have been discovering as he matures, his capacity to sit and listen to your book reading and his ability to understand more complicated stories are increasing. For toddlers, your book selections should be moving away from picture books that encourage labeling and moving toward books that involve some type of sequence of events. Many times, these books represent events that occur in your toddler's life. Book reading now will help your toddler learn more than just words. By reading these types of books to your toddler, you can begin to increase his understanding of more complicated sentence structures and his understanding for how to relate information in a time-ordered, logical manner.

Before you worry about how many times you must read a book to your toddler, relax. We can almost guarantee that your toddler will determine which books should be read repeatedly.

Books, beyond those simple picture books, typically include sentence structures and vocabulary words that may not be as familiar or frequently used as those your toddler hears day to day. Multiple readings of these books provide a new way for your toddler to learn about sentence structure and words. Note here that we say multiple readings. Before you worry about how many times you must read a book to your toddler, relax. We can almost guarantee that your toddler will determine which books should be read repeatedly. For whatever reason, toddlers tend to enjoy certain books over others. These preferred books, and the subsequent multiple readings of those books, then build in the redundancy needed to encourage good learning.

Consider the following example. Nick's dad was reading a children's book featuring two characters from *Sesame Street*. In the book, the text was written in a dialogue format: " 'Let's go to the park!' Bert said. 'Fine idea,' replied Ernie."

After having read the books approximately 5,247 times, Nick's dad, in order to maintain his sanity, decided to drop the *said*s and *replied*s and simply tell the story in the characters' voices. The following exchange ensued:

> DAD (in character's voice): "Let's go to the park!"
>
> NICK: "Bert said."

While Nick was not asked to provide the rest of the written sentence, and indeed that was the point of the reading, he was showing that the multiple readings of this book had helped him learn certain sentence structures and how to say them, at least in these situations where the sentence was "co-created" by him and his dad. This example also shows his awareness that the book was dictating what should be said (but we will talk more about that in chapter 4). What is important overall is that reading to your toddler, just as talking to him throughout the day, is a valuable language-learning experience.

Book reading also helps toddlers better understand how important the sequence of events is for telling stories and how we expect a story to occur in a certain logical, time-ordered sequence. If you are reading about a trip to the zoo, one would expect to read about preparing for the trip, arriving at the zoo, possibly paying for entry, and viewing of the animals. Indeed, there may be more "steps" in the process, but undoubtedly the event will unfold somewhat in this order. By reading books to your toddler, then, you are reemphasizing how events occur.

As you read a story about a familiar event, or are rereading a book that he has heard several times, you can stop and ask your toddler what will happen next. For example, using the zoo trip story from above, you might stop after reading about arriving at the zoo, and either make a "guess" or ask your toddler about what will happen next. This allows him to see that certain events must occur in a certain order. Sometimes it is fun to provide the wrong answer ("Next, they get ready to go") and have your toddler correct you with the right information ("No, Mom. They pay money."). These types of experiences help him to think about and then talk about events he has experienced, doing so in a logical, sequential manner.

Playtime

Your toddler is definitely active. Whoever said running a marathon was easier than following a toddler around during play was right! This is why it is easy to spot the parent of a toddler. If you have been following our advice from chapter 2, you've been trying to follow your toddler's communication lead, focusing on the topics in which she is interested and commenting on her actions and words. As you run around trying to follow this rule of thumb, we have some other suggestions for you to consider that reflect the new language skills your toddler is acquiring.

First, as in all phases of development, you want to be a good modeler of language. This means that when your toddler says a word, phrase, or whole sentence, you want to expand on what she has said. So, if your toddler says, "I like candy," you can say, "You like candy? Yeah, you like all kinds of candy, don't you?" or something to that effect. Remember, by focusing on your toddler's ideas and expanding

on those ideas, you are showing her what she says is important and that she can say even more as her communication
skills increase.

Playtime also is an excellent time to expose your toddler
to new words and phrases. This will happen naturally. As
you play with your toddler, it will be tempting to move into
a "teaching mode." With such a sponge, it seems only appropriate to teach and then test what she is learning. Many
parents at this point try, either because it seems appropriate
or, more likely, because they feel pressure from relatives or
the media, to teach certain concepts, such as colors, opposites, and letters, to name a few. While your toddler most
definitely needs to learn these concepts, *how* she learns
them may be very natural or unnatural depending on the
process.

Take, for example, opposite word pairs, such as *hot* and
cold, *up* and *down*, *big* and *little*. When toddlers are learning these types of words, they typically do not learn them
together. That would indeed be a difficult task. To understand opposite pair words, a toddler must understand that
the word pair represents a continuum, a progression of that
concept, and that each word represents one end of that continuum. For *hot* and *cold*, a toddler must understand that
both words represent temperature and that *hot* is at one
end of that continuum of heat whereas *cold* is at the other
end. Thus, because of this difficult task, most toddlers will
learn to talk about the concept (temperature) with one of the
opposite words (*hot*) before they begin to use the opposite
word. In fact, before acquiring the second member of that
pair, many toddlers will either refrain from referring to the
other end of the continuum or use a phrase such as *not-hot* or
no-big, and so forth.

Like opposites, the same can be said for color terms. During the second and third years of life, many toddlers are
developing an understanding that words like *red*, *green*, and

yellow refer to the color or hue of items. When you think about it, this is no easy task. Color is not an easy concept to talk about, especially because of the great variability in shades (just think about all the different shades of blue in our world). Thus, initially, all your toddler may know about color words is that they are to be used to talk about a feature of an object. Because of this, it is not uncommon for toddlers to label a red sweater as "the blue one." Knowing that your child has already accomplished the great feat of talking about color may help keep you from panicking that your toddler is color blind or won't be ready for school, even though she is only two or three years old.

Finally, letters of the alphabet are particular targets of parental teaching. We would never argue against helping your child learn the letters of the alphabet. As you will see in the next chapter, knowledge of letter names and the sounds they make is highly important. But the same caution about teaching that we gave for other concepts above is true for letter learning as well. Incorporate letters into play instead of drilling your toddler.

So what are we suggesting you do during playtime? Just as the word suggests, during playtime, *play* with your toddler. You can't teach your toddler language, and language is not just colors, numbers, letters, and specific concepts like hot and cold. Incorporate these concepts into play rather than making them the focus of a specific activity—unless, of course, your toddler shows a preference for this. When you are playing with trucks and cars with your toddler, your expansions of his words and phrases can include the color word for that object ("Go truck? Yes, there goes the yellow truck."). You can line up the cars in the garage, confirming you have all of them together ("One, two, three trucks. Yep, they are all here."). You can even comment on similarities in the letters seen on toys ("Look! This truck has a T on the license plate, just like this one does."). Of course, there is nothing wrong with singing songs or saying rhymes that involve these concepts, because, again, the focus is on fun and play rather than on showing success on a parent-devised test. As we state in our major points in the introduction: Don't teach language development, facilitate it.

Outing Times

As you can probably guess, the strategies we have talked about for book reading and playtime are equally useful for times when you go out on the town with your toddler. There are additional strategies you can use during these times, though, that may help strengthen your toddler's understanding and communication of events.

The first time your toddler experiences an event (her first time to eat at a restaurant, her first movie, or her first trip to the circus), all the new people, objects, and actions that she is experiencing can be somewhat overwhelming. Remember your first day in high school or college? It probably was somewhat confusing. What you were supposed to do? What were all the papers you were given called? If you had been required to talk about that first day, we bet it would not have been an easy task. The same is true for your child. However, you can make these initial experiences easier for your toddler to learn and discuss. Before you go to a new place, talk about what will happen. As you are involved in the actual event, discuss with your toddler what is happening. After the event is over, revisit it and remember aloud with your child all the people, objects, and actions that occurred. Finally, do this frequently for the same event. Through repeated exposures and experiences, your toddler will develop a better understanding of the important components of these events, the actions that occur, and how they occur, which will enable her to share this information in a more logical, correctly ordered manner.

Chapter Summary

During the second and third years of life, your toddler has completed a great accomplishment: She has cracked the code for building sentences; she has developed excellent strategies for being a conversationalist; she says her speech sounds correctly. Through your guidance and care, coupled with your knowledge of how language develops, you have helped her along that path of learning. She now is preparing to move into another important phase of the language-learning process. In chapter 4, you will not only learn what else she is developing for her spoken language skills, but you will begin to understand what you can do to help her in the development of her written language skills: reading and writing. Are you as ready as she will be?

4

PREPARING FOR WRITTEN LANGUAGE: SETTING YOUR PRESCHOOLER ON THE RIGHT PATH

DID YOU KNOW?

- Five-year-old children are like mini-adults in their speech and language skills.

- Kindergarten children tell stories with actual plots.

- Rhyming is an important building block for reading.

Pat and Casey both worked out of the home. They had the usual challenges of hardworking parents trying to hold down their jobs while raising their five-year-old daughter. Life was hectic. They worried that they didn't spend enough time with Annie to teach her what she needed to know before going into kindergarten. Sure, they read to her at night, but was that enough? They felt guilty because the time spent with her involved doing everyday routines or errands, with only some time devoted to direct play with her. Because of this guilt, they invented special games or activities to make up for lost "quality" time. When Pat had to take Annie grocery shopping instead of staying home and reading, Pat asked Annie to cross out the items as they put them in the cart. When Casey felt guilty writing the bills instead of playing with Annie, Casey had Annie help put stamps on the envelopes to keep her occupied. When the parents took their daughter to the kindergarten screening day, they were nervous that the teachers would find she knew less than her peers. Imagine their shock when the teachers marveled that Annie knew some of her letters and how to "read" from left to right. Pat and Casey hadn't taught Annie these things. How did she learn all of this?

Your child has learned an incredible amount of language by the time he turns four. In fact, as you will see, he is soon to be considered adultlike in the complexity of his sentence structure and in the ways he interacts with others. His vocabulary continues to become more sophisticated and varied. As your child blossoms into a true conversationalist, you will find that you begin to emphasize another aspect of language, one that you know will be needed as your child enters formal schooling. This new area of language will be the written word.

Although we have talked mostly about what your child is learning about spoken language, and will continue to do that in this chapter, you will find that your child is also beginning to show signs of learning about reading and writing. Some of this learning may be overt. She may "read" books, saying sentences word for word as you have read them in her favorite book a thousand times. She may also begin to write her name or other simple words that she sees frequently. She is acquiring some other skills that will help her with written language; they may not be as obvious, yet they are equally important. These skills include learning to rhyme, knowing the names of letters, and so on. Reading, writing, and spelling skills are rapidly developing in conjunction with spoken language during these years, and this chapter will cover all

She may "read" books, saying sentences word for word as you have read them in her favorite book a thousand times.

the basics of this important phase. There are so many ways that you can help your child develop these written language skills using our easy, everyday activities!

Further Developing Spoken Language Skills

During her fourth and fifth years, your preschooler will be refining certain language skills she has been using for some time while also learning new spoken language skills. These new developments occur in all areas of language, including semantics (meaning), speech sounds, grammar, and social language skills.

Sentence Structure and Grammar

Your child's sentence structures should be quite varied and complex at this age. Many of his sentences should contain more than one verb, such as "I want to go now!" or "I know how to do that." Your child's use of these sentences and his understanding of them are important for several reasons. First, when your child uses these types of sentences, it allows him to convey much more information within shorter amounts of time. More complex relationships among thoughts can be expressed. In addition, by the time your child is about seven years old, he will be reading complex sentences in books. With solid understanding and use of these types of sentences, his ability to understand what he reads will be enhanced.

Along with sentence structure, you also will hear your child use word endings that sound quite mature. Even though your child has been using special endings on words for a year or so, such as the *-ing* ("I'm eating"), the *-s* ("He jumps"; "Billy's swimming"), and the *-ed* ("She walked to the park"), new and more advanced word beginnings and endings will develop. A good example of this occurred one day when Nick was asking his dad to wind up a toy motorcycle. Having discussed that each time the motorcycle raced across the floor it was "rad," he turned to his dad and asked him to wind it up again so that it would go "radly." This example actually demonstrates two points. Nick was learning to attach the *-ly*, an ending that is learned during these years to change an adjective or noun (*friend*) to an adverb (*friendly*). This example also demonstrates another point we have made and will continue to make throughout this book: Your preschooler is not just a little robot, imitating everything you say. Rather, your preschooler is actively learning the rules of speech and language, constructing the rules based on what he hears every day. What a genius!

Speech Sounds

Your preschooler's speech skills also are nearing adult level. She continues to be highly understandable to others. True, she may still be trying to correctly produce her *r*, but she has mastered other difficult sounds like *s*, *z*, *ch*, *sh*, and consonant combinations, such as *st*, *ms*, and the like. By the end of their sixth year, most children will have even corrected their *r*. Children in their fourth and fifth years still may "trip up" on longer words, words that have several syllables in them, like *Cinderella*, *spaghetti*, and *aluminum*. But seriously, how many of us still say *cimmanon* for cinnamon?

Vocabulary

As in the previous four years, your child's vocabulary continues to grow by leaps and bounds every day. In fact, vocabulary development will likely never stop. (We bet you have even learned some new words reading this book!) But your child's development in vocabulary this year is more than just new words. He is increasing his ability to express new meanings. For example, he now is able to use verbs that express communication acts, such as *tell*, *say*, and *talk*. While this may seem insignificant, it is actually quite important. Not only can your child use this new meaning to tattle ("I'm telling Mommy! He said a bad word!"), but it also allows your child to talk about language itself, a skill we will address later in this chapter.

He now begins to use language in different ways, often as subtle ways to get what he wants!

Finally, your child is expanding his meanings of words that he already has learned. For example, your child may have learned the word *first* in relation to his older brother's grade in school. Now he is learning that the same word can signify other meanings, such as being first in line or the first word of a book. Taken as a whole, then, your child's meaning system, semantics, is not only growing in size, but it is deepening in meaning as well. Amazing, isn't it?

Social Language Skills

Perhaps more than in any other area of language, this year your child is really refining his social language skills. While he has already begun using appropriate eye contact, topic skills, and turn-taking skills, he now begins to use language in different ways, often as subtle ways to get what he wants! Children who are four and five years old are developing the ability to use indirect language and hints. These language skills involve implying a certain meaning even when the words used do not state that meaning. A common example is the use of "politeness forms" when requesting an object. For example, during this time your child will learn to ask for music by saying, "Can I turn on the radio?" Now even though the ornery parent or two may say, "I don't know, can you?" we all know that your child is not asking whether he has the potential to turn on the radio. Rather, he is expressing his wants. Because your preschooler has learned that "softening" requests often gets him better results, he begins to construct these types of sentences. Sometimes it seems that these sentences happen more with others than with his own mom and dad. You may experience times when a neighbor or friend says, "Your daughter is so polite. She always asks for things in such a nice way." And you feel yourself asking, "Who? My daughter?"

Besides demonstrating politeness, skills such as using hints and indirect language also allow children to say what they want to say, without saying it specifically. When Nick was four years of age, he was being particularly stubborn about wearing his parka zipped up to the neck. Because it was bitterly cold outside, his mother kept insisting that it be zipped. After battling back and forth (he would unzip, she would insist he zip it up), she stated that he would need to go inside if he unzipped one more time. Not wishing to go inside but still needing to express how he felt, he waited a minute and then began to verbalize his aversion to the jacket: "Ahem, mmm, boy, this jacket is tight. . . . (cough) . . . This jacket makes it hard to breathe . . . (hack)." Through his indirect language and his hinting, he was able to express his dislike of the situation and yet still play outside. As your child reaches this age, you will soon see how he can masterfully manipulate language to meet his needs. And you were excited when he said his first word!

Your child also is developing a much more sophisticated way of responding to requests for clarification. Recall that this skill is highly important for maintaining a conversation. If one person in a conversation asks for clarification and the other person does not respond with an understandable or useful clarification, the conversation goes nowhere (but downhill, that is). Up until now, your child should have been using two highly effective clarification strategies: changing how he says a word (saying it more clearly) and changing the word in question to an easier-to-understand word. Now, during his fourth and fifth years of life, he should be adding a new strategy to his arsenal. When asked to clarify what he just said, your child should also be able to change the whole sentence structure to help another person understand. For example, when Genevieve was four, she was talking to her parents in the car. Noticing a particularly beautiful mountain range out her window, she said, "Look at the Canadia mountains!" Her parents, not quite understanding her, said, "What?" She replied: "Those mountains over there. The Canadia ones. Look at them." Thus, she was able to help her listener understand what she was saying and the conversation continued successfully.

As your child develops in her fourth and fifth years, other social language skills that continue to develop and mature include her ability to maintain a topic (i.e., without your help) and move from topic to topic with very subtle yet understandable ways. This latter skill, sometimes called topic shading, usually occurs when an individual is talking with someone with whom she is quite familiar. For example, "listen" to the following conversation, which occurred in the car between Caitlin and her friend Audrey. Notice how many different topics are covered, yet the movement from one topic to another is very subtle.

CAITLIN: "I want to get some new shoes at the mall."

AUDREY: "Me, too. I saw some new shoes on TV."

CAITLIN: "Yeah, and you know what else? I also saw they have new surprises in kids' meals at McDonald's."

AUDREY: "Yeah, you know, Joey really likes McDonald's, mostly because of the play area."

CAITLIN: "I like that play area, too. Joey is really into Power Ranger stuff, huh?"

AUDREY: "Uh-huh. Some of them are cute, but not as cute as Miss Kitty stuff."

CAITLIN: "Oh, that's my favoritest thing. We went to Seattle and I went to a whole store that had that. Seattle is a fun place to go."

AUDREY: "I love going to Seattle because we always stop and get a TCBY on the way down."

CAITLIN: "Yummy! My favorite flavor there is white chocolate. What about you?"

AUDREY: "My favorite is double-Dutch chocolate."

As you can see, these two friends had quite the conversation. While some may listen to this and be amused about the constant "chatter" between the two young girls, one can look at this short conversational excerpt and actually see how sophisticated it is. Both children took responsibility for keeping the conversation going. Both easily segued from one topic to another. In total, there were five topics covered (the mall/shoes, McDonald's, Joey, Seattle, and TCBY), but because each friend relied on her knowledge of the other and what she already knew, the movement from one topic to the next was smooth and hardly noticeable. In situations such as this, you as a parent are able to view firsthand the incredible social language skills that your child is acquiring and using.

Storytelling Skills

In chapter 3, we talked about your child's ability to link several thoughts and sentences about an event in a time-ordered

Around the age of five, there will seem to be a "plot" to her stories or descriptions of experiences she has had.

fashion. During years four and five, she will begin to expand on this ability. Around the age of five, your child will begin to show some cause and effect in the stories she tells. In other words, there will seem to be a "plot" to her stories or descriptions of experiences she has had. At first, however, this will occur only when she's talking about events with which she has had lots of experiences. Let's provide an example. Consider this story told by Genevieve when she was five. She was asked to tell a story about some children who went to a jungle. She said:

"Once upon a time, there was two kids who went to a jungle. And when they came to the jungle, they had to pay some money. So they didn't have any money, so they went home, get some money, steal money from their mom's purse, come back to the . . . zoo and give him the money and he would give them some food to feed the animals. So they walked along and then that's the end."

As you can read in this example, Genevieve's story has a plot, a cause and effect. In her story, the problem, which was the lack of money, caused the children to get the money, which caused them to be able to get some animal food. This story was not only in the correct time sequence, but it also had the more mature cause and effect that most adults are expecting to hear in a story such as this. One could argue that this story was pretty advanced for someone of Genevieve's age (and her father would agree!), because she was talking about a topic that was not that familiar to her: going to a jungle. But notice what she did. She turned the topic into one with which she had more experience: going to the zoo. (Of course, the hope is that the particular segment about stealing from the mother's purse was *unfamiliar!*)

Your preschooler will continue to grow in her storytelling abilities, as well as her general ability to talk about events, as she matures. Her stories will become more detailed and longer and will include more plots, not unlike the daytime soap operas on TV. Having been parents of teenagers, we can attest to the fact that with age, stories become much more complicated. But that's another book!

Helping Your Preschooler Refine His Spoken Language Skills

As we said earlier, your child is an active constructor of knowledge, figuring out most of the rules of language without your telling him. Granted, this probably would not happen if you weren't such a good model. And so, during the fourth and fifth years, you should continue to do what you have done in the past. Be an active listener and participant in the conversations he wants to have. Follow his lead in conversations, asking open-ended questions ("Tell me more"), which encourage him to elaborate on his topics. If he is still learning to produce certain sounds, provide good, accurate models of words containing the sounds he is misarticulating, without asking him to repeat the words. Talk daily about events and happenings in your life, so he can understand how people tend to talk about situations, especially when there is a causal aspect to the action (problem, action, solution). Remember, your role is not to sit down and teach your child language (could any of us stand to do that?). Instead, your role is to provide lots of good models of speech and language, using encouraging and supportive comments and feedback that create an atmosphere of trust, love, and understanding. This is the context in which we all want to learn, especially children. If you provide this kind of atmosphere, your child should find it much easier to grasp how he is supposed to communicate.

A "New" Language

By the time your child is five years of age, most language experts will say that she is adultlike in her spoken language skills. We agree with this. As you can see from the examples provided earlier, she has become quite the conversationalist. She has taken on the formidable task of learning how to communicate and made the task look easy. She now is gearing up for another difficult task, one that will lay the foundation for everything she does in school. She is getting ready to read and write. In her fourth and fifth years, your child will start to learn about written language in ways that will serve her well as she starts to learn to read, write, and spell.

The second half of this chapter will describe what she is learning about literacy during these years, how this knowledge will help your child when she starts to read and write, and what you can do as a parent to help her in that learning. You likely will notice something else different about how children learn this type of language. Spoken language was learned implicitly; that is, your child was picking up the rules of speech and language without any direct attention or teaching from you about those rules. When it comes to written language, your child will require active attention, instruction, and directed play to acquire this aspect of language. And you can serve as an instructor while continuing to make the learning fun and exciting.

Developing Foundational Skills for Literacy

During the first five years of life, your child is learning to speak language. However, ask him to talk or think about language he is learning, and he most likely will be stymied. What do we mean talk about language? Talking and thinking about language, often referred to as metalinguistics, means being able to treat our words, sentences, and rules of language as the topic of conversation. When we talk about how many words are in a sentence, we are talking about language. When we discuss how another individual has an "accent," we are talking about language. When we talk about a definition of a word, we are talking about language. All of these situations demonstrate metalinguistics, thinking and talking about language. Children five and under show limited abilities to do this metalinguistic thinking and talking.

As you read to her and point to the pictures or the words on the page, she is learning the differences between pictures and words.

During years three and four, your toddler may be showing some precursory skills to metalinguistics, such as using rhyming words or talking about the "funny way" certain people talk. But it won't be until he is closer to six years of age that he begins to understand how one can talk about language itself as a specific topic. Nevertheless, these precursory metalinguistic skills help to lay the foundation for later developing literacy skills. Let's talk about some specific skills.

Knowledge About Print

We hope you've been reading to your preschooler since she was a baby. As you have been reading, you have been talking about the pictures, relating them to your preschooler's life, and providing lots of readings of her favorite books. Perhaps you have noticed lately that your preschooler is starting to make comments about the books you read. She may be pointing to pictures of words you read. She may be tracing the sentences or words with her finger as you read them or as she "pretend" reads. You might observe her trying to write words, asking for letters. She might have even commented on how long her written name is (Genevieve) versus her other friend's (Mary). All of these comments and actions are signs that your preschooler is learning about print, the "stuff" that is written language. This developing knowledge will be a crucial component to developing her reading and writing skills. And the great thing about this is that you have played an important role in causing this to happen.

BOOK READING

During book-reading times, your preschooler will be learning a great deal about books and how they are used that you take for granted. For example, by watching you as you read to her, she is learning how to hold a book, how to turn pages, where the first page is, and how to wait until you are finished reading a page to turn to the next one. As you read to her and point to the pictures or the words on the page, she is learning the differences between pictures and words, how the "white spaces" between the groups of letters represent the end of one word and the beginning of the next, and that the book or reading material dictates to a great extent what words are said. In other words, the book establishes the topic of the conversation. Most parents and adults take these concepts for granted, but they are new to your preschooler and must be learned before she picks up a book to read for herself.

HIGH-PRINT ENVIRONMENTS

When children are in their third, fourth, and fifth years of life, they are not only noticing the objects and people around them, they also are beginning to notice that older individuals use certain objects to communicate with others. They see mom writing a note to an older brother and pinning it on the refrigerator, and they then see the older brother reading the note and performing a chore. They see dad making a grocery list and then using it at the grocery store. They see parents and siblings reading magazines, newspapers, bank

> *Follow his lead in conversations, asking open-ended questions ("Tell me more"), which encourage him to elaborate on his topics.*

statements, e-readers and tablets, and schoolbooks. They see family members typing on the computer and printing out their written product.

What are all these actions showing? Your preschooler is learning that language can be relayed via other modes of communication, *and* he is seeing that there is a purpose to these actions. Preschoolers who see others using the "tools" of written language (pencils, pens, paper, cell phones, computers, books, and so forth), and who observe how and why they are used (to remind, to inform, to pay, and so on), are learning about printed or written language. These types of home environments are called high-print environments because they facilitate the preschooler's ability to understand how and why printed material can be used to communicate. So next time you head off to the hardware store, take your preschooler with you. Show him your list. Point out each item as it is purchased and let him check it off the list. You are helping him learn a great deal about written language and you've got a great conversational partner with you as well.

LETTER KNOWLEDGE

Children as young as three may have some idea that letters represent language and that strings of them are generally used to write down language. It is not uncommon to see three- and four-year-old toddlers attempting to write letters on their artwork or a "letter to Daddy." As children reach the age of five, they have a much better idea of what letters represent. Coinciding with this is their growing understanding of letter names and letter–sound relationships. This letter–sound relationship knowledge, as we mentioned in chapter 1, is part of what we call orthographic knowledge.

As your preschooler enters her sixth year of life and is exposed to more book reading and additional high-print experiences, she will begin to actively use her knowledge of letter names and letter–sound relationships to write language on paper. Letter–name knowledge involves knowing the names of letters when she sees them. Letter–sound relationship means knowing the sound, or sounds, that a letter can make. Most preschoolers learn these letter names early by reading alphabet books or being actively taught letters by their parents. When preschoolers come from high-print environments, they also tend to learn about the "power" of letters: how letters stand for language, how to write them, and how letters differ from other scribbles and scratches made on paper. Encourage your preschooler to express herself in any way she chooses to write. While her inventions in word spellings may seem random or incorrect, she is learning and demonstrating a great deal of knowledge about written language.

Knowledge About Words

Your preschooler has learned many new words since he spoke his first word at the age of one. Indeed, there may be some words you wished he had not learned! However, as good as he is at using a variety of words, he is less able to think and talk about those words, such as defining them, what they look like, and how they are written. Let's go over a few examples.

Most children, before five or six, will be able to use a word or phrase but not be able to define or explain it when questioned. When Nick was three years old, he was playing with his dad, and suddenly said, "Cut it out." When asked what "cut it out" meant, he was unable to answer, even though he had just used that particular phrase correctly and appropriately. When his dad said, "Do you mean, cut it out, like with scissors?" he responded, "Yes." He was unable to think about what he was talking about, much less understand, the dual meaning of the words he was using.

Children before the age of five or six also have a difficult time separating an object from the name of the object. It seems for children in the first four to five years of life, the word that stands for an object is actually considered to be part of the object. For example, when a younger child is asked what a long word is, a typical response might be *hose* or *train* or even *alligator*. In the child's mind, the length of the object represents the length of the word. Using the one of the examples above, *train* would be called a long word because the physical item, train, has many cars attached to it. Thus, the child is not thinking about the word itself (how long it takes to say it, how many letters we use to write it) but rather what the object it represents looks like. You may even see this same confusion in your preschooler's early attempts at spelling. He may spell his dad's name with many letters, but his baby sister's name with only one or two. After all, his dad is bigger so his name should contain more letters. On the other hand, his sister is small so her name should contain only a few letters. Although your preschooler may be making a mistake, his approach makes a lot of sense!

Remember, being able to think and talk about speech sounds is not the same as correctly using speech sounds.

As he moves from his fifth year to his sixth year of life, you will find that your preschooler starts to recognize that words are separate from the objects to which they refer. He will begin to recognize that the length of a word, both in the way it sounds and is written, determines whether we call it long or short. This skill is highly important for literacy development. As he begins to write, his attempts to spell words will more closely represent what the word should look like. Ask your preschooler questions like, "What's a long word?" and "Why is *alligator* a long word?" You will be fascinated with his answer as you begin to determine where he is in developing his metalinguistic knowledge of words.

Knowledge About Sounds

This area of metalinguistics is crucial for children to learn. As you will see, without the ability to think and talk about the sounds of our language, a child is seriously at risk for experiencing difficulties learning to read and write. Remember, being able to think and talk about speech sounds is not the same as correctly using speech sounds (your preschooler has been doing that for a while). Rather, this area of new knowledge will involve actively talking about and playing with speech sounds and parts of words as one would play with a toy. This knowledge of sounds, most often referred to broadly as phonological awareness, will develop gradually, with children first thinking about large chunks of sounds (such as syllables) and then about individual sounds. The sequence of development is fairly similar for almost all children.

Initially, children first start treating the speech sounds of our language as toys when they catch on to rhyming. This may occur as early as three years of age. By five, however, it is expected that preschoolers can rhyme. Rhyming involves thinking of or recognizing two or more words that sound the same at the end of the word. For example, *cat, hat, pat,* and *rat* all rhyme. While this grouping of rhyming words might seem rather simplistic, for a preschooler to recognize this, she must be aware that all four of those words end with the same set of sounds: *at.* She must focus on the word, not the word meaning. This is not an easy task, which is why preschoolers develop these "preliteracy" skills much later than they do their spoken language skills. For example, when Nick was about three years of age, he seemed to have some understanding of rhyming but was missing a crucial component. He would often approach someone (anyone who would listen!) and regale the person with his expertise in rhyming: "I can rhyme. Listen. Elephant. Elephant. See? They rhyme."

After rhyming, the next phonological awareness skill preschoolers generally develop involves knowing the number of words in a sentence. For example, a preschooler might recognize that "I like to eat sandwiches" contains five words. This skill might seem out of place in a discussion of preschoolers' phonological awareness, or knowledge of speech sounds, but it fits here. Perhaps the best way to understand this is to consider the times when you have heard someone speaking a different language than your own. For most of us, we think the person is a "quick talker" and we are hard pressed to understand where one word stops and another begins. This occurs because we are unfamiliar with the language, and we cannot use our knowledge of speech sounds to know which ones complete a word and which ones begin the next.

As your preschooler masters her ability to produce speech and language, she will begin to understand when a word stops and the next one begins. Using the example above, a preschooler without this understanding might say there are only four words in the sentence "I liketo eat sandwiches." In this case, the *to*, which carries very little meaning, is ignored. Similarly, another preschooler with less mature phonological awareness might say there are six words in the sentence "I like to eat sand wiches." Try this with your preschooler. If she is five, there is a good chance she will begin to "get it" and be able to count the number of words she hears in a simple sentence.

Children's phonological awareness continues to develop, such that they are able to count the number of syllables in words. Now most preschoolers (and some adults) are not familiar with what a syllable is. However, if provided an example (*"Baby"*—clap, clap—*"Baby* has two claps in it!"), the preschooler with this phonological awareness skill will catch on.

These early phonological awareness skills lay the foundation for future phonological awareness skills that are crucial for reading and spelling. Later, when your child is about five or six, she will be prepared to think about each speech sound in a word. Thinking about individual sounds is called phonemic awareness because children can actively think about phonemes, or single sounds. The ability to do think about sounds or phonemes, either to break up words into their individual speech sounds or to blend individual sounds together to form a word, is highly important for reading and spelling. That is, as a child begins to read in kindergarten or first grade, she will need to have some understanding that a series of letters represent sounds, and if you blend those sounds together (*c-a-t*), you get a word. Also, your preschooler will need to learn that to spell a word, she needs to think about the individual sounds she hears in the word (*bath* = *b, a, th*), and write down a letter or letters representing those sounds.

Both the skills discussed above and the examples provided help to reemphasize the difference between spoken and written language. When your preschooler was learning to speak, she didn't need to think about the sounds she was making. She didn't need to consider what a word was and whether it was represented by lots of letters or a few letters. However, as she begins to read and write, she will need to actively think about language. No wonder reading and spelling are such difficult tasks! For many children, they are the most challenging tasks of their entire school career. The positive side of this is that you have the potential to make that learning a bit easier. Let's talk about what you can do to ease this transition from learning spoken language to learning written language.

Helping Your Preschooler Learn About Literacy

The second half of this chapter discussed the many skills developing during the fifth and sixth years of life that can lay the groundwork for easier reading and writing development. You have read that unlike the development of spoken language, children need active, directed attention to written language to acquire these prerequisite skills. Does this mean you should be sitting down with your four- or five-year-old, quizzing him on his letters and teaching him rhyming pairs of words? Of course not! Your preschooler wants you to be his parent, not his teacher. However, you can still help your preschooler attend to written language in a way that highlights the important ideas he needs to learn while making this learning fun, enjoyable, and part of everyday situations. You have an important role to play in helping your preschooler learn about written language, but there is no reason you both can't have fun learning. We'll provide you with some ideas, although undoubtedly you will think of others.

There is one other important point to keep in mind, one that we have been emphasizing throughout the last three chapters. As we discuss language games you can play with your preschooler to help him develop these preliteracy skills, you want to repeatedly and frequently model the language concept you are showing your preschooler. Only after that might you occasionally ask your preschooler to demonstrate what he is learning. Keep in mind, for all of the suggestions below, the idea is to provide lots of rich learning experiences with your preschooler, not to "train" him to be a reader or writer. Remember, your role is to be a supportive parent who interacts, not interrogates.

Ideas for Around the House

Pretty much anything you do, in any place within the house, can be a literacy learning experience for you and your

Find some books that involve rhyming. Reading these types of books to your preschooler helps her to focus on the sounds of our language without requiring her to sit through a lesson on rhyming.

preschooler. Whether during more formal literacy situations, like reading to your child, or in less formal situations, such as making meals or doing chores, you can provide activities and experiences that will prove to be beneficial to your preschooler.

READING TIME

Undoubtedly, you've already realized the importance of reading to your preschooler. Reading to your preschooler will help develop both her spoken and written language skills. As we have mentioned before, reading can expand her vocabulary and enable her to learn different ways of saying the same thing. While all children's books are useful for helping your preschooler learn about spoken and written language, you may wish to think about more than the topic of the books as you read to your preschooler. For example, find some books that involve rhyming (titles by Dr. Seuss and Shel Silverstein or any book that emphasizes rhyming). By reading these books repeatedly to your preschooler, chances are she will catch on and begin to provide rhyming words before you can turn the page. Thus, reading these types of books to your preschooler helps her to focus on the sounds of our language without requiring her to sit through a lesson on rhyming.

You also might try to group together other books for reading that seem to contain simple plots involving problems, actions, and solutions. Many children's books will follow this format, perhaps with more than one problem–action–solution sequence. As you read and reread these books to your preschooler, engage her in the book-reading activity by pausing at logical points in the story and talking about what she and you think might happen next. This can help her to develop and use her understanding of cause and effect to predict or infer the plot of a story. If possible or appropriate, relate the story line to her own life. For example, you might engage her in a conversation about her experiences with the topic of the book or, after finishing the book, make up a new story that inserts her as the main character. These types of activities serve to increase her understanding of storytelling and help her prepare for the day when she begins to read books on her own and must "read between the lines" to help make sense of the information.

As you read to your four- and five-year-old preschooler, you also can begin to draw attention to the print on the paper and the speech sounds of our language. For example, as you read, you might, at logical stopping points, comment on how the character's name begins with the same sound as her name ("Kitty . . . That has a *k* sound, just like your name . . . Caitlin. Hmm, we use a *k* or a *c* to write the *k* sound.").

After finishing the book, you can review it, showing and then asking your preschooler about words that begin with certain letters or about words that seem exceptionally long. You also may find yourself occasionally drawing your finger across the sentence as you read to her. As you do this, you might time your pointing with the words you read, so that it becomes clearer where words begin and end. These different types of interactions help increase your preschooler's knowledge of sounds, print, and words.

MEALTIME

Most families, no matter how busy, inevitably end up being together for at least one mealtime a day. Though these times can be hectic amid the bustle of preparing dinner and talking about everyone's day, they also can be used as means for facilitating your preschooler's understanding of written language. For example, when the family is sitting down for breakfast, you can use the milk carton and some cereal as a way to develop knowledge of sounds, words, and print. Consider the following scenario:

> **FATHER:** "Look at this word: *milk*. It sure is a small word. Let's see how many letters are in that word."
>
> **CHILD:** (Father and child pointing to letters) "One, two, three, four. Four."
>
> **FATHER:** "Right! And it is short to say. *Milk* (clap). But look how much milk there is (holding up carton). Even though there is lots of milk, it has a short name. Now look at this word *Cheerios*. Let's count the letters in this word."
>
> **CHILD:** "One, two, three, four, five, six, seven, eight. Eight letters."
>
> **FATHER:** "Wow! Eight letters. And it takes a long time to say: *Cheer* (clap), *ri* (clap), *os* (clap). Three claps. But look at this one tiny Cheerio. It's so small. Even though it has a long name, it is so tiny!"

Simple discussions, such as this one about the length of words, help preschoolers understand that words are not part of the objects they name. This increases their metalinguistic knowledge of print and words.

Other games you might play at mealtime include a rhyming game, thinking of all the words that rhyme with your meal (*egg, leg, beg* . . .). The family can pick a letter of the day and see who can find the most occurrences of that letter on the bread bag. The ideas are endless. The point here is not to turn every mealtime into a quiz or lesson on words, sounds, and letters. Rather, it is to emphasize that a minute here or a minute there directed toward what you know about written language can lead to great payoffs in your preschooler's literacy development.

CHORE TIME

Even though we typically consider chores around the house as more of a burden than a pleasure, we actually can take advantage of those times to provide learning experiences for our children. For example, as you help your preschooler put away her toys, you can arrange the toys on the shelf by the length of the sound of their name rather than by size. As you wash the dishes, you can clap out the number of syllables you hear in the dishes and utensils you put in the dishwasher—"*Knife* (clap), *spat (clap) u (clap) la* (clap)." As you carry the laundry downstairs, use each step to say one word of a sentence—"*We* (step), *are* (step), *almost* (step), *done!* (step)." Your preschooler will be learning to play and talk about language while helping you accomplish the household chores. What a bargain!

Ideas when Traveling

When we were growing up, both of us were part of families who played alphabet games in the car. These games involved finding words on street signs or billboards that began with an *a*, then a *b*, and so on through the alphabet. We played games that required us to rhyme words with objects that one of our siblings saw and called out. Unbeknownst to us, we were learning about print and the sounds letters make as we played these games. It seems that these games have gone by the wayside for many families. Even though we would like to start a movement to bring them back (turn off the DVDs in the family car!), these games are not the only ones that you can play with your preschooler that will help her to learn about written language. In fact, your play with words can occur without any reference to what is outside of the car. When her dad was taking Genevieve to early piano lessons, they would play a game that involved thinking of different definitions of a word. For example:

DAD: "Block. Like blocks kids play with, we live on a block. He's a blockhead."

GENEVIEVE: "Pet. I have a pet. I pet Wendy."

Other games can be those that model and ask children to think of opposites of words (*hot–cold*) or categories of words (dogs: Lab, poodle, wiener dog . . .). These games encourage your preschooler not only to use words in a sentence but to actually think about the words themselves—and thereby practice her metalinguistic skills. And as we have said, these skills provide an excellent groundwork for literacy.

Ideas when Shopping

Shopping can be a time when you just want to buy your groceries or clothes and get home, especially when your preschooler is asking for a pretzel or money to ride the mini-carousel outside the store. However, you again can turn this outing into a fun-filled learning time for your pre-schooler. Before heading off for the store, make a list, but write the list in front of your preschooler. Talk aloud as you write the list. Your list writing might sound like the following:

> *"Let's see . . . We need milk."*
> *(Write* milk.*)*
> *"Hmm, milk has four letters. We also need to get some eggs."*
> *(Write* eggs.*)*
> *"Hey, I hear three sounds—eh, g, z, but I had to write four letters."*

By exposing your preschooler to the way you write lan-guage on paper, and your thought processes and observa-tions about what you write, he will be learning a great deal about print and how we produce it. In other words, he will be learning, indirectly, about spelling.

After completing your list, take it to the store and have your preschooler help you cross off the words as you put the items in your cart. As he does this, you can talk to or ask him about the words. Your discussions might be like the following:

"*Milk.* That doesn't take very long to say, and the word you crossed out is pretty short, even though that's a really big bottle. And look at this. *Macaroni.* That's pretty long there, where I wrote it. It takes a longer time to say it, too. But these macaronis sure are small."

In these kinds of interchanges, your preschooler not only is learning how words are separate from the objects they identify, but he also is learning about the purpose of writing: to inform, to remind, and so on. These simple examples demonstrate that children can learn about language even during the most common, everyday activities.

Chapter Summary

Obviously, the ideas we provide in these different situations are interchangeable (you can play rhyming games during shopping trips or make lists of chores to do around the house). The point is to show how you don't need to buy fancy toys or products to help your preschooler learn to read and write. You have the materials and know-how to do this right now in your home or car. Take advantage of these opportunities. Lay the foundation that will help develop the knowledge and skills she will need to tackle that most difficult of school tasks: reading and writing.

5

READING, WRITING, AND SPELLING: HELPING YOUR CHILD ACHIEVE IN SCHOOL

DID **Y**OU **K**NOW?

....

- Children who can divide words into individual sounds tend to be better readers and spellers.

- Academic reading material is usually organized in predictable ways.

- English spelling is very systematic.

Charlene and Jaxon are the parents of Sam, who is just starting first grade. Sam had a great year in kindergarten, and now they are wondering just how much they should be doing to ensure that his first-grade year is equally positive. They know that it will be critical for Sam to make major advances in reading, but they aren't sure how that will happen and what, if anything, they can do to help. Their friends and family aren't much help. Sam's cousin, Lillie, is only one grade ahead, and she's already reading chapter books, and Charlene knows that Lillie's mom insists that she read at least an hour every day. However, a friend told Charlene that adults should never try to teach children anything about reading or spelling because it will develop "naturally, on its own," and every child will begin reading when he or she is ready. As eager as they are to help Sam, Charlene and Jaxon are at a loss of what to do!

There has been an increased emphasis on reading and academic achievement in the last decade. For example, the passage of federal education legislation, such as No Child Left Behind, and its associated requirements for accountability led to an explosion in the amount of research focused on optimal instructional practices for reading. Parents, and the public in general, are given information yearly about the degree to which their local schools are meeting the required standards of achievement. Although there certainly have been some negative consequences of "high-stakes testing" and somewhat unrealistic achievement goals, the research that has been published over the past several years has provided some very clear direction regarding best practices for teaching reading, writing, and spelling.

In this chapter, we will provide information about how children first learn to decode written words and translate speech into print via spelling. We believe that decoding and spelling are *language* skills, and we describe the various linguistic abilities that contribute to literacy. Reading is more than just recognizing individual words, so we also describe the ways in which reading material is organized. A grasp of these frameworks can have a profound influence on successful reading comprehension and on writing.

Building Blocks of Written Words: Foundations for Reading and Spelling

English words in print often are viewed as random strings that have to be memorized. Many of us have memories of taking home words lists and being drilled by our parents to read or spell them in preparation for a test. But spelling and reading are so much more than memorization. Below we'll review the language building blocks that support reading and spelling.

Awareness of Sounds

Your child has been using sounds to speak for some time. But now he has to do something remarkable: He has to start *thinking* about those sounds. As you may recall from the previous chapter, when a child can think and talk about our speech sounds, it is called phonemic awareness. A child's phonemic awareness *abilities* are measured by giving her tasks such as breaking a word into its individual sounds, taking one or more sounds out of a word and naming the word that remains, or blending individual sounds to form words. Numerous studies have documented the strong link between this skill and reading and writing. It's easy to see why. A young reader is taught to "sound out" words by breaking them into individual letters or chunks of letters, associating sounds with those letters, and finally putting the sounds together to form a word. In early reading, the emphasis is on decoding familiar words so that she can have an "aha" moment when the blended sounds sound like a word she already knows. On the other hand, when asked to spell a word, the child must first divide the word into its individual sounds and then determine which letter or letters should be used to represent each sound. As she gains experience reading and writing words, she no longer has to segment or blend them because she forms mental pictures that allows her recognize (read) or spell words more automatically.

You can help your child develop awareness of sounds by playing games that focus on parts of words. A good example is "match the sound." In this game, someone names a word (e.g., *dog*) and then everyone else takes turns naming a word that starts with the same sound (e.g., *duck, dip, dash, dough, dive*). You can make this game a little harder by asking for matches to the last sound or even the middle vowel. Nick, Caleb, Genevieve, Caitlin, and now Gage can testify about many hours spent playing "first–last" while on family trips in the car. In this game, one player names a word (e.g., *dog*) and the next player has to provide a word that begins with the last sound in the previous word (in this case, *g*, so *goat* or *guess* would work). Remember, spelling doesn't matter; it's the sounds in the words that count. Yes, many happy, positive moments of family bonding were centered on this game—that is, until Nick and Caleb realized that using words such as *fox* would make their sisters scream!

Letter Patterns

It's not enough to know that the word *cat* consists of three sounds. We also must know that the first sound is spelled with a *c*, the second with an *a*, and the last with a *t*. Research has shown that the ability to associate sounds with the letter patterns that represent them is another skill that is strongly related to success in spelling and reading. Sometimes these links are pretty simple, such as knowing that the *b* sound is spelled with the letter *b*. Others are a little more complicated—like knowing that although the second sound in *bed* and *bread* are the same, one is spelled with an *e* and the other is spelled with *ea*. That becomes even trickier when you realize that the "long *e*" sound is spelled *ee* (*beet*), *ea* (*bead*), *ei* (*ceiling*), *ie* (*chief*), *y* (*busy*), and other ways. Now before you throw up your hands and say, "I knew that English spelling is hopeless," let us assure you that research has shown that the majority of spelling patterns are regular, or predictable, if one knows about the principles that govern these patterns. Sarita, a good speller who is quoted in *The Violent* E *and Other Tricky Sounds*, explains,

> *You have to, like, have ways of learning. You can't, um, like, try to keep memorizing the words, like look at the word and try to keep memorizing in your head, because then you're never going to know. You can't remember every single word in your head.* (Hughes and Seare, 1997)

So how does a child gain optimal knowledge of these principles? First, let us tell you what does *not* work. Giving a child a list of words on Monday and telling her to memorize them by practicing them verbally and writing them 100 times each may result in her making a good grade on the Friday Spelling Test; however, within a very short time, there will be little evidence that she ever studied many of those words. She'll likely have another test on many of the very same words during the next grades, too. So, if this doesn't work, why do teachers keep using this method?

An interesting study was conducted a few years ago by researchers who surveyed teachers to determine the methods they were using to teach spelling. They found that most teachers did very little to help their students develop strategies for spelling, and this was mainly because the university training programs from which they had come didn't focus on spelling strategies either. So it becomes an unproductive cycle: Universities don't focus on how to teach patterns for spelling (and even sometimes for reading), so the teachers don't know about them, so they don't teach their students about them, and so forth. Instead, the old standard Friday Spelling Test continues to reign. We've been doing research in this area for the past decade, and almost without exception, teachers welcome learning about strategy instruction and want to apply it with their students. When they do, students' skills tend to improve. Interestingly, the teachers sometimes tell us that the parents are concerned because they no longer use the Friday Spelling Test. They have to emphasize to the parents that they are not abandoning spelling; quite the contrary, they are teaching it in meaningful ways.

What are these meaningful ways to teach spelling or letter patterns? We believe that the principles aren't just about spelling; rather, they are strategies for decoding individual words in reading as well. It would be great if all we had to do was to say something like this to a student: "Billy, when you hear this sound (make the first sound in the word *apple*), spell it with an *a*. When you hear this sound (make the first sound in the word *ate*), you either spell it with an "*a*-consonant-*e*" pattern, *ai*, *ay*, *ey*, or even sometimes with a single *a* as long as it's in a multisyllabic word. Got that? Okay, let's move on to the next sound."

Unfortunately, this doesn't work either! In fact, this method probably wouldn't be any more effective than the Friday Spelling Test method. Instead, the goal is to help the student discover the pattern herself in meaningful ways. We refer to this as word study, and it requires the teacher to carefully arrange activities that contrast a new spelling pattern with the incorrect, less developmentally sophisticated one that students are currently using. For example, a child may initially use the letter *e* to spell words like *eat*, *beet*, and *chief*. After all, the name of that letter is the same as the sound he's trying to spell—pretty smart, huh? Well, it is clever, but the student must move past that strategy in order to spell these words correctly. So the teacher might arrange a sorting activity using the following words printed on individual index cards: *bed*, *bead*, *egg*, *fed*, *bee*, *let*, *jet*, *eat*, *meet*, and *sea*. She would make sure that the child was aware of the difference between the two sounds *eh* and *ee*, and label a basket for the words that have the *eh* sound and another for words that have the *ee* sound. The *eh* is often labeled the "short *e*" sound and the *ee* the "long *e*" sound. Hopefully sorting by sounds would result in the following two lists:

"Short *e*" Sound (*eh*)	**"Long *e*" Sound (*ee*)**
bed	bead
egg	bee
fed	eat
let	meet
jet	sea

After the sort is completed, the teacher can ask the student to read the words in each list, confirming that they share the same vowel sound. She then asks the student to identify something different about the spellings of the short versus the long. At this point, we want the child to recognize that the long vowel patterns involve two vowel letters rather than the single *e*. We encourage the child to put that principle into his own words, write it in his word-study journal, and pick two or three key words to help him remember the principle. We then follow this activity by reading a short story that includes several words with the "long *e*" sound and a writing activity that will allow him to use his new pattern in authentic writing.

We certainly acknowledge that some of the letter patterns are a little more obscure than others. Many times they are dependent upon position in the word. You've probably read about George Bernard Shaw's exasperated claim that "fish" could be spelled "ghoti" since the *f* sound is spelled *gh* in *rough*, the "short *i*" sound is spelled *o* in *women*, and the *sh* sound is spelled with a *ti* in *nation*. However, appreciation for word position influences would refute Mr. Shaw's claim. The *gh* is never used for the *f* sound at the beginning of words, and the *ti* is never used for the *sh* sound at the end of words. If these spelling principles are incorporated into word study, a great deal of the perceived "arbitrariness" of English spelling will disappear.

Vocabulary and Word Parts

Julie has a clear memory of reading with her first-grade teacher and confronting the word *eyes*. She pronounced it as "ee-yes" and wondered why the teacher chuckled. She had made an admirable attempt to break the word into pieces that she knew; unfortunately, the pieces weren't the correct ones. Think about how we spell the rhyming words *act* versus *backed*. The last sound of the second word is spelled with an *-ed* rather than *t* because of the meaning (i.e., past tense) that it represents. As early as grade 1, children begin to develop an appreciation for prefixes (e.g., *un-*, *pre-*, *re-*), suffixes (e.g., *-ly*, *-ed*, *-ing*, *-tion*), and other aspects of combining word parts into related words. This understanding, which is called morphological awareness, plays a critical role in spelling and reading starting around grade 3.

Much like they learn to appreciate that letters and letter combinations represent sounds in words, students learn to associate spellings with larger chunks of language that have meaning (called morphemes) that they represent. Once again, simply giving a student a list of words that contain various extra word beginnings and endings (e.g., words that end with *-ation* like *application, combination, information, occupation, presentation*) or word relatives (i.e., words that share the same base portion, such as *electric, electricity, electrician*) and asking him to memorize it for an upcoming test does not work. Instead, we use word study to help a student discover the principles underlying the use of the prefix or suffix or base part of the word. We may use a sorting game, this time with base words and their associated modifications with a given prefix or suffix. Using the example lists just provided, the sort may result in these two lists:

Base Word	Relative with "ation"
apply	application
combine	combination
inform	information
present	presentation
occupy	occupation

Using the sorted lists, the teacher would then ask the students to brainstorm about characteristics that words in the first list have in common (i.e., they are all verbs) and then lead them to discover that the words in the second list are all nouns that result from modifications associated with the base verb (e.g., if one *applies*, the result is an *application*; if one *combines*, the result is a *combination*). This works beautifully until the students come to the last pair in the list. Although it's true that if an army *occupies*, the result is an *occupation*, that's not the first meaning that typically comes to mind for that word. That can lead to a great discussion of how meaning often depends on context, how some "word relatives" are closer in meaning than others, and how a term for a person's job could be related to the word *occupy*. The key to word study, whether it be about associating letter patterns with sounds in base words or spellings with word parts, is to celebrate the way that the richness of language is represented in written words! Most spellings make sense, and for the ones that don't, we can employ some special strategies for remembering. That's the topic of the next section.

Mental Pictures

Have you ever wondered when and how a young reader stops needing to sound out words? Parents of young readers are ecstatic when they hear their child transform from a halting "d-d-d-uh-uh-k-k, oh that's duck!" to "The duck swam in the water." How does that happen? Miraculous! Once again, we'll start by telling you how it does *not* happen. Of course, by now you probably know what we are going to say. It does not happen by rote memorization, that is, staring at each word within a group of words for two minutes or writing each one of them 50 or even 100 times. Instead, a student develops a "mental picture" of an entire word (likely in the case of *duck*) or parts of words as an outgrowth of adequate skills in phonemic awareness, letter pattern knowledge, and morphological awareness. Through lots of time reading and good word study, this ability does more or less miraculously take place.

There are a few things, though, that a teacher and parent can do to help students develop mental pictures of words. Not to sound like a broken record, but the most important thing to do is to ensure that your student is developing a healthy appreciation for sounds, letter patterns, and word parts. Once that's in place, the remaining pieces that are required to "remember" are actually quite few. Take, for example, the word *graph*. The student has to first recognize that there are four sounds in the word, and then she can use knowledge of straightforward sound-to-letter relationships to get the *g*, *r*, and the *a*. That leaves her the need to pay special attention only to the fact that the *f* sound is spelled with a *ph* in this word rather than the more typical *f* or *ff*. We've used a variety of techniques to make these portions of words that can be spelled a variety of ways more salient, or noticeable. Examples include color coding the pattern and finger tracing. We also sometimes ask students to "take a mental picture" (i.e., really think about what the word, specifically that portion of the word, looks like) and then spell it backward. We are always adamant, however, to point out that such techniques are used *after* basic awareness of sounds and spelling are in place. *That is, we never start with memorizing!* We "resort" to memorizing only those parts of words that are not readily spelled with straightforward associations among sound, meaning, and spellings.

Frameworks for Organizing Text

How many times have you watched a movie or TV show or read a book that begins with a scene, only to follow that scene with a title, "X days (hours) earlier . . ."? If we read or see something that happened at point D and then get information on what happened at points A through C later, how do we put all of it together to make sense? The answer is that we have a knowledge, a framework, for what to expect in stories. As we described in chapter 4, children in the late preschool years develop basic storytelling skills that allow them to provide tales with simple plots. That is, they mention characters, a problem, and how the problem is solved. During the school years, your student will develop an appreciation for a framework that governs stories that includes more and more detail. She will use this framework not only to develop stories that she tells and writes herself, but she'll also use it to understand stories that she hears and reads.

Stories (Narratives)

What are the components of a simple story framework? First, there is the *setting*, which includes a description of the characters in the story and sometimes where and when the story takes place. Next there is a *problem*, or complication. This is sometimes referred to as the focal point of the story. After seeing the first *Jurassic Park* movie, Julie commented to Caleb, who was nine years old at the time, that everything would have been a lot better if they had just stuck to cloning leaf eaters. Caleb replied, "Mom, that's silly. Without the meat eaters, there couldn't have been a movie." He had a good point: Without a problem to solve, the story isn't very interesting!

Next, the characters typically react to the problem with their *feelings* about the situation and/or *plans* to solve it.

Feelings and plans must be put into action, so a good story next describes the *attempt(s)* to solve the problem and their associated *consequences* (were they successful or not?). Finally, the story ends with a *resolution*, which provides a sense of closure to the story. Using this framework, we can dissect a popular children's story/movie, *Cinderella*.

SETTING   Cinderella, a kind girl, lives with her mean stepmother and stepsisters.

PROBLEM   Cinderella doesn't have anyone who really loves her; she has to do all of the household chores by herself.

CHARACTER FEELINGS/GOAL   She doesn't mind the chores, but she's lonely. She thinks if she could go to the Prince's Ball, her life would get better.

ATTEMPT   She finishes all of her chores in time and finds a dress to wear.

CONSEQUENCE   Her stepmother and stepsisters destroy the dress and tell her she can't go.

ATTEMPT   Her fairy godmother gives her some fancy clothes, shoes, and a carriage to go to the ball.

CONSEQUENCE   Cinderella meets the prince, but she has to leave by midnight, so she doesn't get to make future plans with him.

PROBLEM   The prince wants to find his new love. He decides to use the slipper to find her.

ATTEMPT   He tries the slipper on every young woman in the kingdom in an effort to find his true love.

CONSEQUENCE   The slipper fits Cinderella.

RESOLUTION   They marry and live happily ever after.

Try to imagine reading this story without the part about the mean stepmother who makes Cinderella do all of the work by herself. That might make us feel a little less concerned about Cinderella needing to get to the ball. What if we left out the part about her losing the slipper? A royal prince traveling all over his kingdom making young women try on a shoe would sound strange at best. People with sufficient experience with this classic story mode know to expect at least one problem in a story as well as other events that happen when the characters try to solve it. These expectations allow a listener or reader to "fill in the blanks" either with information directly provided in the story or inferred via reasonable deductions.

Students in early elementary grades are soon reading "chapter books" and other literature best characterized as narratives. These narratives become more complex by adding additional problems, which can occur when the first problem is solved or even in the midst of solving the original problem. They also can be more challenging when components are not provided but rather most be inferred by the reader or listener.

You can use this information about the way that stories are organized to help your student comprehend what she is reading. We often begin by making a chart with all of the story components in one column (much like the Cinderella example above) and then have the student fill in the second column as she reads the story. This approach gives us an opportunity to discuss what information is directly provided and what must be inferred. We often encourage students to "put themselves in the place of the characters" and discuss what they might do, how they might feel, and so on. Such strategies to get readers actively involved in what they are reading have been shown to result in better comprehension skills.

Being knowledgeable about stories is important for communication, both when students are writing and when they are reading. There are other ways, though, that information is expressed in writing. These types of frameworks may be less familiar to students. In fact, some of these mostly *only* occur within books they read in their classrooms.

Textbooks

Most of us remember learning about the life cycle of a frog. We read about how they start as eggs, then develop into tadpoles, then become some sort of intermediate being called a froglet, and ultimately turn into adult frogs. This type of information is different from the narratives previously discussed. Students don't read about some specific character (e.g., Frances the Frog) who has a problem (needing to survive), develops a plan to fix it (thinks she'll start as an egg and turn into a tadpole), and ultimately solves it (makes it to adulthood and has eggs of her own). Instead, this information is provided in what is sometimes referred to as expository text.

Books for academic subjects, such as science, health, and geography, are often organized with several characteristics that help the reader know how to recognize the pieces that deserve special focus. The books are divided into units, which are then further divided into chapters. The chapters have special text markers, such as boldface words, section headings, pictures and other graphics, and questions at the beginning that emphasize the key elements of the information.

You can help your student to get the most out of her reading and other homework assignments by modeling how to use these "cues" to ensure you pay attention to most important material. For example, a third-grade social studies textbook has the following structure.

UNIT 5: MANY CULTURES, ONE COUNTRY
Chapter 10: People and Culture
Lesson 1: Our Country's People
Special Days and Special People
A Polish Hero in America
Juneteenth
Community Birthdays
Remembering Important Times
Celebrating America

If you looked at the pages of this particular chapter, you would see inset boxes that had key vocabulary, a summary at the beginning and end of the lesson, and a lesson review. All of these heading, subheadings, inset boxes, and so forth help the reader have an idea of what the important points are for that lesson and what to expect in each section. With these "cues," readers can be prepared to understand what the book author wants him to remember and link information together from across the lesson.

Academic "Stories"

Young readers "cut their literacy teeth" on fictional stories about talking animals, fantasy characters, and so forth. However, they also will encounter factual information that is presented in story form. Some of these early stories are simple sequences of events that occur. For example, young students may read a lesson called "Life on a Dairy Farm." They will learn that the farmers wake up very early, have breakfast, feed and milk the cows, and then clean the barns and equipment. This simple sequence is repeated on most days. A history lesson about Christopher Columbus's voyage to America also might involve a sequence (i.e., Columbus was given three ships by the Spanish royalty, he and his crew crossed the ocean in the *Niña*, *Pinta*, and *Santa Maria*, and they landed in North America, even though they thought it was India). We use the framework "first-second-(next, if applicable)-last" to help young children focus on the important elements in this type of reading material.

Sequential stories also characterize text that focuses on how to accomplish a task. For example, recipes provide great opportunities for young readers to follow simple instructions. There are numerous cookbooks that are specifically written for young readers, and many packaged foods (e.g., cake mixes) employ simple language and graphics. With just a little help (and maybe a lot of patience) from you, your child can bake an impressive batch of brownies or cupcakes.

Writing

Our sons and daughters are now in their 20s, and some of our most treasured artifacts from their childhood are samples of their writing. From scribbled notes for holidays to emails and text messages, written communication played a very important role in our everyday interactions.

We described the way that spelling develops and things that you can do to help your child spell in the first section of this chapter. However, writing skills involve more than just knowing how to spell accurately. Like reading, writing emerges via very basic skills and develops well into adulthood. The earliest forms of writing are scribbles and drawing. In fact, the early writing done by first graders typically includes, and even focuses on, associated drawings. Later, the use of drawings to supplement texts will decrease. In addition to simple stories, children will write to describe objects or events and complete simple worksheets. An example is provided in Figure 1 at the end of the chapter, which Caitlin did as a Mother's Day present while in first grade. Certainly the capitalization and spelling are not perfect, but the answers do seem to be reasonable completions for the sentences. In fact, her mom continues to remind her about the enduring truth value of her response to item 3!

As emphasized in chapter 4, the most important thing parents can do to facilitate writing skills is to model how they use writing in everyday activities. In the early elementary years, parents can also emphasize the communicative value of writing by allowing the child to prepare written notes and emails for family members and friends. Text messaging and social-networking websites provide high motivation for children to write, and the influences of these technologies are described in greater detail in chapter 8. In a nutshell, the use of texting has been associated with gains in literacy skills. That's a good thing, even though we sometimes go bonkers with the *amount* of texting some children do!

Not too many people, especially young students, think writing is easy. These days they certainly are happy to text a friend or update a status on Facebook. However, writing a formal report or essay for school is another matter, and most students, regardless of the grade level, find such assignments daunting. We agree. Writing this book was no piece of cake! But one strategy we learned and used, and one that you can help your student learn, is the three-step writing process of Plan, Write, and Review. The planning step is pretty self-explanatory but is quite often completely ignored. In this step, we actually plan out what we want to communicate before we start writing. We might use some structured, graphic organizer (your child will likely learn some of these in school), or just brainstorm and jot down ideas on a paper. Either way, we get our thoughts out about our writing assignment before we actually put pen to paper or fingers to keyboard.

Once we have a plan, we begin writing. As we write, our goal is to get our thoughts down on to the paper or the computer screen without a lot of self-editing. In other words, the idea is to just get as much information on the paper or screen as we can. After writing, we then review what we have written, ensuring not only that our written composition sounds good but also that we covered everything we planned in the first step. Invariably, we end up going back to the writing step and then again to the reviewing step until we get our writing composition to just the place we want it to be.

This idea of planning, writing, and reviewing is such an important process; so many students are asked to write and just start writing before they have thought about *what* they want to say (what are the main points?), *how* they want to say it (should I write a narrative, a compare-and-contrast essay, or a sequence?), and *who* their audience is (who will be reading the composition?). The outcome of writing can really change depending on the what, how, and who of the writing process. Additionally, when students go back and check whether what they wrote reflects their plan and the ideas they want to convey, invariably their written compositions are much higher in quality.

We recommend that you communicate closely with your student's teacher so that you are aware of how she is helping your student learn the writing process and the kinds of writing activities that she is expecting your student to do at school, as well as what you should expect for her writing "products." This knowledge will equip you to provide her with similar activities at home, where you can give her optimal support and encouragement.

Chapter Summary

Watching your child develop reading, spelling, and writing skills is tremendously exciting. You know that these abilities will allow her not only to succeed in school but also to gain hours of enjoyment from reading novels or magazines. Interacting with friends via email or texting will contribute to your student's social development. Writing may offer an avenue for her to learn more about herself and gain insight into her likes, dislikes, choices, hopes, and dreams. Our experiences with our own children's writing have ranged from interactive journals when they were preschoolers to getting their text messages (and learning how to send texts ourselves!) to proofing essays that accompanied applications to graduate or medical school. We hope that by reading this chapter you are set to enjoy the ways in which your student's reading, spelling, and writing skills develop across her academic life.

Top 10 Reasons Why I Love My MOM

10 I love my Mom because she reads me ___BOOKS___

9 I love my Mom because she helps me ___Make my BeD___

8 I love my Mom when she makes me laugh by ___telling me jokes___

7 I love my Mom because she taught me how to ___count___

6 I love to hear my Mom sing ___songs___

5 I love my Mom because she finds time to ___Make cookies___

4 I know my Mom cares because she ___Loves me___

3 I know my Mom is smart because she ___KNOWS MORE THAN ME___

2 I love my Mom because she works so hard at ___CLEANING THE Ho___

1 I love my Mom because she's the BEST MOM EVER!

HAPPY MOTHER'S DAY, MOM!

LOVE, CAITLIN

Grade 1

Figure 1. An example of Caitlin's writing in grade 1.

6

THE INFLUENCE OF GENDER AND BIRTH ORDER ON LANGUAGE DEVELOPMENT

D ID Y OU K NOW ?

- Many parents talk differently to girls versus to boys.

- Younger children actually learn valuable language skills when they are around their older siblings.

- "Twin talk" is somewhat of a myth.

Yu-Chun and Brandon were excited. Their second child, a daughter, had been born. They felt they knew what to expect: feeding, bathing, diapering, clothing, diapering, and feeding again. This would be second nature to them. But the one factor that was new was that this second child created a sibling for their three-year-old son. How would he react? Had they prepared him enough? They had talked with him many times about the new baby coming into his life. He had been prepped on what it was like to hear crying at odd hours of the day and night. They had even "borrowed" a friend's baby for an afternoon, so he could see what it was like to have an infant around the house. Now today was the big day. He was meeting his little sister for the first time. He entered the birth room with his father. There, on his mother's lap, was his new sister. He gazed on her, looked up at his parents and then said, "She's not talking!" Apparently, they had forgotten one little detail!

Just like other parents, we were somewhat apprehensive when each of our children was born. With our firstborn child, we wondered if we had the type of parenting skills and instincts that would help our baby grow physically and mentally. With the arrival of our second-born child, we wondered how the older child would handle the presence of the younger child. Just like you are doing now, we read what we could on how parents and siblings affect the growth and development of children. We found some fascinating information, including how gender, birth order, and siblings affect language development, which we will share with you in this chapter. Before we begin, though, we have two points to make.

All children are unique—just when you think you know everything, a child will throw you for a loop!

As you read this chapter, it will be important for you to remember that the information we report on the effects of gender, birth order, and siblings on language development is what researchers have found *in general*. While studies suggest that girls generally acquire certain words before boys and that firstborns typically use a certain style of language, these findings are not definite in every situation. Thus, it is very likely, as you will see from some of our examples with our own children, that your child may not follow the patterns or strategies of language for his gender or birth order we describe. This should not be a cause for concern. All children are unique, and one thing we have learned in our professional and parental experiences is just when you think you know everything, a child will throw you for a loop! Use this information to gain a deeper understanding of how the intriguing process of language acquisition *can* occur. We think that the more you read about the process of language development, the more fascinated and impressed you will become with what your child is learning and *how* he is doing it.

Our second point is to remind you of something you read in chapter 2. As you recall, we talked about how children may approach early language development using different styles. The baby with a referential style approaches learning language by focusing more on nouns and playing naming games. A baby with an expressive style likes to play social-interaction games and uses many more words that describe actions or serve to help the baby interact (*please, more, all gone*). We return to this topic now because these styles of language development are often associated with children of a specific gender or birth order, though not necessarily 100 percent of the time. Nevertheless, it is helpful to keep in mind these styles and what they mean as you read the rest of this chapter.

Language is one of the most crucial areas of development in a child's life. The fact that gender, birth order, and siblings may influence it is worthy of note. We have said all along that you are one of the most important aspects of your child's language development. This chapter should help you understand this fact even more, while helping you to learn how certain biological and familial factors also influence your child's language development. Let's get started.

Gender Effects on Language Development

Perhaps one of the most frequently asked questions we receive when we lecture on language development is, do girls and boys develop language differently? The answer is both yes and no. There *are* some differences in how many, but not all, boys approach language learning when they are compared to many, but not all, girls. However, when you look at the greater picture (i.e., the complete development of language), there are many more similarities than differences. Both genders acquire language skills along the same timeline. Both become active, engaging conversationalists. True, there may be some differences in interactional styles when you compare adult men and women (after all, they *are* from different planets!); however, the difference between the sexes during the first eight years of life is not vast.

Differences Between Girls and Boys

Researchers have attempted to find differences between girls and boys by administering formal language tests and determining whether the two sexes differ in their scores. In some studies, girls have performed better on tests that focus on expressive language, or how advanced they are in what they can say. However, other studies have not found similar results. For the most part, research that has examined whether boys and girls understand language differently has consistently yielded no differences. Thus, on very general measures of language skills, there appear to be no differences between boys' and girls' language skills. However, other studies that have focused on specific skills have found some slight differences.

During the first few years of life, differences between boys and girls may be apparent when their word meanings are examined. For example, research has shown that girls are more likely to begin using emotion words (e.g., *love, like, sad, happy*) before boys do. Obviously, boys are not considered to be delayed in their use of these words, and ultimately they do use them. However, there may be a time delay between when girls begin using these words and boys first say them.

Girls are typically first to use language to collaborate with their peers to solve problems during play situations. When confronted with a situation that requires some strategy as a means of solving a problem, preschool girls are more likely to talk about possible solutions with one another. They may initiate more turns in a conversation about the problem and ask for help more frequently. They also tend to describe how they solved a problem as they accomplish the task. On the other hand, preschool boys are more likely to attempt to work through problems with actions. Over time, boys also begin problem solving by talking with their peers. Even though there are initial differences in how the two genders try to solve problems (using language versus acting on the problem), their successes in solving problems are similar.

One additional potential difference between boys and girls is the style of language development they tend to use. Studies have shown that approximately 78 percent of all girls have a referential style of language acquisition, whereas approximately 60 percent of all boys have an expressive style. Thus, girls are likely to use more nouns than boys, show a preference for naming games, and demonstrate clearer speech than boys.

Possible Causes for Gender Effects on Language Development

What might lead to these subtle differences in the language development of boys and girls? Not surprisingly, it appears, at least in part, to come back to . . . you! When researchers have studied parents (mostly moms) interacting with their two- or three-year-old children, they have observed that parents use different types of language with boys than with girls.

Mothers of two-year-olds tend to ask more open-ended questions of their daughters, use more child-directed speech (see chapter 2 for our discussion of child-directed speech [CDS]), and produce longer and more complex sentences than they do with their sons. They also just talk more to girls than they do to boys. When mothers are talking to their two-year-old sons, they use language more to direct their sons than they do with their daughters. They also may be less articulate than they are with their daughters.

The differences in parent talk aimed at boys and girls also extend to the specific situations where language is used. In a number of studies, researchers have examined where parents are more likely to initiate or begin conversations with their children. In studies of parents and their three-year-old children, research has shown that parents are most likely to initiate conversation with their boys in play situations than in other situations. However, with their daughters, they are more likely to initiate conversations during non-play times and in situations that require help.

How do these research findings about parent–child interactions tie into the subtle differences between boys and girls? When parents initiate conversation more to their boys in play situations, they likely are talking about what is occurring at that moment in time. Thus, their language will naturally be less complex and less abstract than if they were talking about topics out of their sons' present surroundings. Chances are their language is about the actions occurring rather than on naming of objects. Parents also may not feel compelled to be particularly articulate in these types of informal situations. This may explain why boys develop the use of language to talk about emotions and to solve problems later than girls. These types of language skills and meanings just may not occur as much in these parent–child interactions. It also suggests that parents are matching their sons' style of acquisition, focusing more on interactions and less on naming.

However, when parents initiate more language during non-play times with their daughters, they likely are using more complex and lengthier sentences to talk about situations and events out of the present, including talking about feelings. By asking questions of their daughters, they also may be modeling how we use language to solve problems as well as focusing on labeling of objects or people. This latter interaction would match many daughters' preferences for nouns. Thus, the way parents interact with their children, and when they choose to do this the most, may occur because parents are matching their children's style preferences. This, in turn, may set the stage for when girls and boys acquire certain language skills.

Finally, one cannot overlook the actual play activities of boys and girls as an additional explanation for why there might be subtle differences between the sexes in language development. When children are playing with dolls, there is a greater chance that the language used during that play will involve more nouns and more questions. When children are engaged in play with vehicles, there is a greater chance that creative sounds or noises will be used and fewer actual real words will be produced.

Of course, we don't want to suggest that play with dolls is "girl play" and that play with cars and trucks is "boy play." Indeed, for all of our children, we made all types of toys available. However, there does seem to be some relationship between dolls and girls and cars and boys. Perhaps children are biased by parents who purchase their toys, by the media that promote certain stereotypes, or even by some basic biological differences. Nevertheless, boys *tend* to play more with trucks and cars, and girls *tend* to play more with dolls. Thus, the actual play situations may also influence their language development. Whether the play influences the style of language the child uses or the style of language influences the play is unknown.

An experience from a holiday gift exchange several years ago illustrates the differences in boy–girl language seen in one of our households. It was a tradition to allow the children to open their presents from each other on Christmas

Eve and save the rest of the gifts for the next morning. Caleb received a Godzilla action figure from his sister, and Caitlin received a Barbie doll from her brother. About an hour after the exchange, their parents walked in quietly to observe their play. At first, they were surprised to see that Caleb was playing with Barbie and Caitlin was playing with Godzilla. As they listened carefully, however, the play itself wasn't surprising after all . . .

Caleb had Barbie by the fireplace yelling (accompanied by the sounds of screaming, gunfire, bombs exploding, etc.), "Get back from the building, everyone! The bomb has gone off! The bomb has gone off!" More screaming ensued.

Godzilla, on the other hand, was over by the coffee table, saying to baby Jesus and the rest of the characters from the manger scene, "Hi. What a nice baby! Do you need a blanket to keep you warm? Will you be my new friend?"

Summary of Gender Effects

The bottom line regarding the effect of gender on language development is that there are more similarities than differences in how boys and girls acquire their language skills. Any subtle, temporary differences may be due to how and when parents interact with their children, as well as the types of play situations in which the children engage. So enjoy your son or daughter, expose him or her to different types of play situations, and interact with your child in a variety of situations. This will only serve to increase the experiences and language models from which your child can benefit.

Also, remember that for all of the differences we discussed, not all girls demonstrate a certain trait and not all boys use a certain language strategy. In other words, do not be concerned if your daughter has a "male strategy" or your son has a language skill attributed to young girls. What we want you to take from this review is simply that there are some aspects of language development that differ between some boys and girls and that, knowing this information, you may be able to spot those difference in your son or daughter. The differences will not be problems, just alternative ways of achieving the same goal: language development.

Enjoy your daughter or son, expose him or her
to different types of play situations, and interact
with your child in a variety of situations.

Birth Order, Siblings, and Language Development

Both of us have one son and one daughter. For each of us, our son was the firstborn and our daughter was the second born. During the second pregnancies, we were somewhat uncertain as to how our sons would deal with the new arrivals. Because of this, we did everything possible to prepare them—Nick is Kenn's son, Caleb is Julie's son—for their new siblings. We talked about the need for Mommy and Daddy to attend more to the baby's needs at first, that there might be crying at night (and this wouldn't be just from the baby!), and so on. Nick seemed to take it all in stride. He often took interested visitors on tours of the baby's room. In Caleb's case, he, too, took the process seriously. He was adamant throughout the pregnancy that the new child would be a girl, even correcting the obstetrician. During ultrasounds, when the physician would point out "his" head, Caleb would butt in and say, "There's *her* head!" Both of us were sure our sons were not only incredibly prepared for the new arrivals but equally excited about the prospect of a sibling.

When the blessed days arrived, however, both boys reacted in ways that we could not have foreseen. Even though Kenn was sure he had prepared Nick for his new baby sister and that he would greet her with open arms, Nick's first comment on seeing her was, "*Now* can we go to McDonald's?" Caleb's reaction was somewhat delayed compared to Nick's but decidedly more straightforward. After approximately two weeks of having his baby sister in the house, he hung a picture on the door of a baby with a circle around it and a slash through it (the universal sign for prohibited). About the same time, he said, "I know I love her, but do we have to *keep* her?" Thus, both boys' enthusiasm regarding the arrival of their new baby sisters quickly dissolved with the actual appearance of the infant.

Just as parents may not be able to completely control how their child will react to the birth of a sibling, so, too, will parents have little control over how the language environments differ between that of their firstborn and subsequent children. There has been considerable study of the language skills and the communicative environment of children who are firstborn or later born. The findings suggest that both parents and siblings may be at the root of differences in language development based on birth order. As you will see, the manner in which parents and siblings interact with one another may be intricately tied to the situational factors that are more than likely out of a parent's control.

Differences Between Firstborn and Later-Born Children

Some studies have shown that firstborn children are more likely to have larger vocabularies during their second year of life and reach the 50-word milestone (when most toddlers

> *Firstborn children are more likely to have larger vocabularies during their second year of life than are later-born children.*

begin to use two-word sentences, the first appearance of syntax use) sooner than later-born children.

In addition, about two-thirds of firstborn children use a referential style of language acquisition, whereas about two-thirds of later-born children take on an expressive style of language development. Nick and Genevieve did not follow this particular scenario. Nick, the firstborn, was very much an expressive language learner. Genevieve seemed to be referential from the very beginning. Of course, it may have been in their case that gender "won" over birth order. However, both Caleb and Caitlin were referential. This does not fit the typical pattern in that Caleb is a male and Caitlin is second born. Thus, as we have stated all along, research findings in these areas provide tendencies but not absolutes.

Other studies have found additional differences between siblings. Children who are later born have been shown to develop certain conversational skills earlier than did their firstborn siblings. For example, later-born children are more likely to stay on topic by relating what they say to what others are saying. This is a particularly important conversational skill. We're sure you have been in conversations with someone where the balance of the conversation seems one-sided. The individual seems to talk more about what she is interested in and less about what you are discussing. None of us particularly like these types of situations, because we intuitively expect our listener to react to and expand on the topic we have begun. Thus, using contingent sentences, or relating one's sentences to others' remarks in conversations, is a crucial skill to develop, and it is one that later-born children seem to master sooner. Perhaps it is not surprising, then, that other studies have found that later-born children may be more successful early on in developing friendships with peers.

Possible Causes for Language Differences in Siblings

The differences noted between firstborn children and later-born children is likely due to a several factors, including the fact that no two children seem to be *exactly* the same in how they learn language. However, the differences in sibling language development are likely due to the very real differences in the language environment in which they are raised. In other words, the situation in which firstborn children are originally raised is unlike that of later-born children. These differences, then, often center on the parent and the siblings.

At least until a second child is born, a firstborn child is often the only child in the home. This means that, in most cases, the child has the relatively undivided attention of his mother and father. On the other hand, the second-born child has at least one more member in the household than the firstborn child had. Because of this, firstborn children tend to have more one-on-one parent–child time than do later-born children. Researchers have found that parents of firstborn children are more likely to use more complex sentences and ask fewer direct questions than are parents who have more than one child. Parents of one child are also likely to provide more helpful support, that of CDS discussed in chapter 2, than parents with more than one child. Thus, firstborn children, at least while they are the only child, are likely to receive a high degree of language models that are extremely helpful for language development.

When there is more than one child in the home, parent language interactions tend to address less of their input directly to each child. So, for example, even though with a second child parents have doubled their number of children, they do not double the amount of language they use with their children. When parents are addressing several children, they are more likely to be directive than when addressing firstborn children or an only child.

Of course, one could argue that parents do not need to double their language input when they have more than one child, because the later-born children are receiving language models from their older siblings. Researchers have been intrigued about this possibility and have studied the language input of older children to their younger siblings. Studies have shown that the age of the older sibling influences the quality of the language input to the younger sibling. In general, the greater the age gap between children (i.e., the older the firstborn sibling is when the younger child is beginning to acquire language), the more facilitative the input to the younger child. If, for example, the older sibling is school age, then there is a good chance that he will use CDS with his younger sibling. However, if the older child is a preschooler himself, the use of CDS to support the language development of his younger sibling decreases dramatically. Interestingly, some child language experts have suggested that this still could be helpful for the child. It may be that the less-than-perfect input and modeling by the slightly older sibling prepares the younger sibling for talking with strangers, who by definition may not be as tuned in to the child's language level and needs.

At first, this information on siblings may make it seem as though later-born children do not experience many benefits from the language environment in which they are born. They are likely receiving fewer one-on-one language models than their older sibling. However, there are definite positive attributes to the language environment for later-born children to which firstborn children have much less exposure. For example, later-born children have many more early experiences with multiple-person conversations. That is, because of the presence of at least one older sibling, later-born children hear and partake in more conversations where two or more individuals are talking. This can be helpful in a number of ways.

In two-person conversations, it is fairly easy to take turns. When one person stops talking, the other can begin. In multiple-person conversations, each individual has to negotiate her turn to speak. Being part of a multiple-person conversation means each person must pay close attention to the others' signals as to when they are finished with their thought or when they want to jump into the conversation. These signals involve changes in the rate or melody of their voice, the language they are using (e.g., a question), and their body language (e.g., hand gestures, eye contact, etc.).

As a mature language user, you have come to understand the signals for when you can talk in a multiple-person conversation. Because later-born children are part of multiple-person conversations, they must quickly learn these signals as well. Research has shown that later-born children acquire these conversational skills earlier than do their older siblings.

We should warn you that the rules for negotiating multiple-speaker turns become inordinately more complex during car trips and when parents are on the phone. Those two situations seem to have a mysterious influence on your children's desire to tell you something *right then*! We ultimately resorted at times to very explicit strategies for car talk: "Nick may say two things. Okay, now it's Genevieve's turn. You can say your two things." Occasionally, Kenn was also given a turn to talk.

Research has shown that later-born children acquire certain conversational skills earlier than do their older siblings.

Being part of multiple-person conversations also has other advantages. In multiple-person conversations, there are many more chances for children to hear pronouns (e.g., *she, he, him, her*) being used. This may seem odd, but it makes sense when you consider the circumstances. In one-on-one parent–child interactions, parents are more likely to talk about the here and now. Thus, much of the talk will be focused on the child and what he is doing. Also, parents are more likely to refer to themselves by their label, Mommy or Daddy, in these situations ("Give it to Mommy"). However, in multiple-person conversations, the extra individuals lead to an increase in the use of pronouns. Parents also tend to use more pronouns for themselves ("Give it to me") than in one-on-one situations. Not surprisingly, then, later-born children learn to use pronouns earlier than their older siblings. This may seem trivial, but understanding and using pronouns is not an easy task for children. Thus, being a later-born child definitely is a plus in this area of language development.

Finally, even though parents are not talking more when they have more than one child, the conversations they have with their children may be longer in length. This may be an advantage for the later-born children. Learning about language in conversations with multiple persons is not an easy task, as we stated above. With longer episodes of multiple-person conversations, later-born children in essence have longer "lessons" or models from which to develop their understanding of how to use language with others.

The Special Circumstance of Multiple Births

Some children fit into both categories: firstborn and born into a sibling situation. This occurs, of course, when a child is part of a multiple birth. Because most of the research on multiple births has focused on twins, the information we present is largely based on these studies. However, with the increase in larger multiple births, and the slowly increasing number of research studies conducted with them, we expect to know more about language development and larger groups of children, such as triplets, quadruplets, and quintuplets. Until then, the limited information on larger multiple births suggest that the information we relay below holds true for them as well, with the possible exception that larger multiple-birth situations put children more at risk for language delays.

Initially, twins may lag behind single-birth children in their language development. Part of this could be due to biological or medical reasons, such as preterm birth. With some preterm births, accompanying medical complications may interfere with a child's development in many areas, including language. In cases of premature birth for any child, it is wise to determine whether she is reaching her language milestones based on calculating her age from her full-term due date or from her actual birth date. By adjusting in this way, what may appear to be a delay will not be.

Nevertheless, there is some research that suggests that twins may lag behind single-birth children even when compensations are taken into account. Twins have been shown to have smaller vocabularies during the second year of life and demonstrate less joint attention with their mothers. Others have delays in other areas, such as their speech development and grammar. Some language specialists have suggested these possible delays occur because twins are sufficient company for one another and adult interaction is not needed. While this may seem obvious, other studies have found that most twins prefer to interact with their parents rather than with the other child. Some experts have suggested that possible delays are due to the lack of one-on-one situations. By definition, twins do not have the same experience with parents that only or firstborn children have. However, as we discussed, this is not necessarily a disadvantage, especially when one considers the multiple-person conversational skills that twins learn early on. Thus, just as later-born children have advantages in language environment compared to firstborn children, so, too, do children from multiple births.

It is not uncommon to hear people talk about "twin talk." Twin talk has become somewhat of an urban legend. With twin talk, twins are reportedly speaking a new and self-created language with one another, a language that no other individual understands. In fact, a popular video of two twins "talking" went viral on the popular site YouTube. As you might imagine, this "phenomenon" has definitely piqued the interest of language researchers. What they have found has considerably put into question the existence of twin talk, at least as described by popular media.

Researchers have studied twins who reportedly use twin talk. Specifically, they have examined how the siblings interact with one another and the actual speech sounds they use. They have found that twins are more likely than single-born children to imitate and respond to the vocal play (non-language sounds, such as babbling and other creative noises) their sibling is using. Through imitation and repetition of vocal play, each twin is learning how to produce sounds like her twin, while simultaneously learning to make speech sounds like her parents. The result may be an initial different knowledge of speech sounds. In fact, twins who have been thought to be using twin talk have been found to have delayed speech development. This is not to say that all twins develop speech and language delays. However, what it does suggest is that few if any sets of multiple-birth siblings are creating a language known only to them.

Summary of Birth Order Differences

Even though there are some noticeable differences between firstborn and later-born children, it is important to realize that these differences do not lead to greater likelihood of language problems. There is no research to suggest that birth order is tied to language-learning problems. Indeed, as we mentioned in our discussion of gender effects on language development, there are more similarities than differences in language acquisition among siblings.

We frequently hear that a younger sibling is not talking because his older siblings talk for him. Indeed, this could be the case. However, just because older siblings talk for a younger one does not mean one should not expect the younger child to talk. Our advice for this particular situation is not to assume that a child who is not talking or who is delayed in his language skills *could* talk if his siblings didn't talk for him. Instead, if a child is not using the language skills we outlined in chapters 1 to 5 when he should be, parents should seek professional advice. We talk about how to do this in chapter 11.

Chapter Summary

In our personal lives, we have experienced what it is like to parent sons and daughters, firstborn children and second-born children. We have seen in both our personal and professional lives how gender and birth order can influence language development in different yet exciting ways. We hope that this chapter has provided some answers to questions you had about the effects of gender and birth order on language acquisition. We hope that, as we did, you find these differences both fascinating and worthy of observation.

Gender, birth order, and siblings are not the only influences that can impact language development. Other family variables, such as language, dialect, and culture, may influence language development as well. Our next chapter adds to your growing body of knowledge by explaining how your language, your culture, and your thoughts on the importance of these factors can affect how your child learns language.

7

THE INFLUENCE
OF CULTURE
ON LANGUAGE

D*ID* Y*OU* K*NOW*?

- Most children can learn two languages as easily as they can learn one.

- Children learning two languages at once benefit when the languages are spoken by different adults.

- Everyone has a dialect.

John and Maria are the proud parents of a 13-month-old girl. Even though little Grace is beginning to use some words, her parents are nervous about her speech and language development. When speaking to Grace, John uses English. On the other hand, Maria, whose native language is Spanish, has been speaking Spanish to Grace since birth. However, both parents are now worried that they might be confusing their daughter, setting her up for a difficult time in learning language. They wonder if they are "harming" their daughter's chances of speaking Standard American English (SAE) and setting her up for difficulties in school and possible ridicule. They've gone to a speech-language pathologist to ask how they can "talk better" to their child.

John and Maria's concerns are not unique. In chapters 1 to 5, we presented a review of how children develop speech and language during the first eight years of life, based on research conducted mainly with children in the United States. Unlike what one might assume, however, these children were learning variations of SAE. Some children were learning speech and language influenced by the regional variations of English used where they live (e.g., Southern English, African American English, Middle Atlantic English), whereas others were learning English in addition, or secondary, to another language. In fact, children in the United States do not learn a strict, "pure" version of English. Rather, all children are learning a variation of SAE. Thus, instead of feeling that their situation is rare, John and Maria will come to realize that they are much more typical than they thought.

In this chapter, we will provide information about the variations that may occur in language development because of cultural, geographical, and family influences, as well as about the purpose for which language is used. This discussion includes how language acquisition differs because of additional languages being learned or dialects in the parents' speech. We also talk about the benefits of bilingual development as well as fears parents often express when raising their children bilingually. We include in this chapter important factors to consider when raising your child in a bilingual or bidialectal home. The topic of this chapter is not only an important one for you and your young, developing child, but it is also a serious social topic as well. As you will see, we will try to disperse the common myths and prejudices some individuals hold when they encounter others who speak somewhat differently than they do.

Cultural and Linguistic Variations in Language Acquisition

When you were growing up, you probably encountered other children and their parents who communicated somewhat differently than you did. It may have been that these were families whose first language was not English. These families were speaking English, albeit a variation of the English you spoke. Others may have been families who had moved from another part of the country and brought with them the sounds and vocabulary specific to that region. We are betting that after a few days of attending to the differences between their speech and language and yours, you stopped noticing the variations. This is exactly what happens to most people. Awareness of variations in the way speech is produced or language is used quickly fades when a communication partner decides to listen for meaning rather than differences. Nevertheless, it is helpful to review what the effects are of growing up in a home where the English language is not the main language, or the only language, being learned. It is also important to talk about what differences in dialects might mean. This discussion should help us be better informed about the wide range of typical variations in our English language as well as dispel myths about these variations.

Growing Up with Two or More Languages

John and Maria's concerns for Grace are those often held by many parents of children who are learning English as a second language to the primary language in the home. Children may learn to speak English either simultaneously or sequentially. Simultaneous language development is when a child is learning more than one language at a time, as was the case with Grace. Sequential language development is when a child learns one language initially and then at a later date learns a second language. This may occur during the early years (three to five years) when the child is still learning the first language, or it may occur when she attends formal school, after she has acquired a great deal of the first language. In either case, it is important to know how best to expose the child to the second language.

SIMULTANEOUS BILINGUAL DEVELOPMENT

A great deal is known about children who are learning more than one language at a time. Studies have shown that as children learn two or more languages, there is a good chance that they express a concept in one language, but not the other. That is, children are exposed to different languages and usually those languages are attached to different people and purposes. So children learn the words that are used for those interactions that may be different. For example, the words used at home in French may be different from the words used in the Italian-speaking day care center. So the child might know the words for "ham and eggs" in French because that is what her mother prepares but will know the word for "paint" or "clay" in Italian because those are materials used in the day care center. If you were to count the words in each language's vocabulary, it might seem, at times, that there are fewer words than in the vocabularies of children learning only one language. But wait! Remember, when you combine *all* the words the child knows in both languages, often he has many more words in the two vocabularies than a child who speaks one language has in his.

Initially, children may use words from the two different languages in one phrase or sentence when they are communicating, although they may also use only words from the language that their communication partner knows. This latter situation may occur when it is very clear to the child what particular language a specific individual speaks. For example, it may be that Grace would use English when speaking to her father and Spanish when conversing with her mother.

Although children may initially blend the sounds from each language as they start to talk, they quickly learn to differentiate which sounds go with which language. Granted, many sounds may be shared by both languages. However, there will be some speech sounds that are used in one language and not the other. In these cases, children by the age of three are usually differentiating the speech sounds of each language.

As children develop further, they learn to recognize how two words, spoken differently in each language, have the same meaning. They begin demonstrating the ability to relate a word in one language (*dog*) to the corresponding word in the second language (*perro*). When Caleb was two, he had a wonderful nanny, Celia, who spoke only Spanish and lived in the family home. Celia stayed with the family until Caleb was five years old. During that time, he acquired both Spanish and English, as Caleb's parents asked the nanny to speak only Spanish to him. His appreciation for the difference in word use in the two languages was demonstrated one afternoon when he was almost three years old. He was walking by a large fountain, and he pointed and said, "Water." He then added, "Celia say *agua*." This statement not only illustrated Caleb's appreciation for the notion of distinct languages but also his knowledge that words actually stand for objects, an early metalinguistic skill (see chapter 4).

While this ability to recognize the similarities and differences in words and how they sound develops relatively early on, children will likely need more time to learn the more complex differences, such as the syntax, or word order, of the two languages. At first, children learn simple sentence structures in both languages ("I like ice cream"), but as they begin to tackle more complex syntax, children will likely learn how to say longer and trickier sentences in one language before the other.

Generally, between the ages of five and seven, a child learning two languages simultaneously will have mastered both languages, understanding and using the different words, speech sounds, and sentence types of each language. This assumes, of course, that the child has been exposed to both languages equally and had comparable experiences in both. There may be some continued blending of the two languages when he speaks, but this is likely to occur when he is uncertain about a word in one language and uses a more familiar word in the other language to complete his thought, just as many adults do. In fact, after five years of age, children may mix a word from one language into another because that is what they have observed adults to do. This ability to mix words for different purposes and situations is actually considered a high-level linguistic skill.

Generally, between the ages of five and seven,
a child learning two languages simultaneously
will have mastered both languages.

As a child is learning two languages simultaneously, it will be helpful for the parents to expose the child to the different languages by using each language in its own separate context. For example, the situation in which little Grace was learning Spanish and English was ideal. In her case, her father was speaking to her in English and her mother was speaking to her in Spanish. This is what happened with Caleb. His nanny, Celia, spoke only Spanish to him, while his parents spoke only English. Other parents may set up situations where one language is spoken in one situation (e.g., Spanish is spoken by both parents when they are at Grandma's house) and the other language is spoken in another situation (English is spoken in the home). By separating the languages into clear-cut situations or with specific individuals, the learning of that language is considered easier because it gives the child the opportunity to experience each language system separately and completely.

Children learning two languages simultaneously will become successful communicators in each language in about the same amount of time as children learning only one language. Thus, although some parents fear that bilingual language learning can cause a slow rate of development, children are adept at learning two (or more) languages without any difficulties or lingering inefficiencies. In fact, children who are multiple-language learners may have several advantages over monolingually developing children. Some studies suggest that children learning more than one language may perform higher on formal vocabulary tests and develop some metalinguistic skills earlier than their monolingual peers. They also outperform other children (children who are monolingual or learn a second language later) as they begin to learn to read. As the country becomes more and more multilingual, individuals who can speak more than one language will have expanded opportunities to communicate with many more individuals and likely understand other people's points of view in more empathetic ways.

SEQUENTIAL BILINGUAL DEVELOPMENT

In other situations, children learn to speak one language at home and then must learn a second language in a child care situation or at school. When children begin learning a second language after the age of three, they are considered to be learning the two languages sequentially. How children learn the second language, and the manner in which the first language is respected, may determine how well both languages are learned, used, and maintained.

Some children may learn a second language mainly through social interactions with peers who speak that second language. In these cases, a monolingual child typically begins to learn a second language by developing social connections with her peers and relying on standard words or phrases to interact with these friends. She may quickly learn to say *okay*, *I don't know*, and other key phrases to simulate adequate language use in the second language and give the appearance of being engaged in the conversation. In these initial language-learning situations, some children will actively try new words and phrases in the second language, supplementing these language attempts with other means of communication (gestures, facial expressions, and so on) to get their meaning across. Other children may be more hesitant to jump right in, preferring to listen and learn the language before being too active in conversations. In either case, the children are carefully listening to what their peers say, analyzing the play situations, and searching for commonly used words and phrases that seem to relate to what is being done at the moment.

After some time, children will decide to communicate with their peers in the new language, regardless of their level of capabilities. The urge to socialize through language becomes too strong to not communicate. We love that finding! It fits with our theme for this entire book: Language is a tool for interaction! When children reach this point, it may be that because of their level of competence, they produce language that is a blend of the two languages. This blended language may contain words and sentence structures from both languages as well as some language invented by the child herself. This is a time when the child's capabilities may seem to change daily, as she struggles to meet the demands of communication with a level of competency that remains somewhat limited.

Finally, children begin to pay more attention to the

language being learned and the importance of following the rules of the new language. This may occur because, as a second language learner slightly older than the child who learned two languages simultaneously, this learner has the ability to *think* about language. In other words, the child can use her metalinguistic skills to analyze what the rules are for the second language and take a more direct role in learning the new language.

This type of sequential language development occurs when no active or direct adult attention is given to helping the child learn the second language. In cases where a child is learning a second language in a more formal situation, such as a classroom, the same type of development may or may not occur. Often, when children are required to learn a new language in a formal classroom environment, their feelings about the individuals who speak that language and their desire to communicate with them may affect how well the children learn the new language. Likewise, if the adult providing the more formal "language instruction" matches the learning style of the children, better language development should occur. For example, if a child is ready for direct instruction in language development because she has the metalinguistic skills to understand discussions *about* language, language development may be successful.

One cautionary note is important here. Even in cases where children are more aware of language and thus open to a more direct, formal approach to learning a second language, it may be that the language learned initially does not immediately prepare them for complex language situations like the classroom. This is because the language used in the classroom does not have all the extra cues (facial expressions, gestures toward the conversational topic, familiar vocabulary) that are present in regular conversational situations. Thus, the use and understanding of a second language to converse with peers does not immediately guarantee that a child will follow the language used by teachers in classrooms when they are instructing children in their lessons. It may take up to seven additional years to become proficient enough to use and comprehend the complex language used in classrooms.

Sequential language development, whether it is acquired through formal or informal means, may be affected by a number of factors. First, the age of the child when she is learning the second language can affect how well it is learned. Studies suggest that children who learn a second language after their early teen years are less likely to acquire nativelike speech patterns in the second language (i.e., with pronunciation and intonation similar to the native language). Preteen children are more apt to acquire both languages completely. However, other factors may have a stronger effect on bilingual language development than age, including motivation, perceived need to use the language, the use of the language by siblings at home, the parents' social mobility, political agendas in the community, and so forth.

The timing in which a second language is introduced relative to the first language may affect development in both languages. If a child is *formally* taught a second language after the first language has begun to be learned but before it is completely learned, the result may be an impact on the development and use of the first language. However, as we mentioned above, if a child is more mature in her first language and has the metalinguistic skills to think about the second language, the second language may be acquired more easily without any delay in the first language.

One final factor that can affect sequential bilingual development is the amount of respect or importance attributed to each language. Unfortunately, some children may be placed in second language-learning experiences where the first language is devalued in comparison to the new language being learned. In cases such as this, it is possible that the child will decrease her use of the first language, resulting not only in a loss of skills within that first language but also in a loss or lack of appreciation for the cultural and familial aspects of that first language. This is unfortunate because the first language typically represents the traditions and customs of the family. To diminish the importance of the home language is to devalue the importance of the family and its culture. This indeed would be a terrible mistake.

Bilingual Language Development: What Should Parents Do?

As you can see from this review of bilingual language development, children are incredibly good language learners and not just with one language. You may be considering whether your child should learn more than one language. As you consider this possibility, keep in mind several key points. First, if you choose to provide a simultaneous, bilingual language-learning environment for your child, determine who will speak one language and who will speak the other. If one parent is speaking both languages, it is better to keep the boundaries clear, always using complete expressions in one language without mixing both languages in one sentence or thought. Remember, the clearer the boundaries between the two languages, the easier the learning. For example, Caleb expected to use Spanish with Celia and English with his mom and dad. He kept these "language boundaries" quite distinct for about two years. Then, much to the dismay of his mom, this began to change. Even though Celia never spoke English directly to Caleb, he seemed to realize that her English skills were improving because he heard her conversing with others in English. Gradually, he began speaking English more frequently to Celia. Interestingly, the style of English he used with Celia was different from the English used with others. When he spoke to Celia, he used many of the grammatical and phonological variations that Celia used as a native Spanish speaker acquiring English as a second language. At the same time, his language use was characterized by the use of a variety of English typical of persons living in Mississippi, as he and his family were living in Mississippi at the time. As you might imagine, he was certainly an interesting little "case study," and many of his mom's graduate students used him as a research project!

Children are incredibly good language learners and not just with one language.

You may wish to take a different route for your child and expose him to a second language *after* he has already learned much of his first language (after three years of age). If so, consider the information we have provided in regard to how your child will learn that second language. If you intend to expose him to the second language through interactions with his preschool peers, then let him learn through his social interactions with these friends and don't feel you have to *teach* him the language for him to be a successful communicator and play partner.

However, if your child will be learning a second language in a more formal situation that involves active teaching of the language, investigate the instructors and their method of teaching. For preschool children, you should determine whether the instructors allow the children to learn the language through "hands-on" activities, with little specific drilling of language rules. For older children, you should determine whether the instructors encourage the children to use their metalinguistic skills to help them learn new rules in the second language. Finally, regardless of age, you will want to determine whether the instructors encourage the children to maintain and respect their first language as they go about the task of acquiring the second one. If the scenarios just discussed appear to be the case, then chances are good that you have selected an appropriate language-learning environment for your child.

Learning more than one language will not put your child at risk for language-learning problems. As long as your child has ample time exposure to the languages (20-plus hours per week per language) and you use those good parenting language skills we covered in chapters 1 to 5, there is no reason to expect anything but good language development from your bilingually developing child.

Variations in Dialect

We have reviewed what is known about bilingual language development and provided you with some examples of what you can do to help your child learn more than one language in an efficient and worthwhile manner. As you undoubtedly know from your own experiences, another possible variation in language development has to do with the dialect(s) a child hears and uses in her speech and language.

When people consider the language used in America, many think of SAE. However, SAE is rarely used by individuals when speaking. In fact, the most common place one finds SAE is in written language (e.g., in books, on the Internet, and so on) and in televised newscasts (but even this seems to be decreasing). In reality, American English is represented by many different dialects. A dialect is a manner of speaking that is used by a specific group or population. Dialects are variations in speech sounds, words, word endings, sentences, and word use within a language that occur due to a number of different variables, including geographic region (e.g., New England English), culture (African American English), and learning English as a second language (Spanish-influenced English where the first language is influencing the use of English). Most dialects have evolved over time, influenced by different languages used in a particular region or culture and a historical "massaging" of the language used. Unfortunately, a lack of knowledge of the manner in which various dialects emerge has led to misconceptions of and biases against speakers of certain dialects.

Dialect Misconceptions

Some individuals assume that if a person belongs to a certain ethnic or cultural group, then that person will use characteristics of the dialect typically associated with that group. For example, it may be that when an African American who speaks African American English encounters another African American, the assumption is that they share a common dialect. Of course, this may or may not be true. In this case, the dialects spoken by African Americans will be influenced by their culture, the region of the country they are from, and others with whom they have come in contact. African Americans from the southern states of the United States will sound different from those in the Northeast. Thus, there are likely to be differences in the dialect spoken by members of the same race.

Conversely, it may be that when some individuals hear a person using a certain dialect, they assume that person is from a certain cultural background. In fact, the person may be from a specific region of the United States that contains a large population from a specific culture. An example of this may be when an individual who has grown up in New York City is assumed to be Jewish because of the Yiddish influences on the New York City dialect. In either case, the assumptions can lead to errors in judgment and communication.

Another misconception about dialects is that certain dialects always reflect that the speaker is using English as the second language. For example, when individuals hear others using Spanish-influenced English, they may assume that this particular dialect reflects the effects of the user's first language (Spanish) on the second language (English). While this may be the case, the dialect also may be due to home environment and culture. That is, children growing up in communities in Texas, for example, may be acquiring a variation that reflects the amalgamation of English and Spanish that has been happening for generations.

Finally, perhaps the most common and damaging misconception about certain dialects is that they do not represent accurate or "proper" English. Some individuals view certain regional dialects as inappropriate and lacking the rules of SAE. For example, the use of multiple "helping verbs" used by some individuals who speak Southern English (e.g., "I might could go") is thought to be improper grammar. One of us must confess that she did not know that the grammar of SAE prohibited such combinations until she was in her doctoral program! It was used all the time in her hometown in Arkansas. In fact, the grammatical rule was covered in one of her doctoral seminars and she protested that the professor was mistaken! She explained to the professor and the other students that she used that series of words all that time ("I might could do that report"; "I might could have that finished by March"), to which they replied, "We know you do . . . !"

Others may view certain dialectal rules of African American English as incomplete SAE, such as when an African American speaker says, "She got five dog." Some individuals might even note that most African American English speakers don't use African American English all the time, and consider them "lazy" when they use African American English. What is missing in these views is an understanding of the rules underlying these dialects. Dialects represent differences, not errors, and they have very specific rules for the sounds, words, word endings, word use, and sentence structures to be used. In addition, in some dialects, such as African American English, the rules are used variably. For example, in some cases, the plural -*s* might be left off a noun (*dog* for *dogs*) but in other cases, not. That's the rule or pattern, not a form of laziness. Without an understanding of the notion that the English language is made up of *many* different variations, and that these dialects have rules or patterns that differ in type and use, prejudices or biases may be formed.

Dialect Biases

Unfortunately, when you think about some of the dialects just discussed, as well as others found within the United States, you probably can recall a joke or two that use particular dialects to make fun of speakers of those dialects. Why does this occur? To be blunt, it often arises out of ignorance and intolerance. It seems some individuals have a difficult time accepting speech and language that differ from their own. They assume that others are not speaking "proper English" when, in fact, the same can be said about their own dialect as well. Other than what might appear in print, proper English is a rare entity, one that some may strive for, but few achieve, simply because of the regional or cultural dialects people bring to the task of talking.

When individuals choose to make fun of dialects or those who use them, they are, in essence, making fun of cultures, families, and traditions. While some may think such jokes are harmless, one has to question the effects of these jokes on the young children who are using the dialects as part of their language. Language is an integral part of one's self-image. Hearing jokes or puns aimed at belittling certain dialects can lead to decreased self-image and self-esteem for young children. As we have said throughout this book, language is part of the individual. In this case, then, dialect also is an integral part of the individual. When our children were exposed to jokes or comments that poked fun at others' language or dialects, we encouraged our children, through modeling, to turn the potentially hurtful comments into positives, such as "He sounds just like Blake Shelton" or "I like the way he talks—he uses cool words!" Statements such as these help to recognize the importance of diversity in language and dialect and give it the proper respect it deserves.

Dialectal Variations in Language: What Should Parents Do?

Some parents may wonder whether the dialects they "pass on" to their children will affect their language development or, during the school years, their academic achievements. For example, we have had parents ask whether their children's dialects will affect their ability to read or spell correctly. Will their children be able to read or spell words that are said differently in their dialect? Our answer is always the same: Dialects do not limit language development, either in the preschool years or in later school years. First, most children, even if they use a particular dialect, are hearing a variety of dialects used by peers and individuals in the media (e.g., television, movies, etc.). And remember, with some dialects, the particular patterns don't occur 100 percent of the time. In addition, children typically are seeing only one version of English in print. Thus, all children are growing up in multiple-dialectal communities. What we think we hear (i.e., everyone using SAE) just is not the case. We all are multidialectal in reality.

We are not suggesting that parents should not expose their children to what we know as standard English or discourage them from learning it. All children will need to understand and use the standard English used for academic purposes in the school setting. Thus, for children who speak a nonstandard dialect of English, it will be important for them to add a version of SAE to their repertoire without abandoning their nonstandard dialect. They also will need to learn when to use one dialect versus another. This is called code shifting; children learn to switch from one code (the dialect of the home) to another code (the dialect of the classroom). A recent situation we encountered is a good example of this notion of code switching.

A student recently asked us how we would respond to the pronunciation of the word *picture* as *pitcher*. Apparently, a speech and debate teacher had deducted points because the student had used that pronunciation during a class presentation. We responded that we thought it would have been best to initially talk to the student about formal and informal pronunciations and the situations in which to use each. Then, we would have helped the student to see that a class presentation represents a setting that generally calls for standard English pronunciations. After developing the student's understanding of situational influences on pronunciation choices, we would hold him accountable for the production indicated by the setting. In other words, we would have discussed and coached first, and then in subsequent presentations we would have expected him to use the SAE pronunciation, *picture*.

We believe that parents can be excellent models
for their children when it comes to understanding
and respecting others' dialects.

A parent's worry about the effects of a child's dialect on language, social, and academic development generally occurs because of a lack of knowledge about dialects. We hope this discussion of dialects has filled in some missing information. As we hope you have learned, we believe that parents can be excellent models for their children when it comes to understanding and respecting others' dialects. The value and importance a parent places on the communication abilities of any individual, regardless of his language abilities and dialect, will set an example for the child to follow.

Culture and Language Development

As you have seen, the language of the family can play a large part in children's language learning. Parents who speak more than one language can provide additional experiences for their children during the language-learning years. Children learn more than just the speech sounds, words, and sentence structures of the family. They also learn the family's culture. In many cases, culture has an equally strong influence on language development, yet in ways that may not be as obvious as the way the family *speaks*. Differences in culture also may influence the manner in which children learn to talk.

In the popular media, such as television and movies, it is fairly common to see parents interacting with their children, talking to them and with them, focusing on what seems to be most important at the time. Indeed, in chapters 1 to 5, we have encouraged you to pay attention to your child's interests and converse about those topics. However, it is equally important to be aware of the type of upbringing you experienced, based on your particular cultural background, and how that upbringing may influence your interactions with your child. In addition, it is helpful to know your spouse's or your child's caregiver's cultural background so as to best understand how these adults interact with young, developing children.

You or those around you may have come from a family or culture that did not encourage active communication with young children. Some cultures prefer that children remain silent and not talk with parents or other adults frequently. Although this may sound like the old adage "Children should be seen and not heard," it is not that a cultural preference for quiet children means that children are not to be learning. Rather, a culture such as this places importance on reflection on what adults say and puts more emphasis on understanding language than using it. Children raised in those environments are equally good communicators as those from other cultures.

Some cultures may value storytelling; however, the structure of these stories may differ in form and purpose than those children encounter in popular books. For example, stories in popular books generally introduce main characters and move to some type of cause-and-effect plot. Many times, the purpose of the story is to entertain. However, people from other cultures tell tales or stories that are more historical in nature and serve to pass down their history.

Other cultural variations include how much parents require children to imitate them and how much they model conversational skills for their children. Some cultures encourage children to imitate everything that a parent says, rather than, as we suggested earlier, providing good language models and allowing the child to *choose* whether she will repeat some part of what the adult has said. Other cultures leave the learning of social language skills to friends or siblings rather than to parent models. Still other cultures discourage eye contact with a conversational partner who is considered to be a superior. The differences in how cultures provide language-learning experiences to children can be many.

You may recognize some of these traits in your upbringing or that of your spouse or others who are raising young children such as yours. What are the implications of cultural variations on language development? In reality, not much! Children are naturally adept at learning language, regardless of the style of parent interaction or expectations. However, knowing and recognizing differences between parent–child interactions is important for two reasons.

First, if you find yourself following one of these traits, appreciate it for the value it represents in that culture. You are handing down to your child a significant part of you—your culture. Second, recognize that as your child nears his fifth year of life, if not sooner, he will be entering a more formal educational setting, such as preschool, kindergarten, and eventually, first grade. Knowing this, you can prepare him for these more "mainstream" situations by modeling and encouraging the use of language that is consistent with the "rules" of the school culture. Again, as we said earlier, this does not mean you should abandon your culture. Instead, you can *add* to your child's experiences and background by exposing him to the type of language use that may be expected in these more formal situations. Reviewing some of the suggestions we mentioned in chapters 1 to 5 should help with this endeavor.

Chapter Summary

Growing up in bilingual or bidialectal homes does not put a child at greater risk for language-learning difficulties. These children will not be slower to develop language nor will it be a "harder" task. Quite the contrary, children who learn more than one language are perhaps better prepared to meet the demands of a multicultural, multilingual society. By understanding and promoting the importance of each language and dialect, parents have the capability of helping their children develop into respectful, knowledgeable citizens who honor differences and variations in others' language and styles of communication.

8

THE INFLUENCE OF MEDIA ON LANGUAGE DEVELOPMENT

D ID Y OU K NOW ?

• The American Academy of Pediatrics recommend that preschool children watch no more than two hours of supervised television each day.

• Computers may help or hinder language development.

• Video games may be one tool for children to practice their social language skills.

• Proficient use of "text-isms" does not hinder spelling and academic writing.

Helen and Tom allowed their children to play video games for one hour a day and watch television for one and a half hours a day. Although they encouraged their children to do other things, such as read and play outside, it seemed that the children preferred the television or video game player to anything else. The more the parents watched their children engaged in these activities, the more they worried. When the children were watching television or playing video games, they almost seemed like zombies. The children never talked or seemed to acknowledge others around them. When Helen suggested that

> *Your child will be somewhat out of the loop if he cannot contribute to conversations on these media or demonstrate some competence with them.*

perhaps television and video games should be discontinued, the children protested loudly. Even Tom wondered if that would be best. How would the children fit in with other children if they weren't aware of the latest television shows or video games? Both parents were confused and felt helpless.

Television, computers, videos, texting—your child has so many types of "media" available at the push of a remote, the click of a mouse, or the tap of a telephone keypad. Media use by children is higher than ever. Children between ages two and five average more than 4.5 hours per day watching television, movies, or playing video games. If music and other audio media are included, the average person between 8 and 18 years of age spends almost 7.5 hours per day, 7 days a week using media! Of particular interest is that the media exposure is "multiplied" via multitasking. That is, young people tend to watch television, listen to music, and work (or talk) on their computer all at the same time. Current media technology has resulted in a change in the way that TV is viewed. Almost half of the programming watched today is online, time-shifted (i.e., recorded earlier), or on DVD or mobile. But are these types of media "good" for your child? Do they affect language development in a positive way? These not only are questions parents have asked us professionally but they also are questions we have asked ourselves in regard to our own children.

On the one hand, it seems unreasonable not to allow your child to experience these different types of media. Most of his peers use these media, and your child will be somewhat out of the loop if he cannot contribute to conversations on these media or demonstrate some competence with them. On the other hand, these media have the potential to dominate your child's life to the extent that significant and important social interactions among his peers and adults may not occur.

As with the information on language development, we feel that your best tool for making decisions about what media your child should use and how much he should use them is a solid knowledge base about the effects of media on language development. With this knowledge in hand, you can begin to make intelligent and informed decisions about how your child uses different media. You also can become an expert in developing rich learning experiences that use these various media. Television, computers, and video games are powerful entities in your child's life. It's important that you control them so that they don't control your child.

Research on Media and Language Development

One thing you should keep in mind as we talk about the effects of media on language development is that there have been many studies published and their results sometimes provide different views of the media. Some research suggests that the media can be helpful to your child's language and social development. Other studies bemoan the harmful effects of media on language development. In our opinion, the main factor that determines whether any type of media will be harmful to your child's growth is *you*. Just as your child is learning about the world around her through your language models and the daily situations to which you expose her, so, too, will she learn about language and the world of the media by what you allow her to view and how you interact with her as she uses the media.

This chapter will provide some specific information about the effects of television, computers, video games, and texting on your child's language development. And we conclude with some suggestions for how you can best take advantage of these media to help your child grow and learn while simultaneously ensuring that these media don't negatively affect your child's growth as a good communicator.

Television and Language Development

In 1949, 10 years after being introduced to the general public, televisions were present in only 2 percent of American households. In the last decade, that number jumped to 98.9 percent, and 66 percent of American households have three or more TVs. Over the past year, the number of households having a television set decreased slightly, falling to 96.7 percent; however, the Nielsen Company suggests that the decline was likely due to many young people preferring to watch television shows and movies from the Internet. Half of American households report that the TV is on most of the time.

The average American child watches 1,680 minutes of television per week, whereas she spends about 3.5 minutes in meaningful conversation with her parents. Almost three out of every four young people between ages 8 and 18 have a TV in their room, and many have access to DVD players, video games, and premium cable channels on their personal TVs. In fact, other than sleeping, the average child spends more time watching television than at any other activity throughout the day. That's a lot of television! No wonder we as parents question its influence on our children. Although these average viewing times are probably excessive, you will see that television has some positive features that may aid your child's language development. However, like most other things, it also may lead to negative outcomes.

How Might Television Help Language Development?

Children are active viewers of television. Their little minds are often engaged in the actions and characters in the shows they watch. They like to discuss what they see and can recognize some of the objects and events on television as representations of those same objects and events in their own lives. In essence, the television can be, in some cases, the equivalent of a moving picture book. Thus, just as books can facilitate your child's language development, television has equal potential. However, just as your child needs your help in learning from books, he also needs your help to learn from television.

TELEVISION MAY PROVIDE SPEECH AND LANGUAGE MODELS

In the past, child language specialists have studied the type of language used in popular young children's shows, such as *Sesame Street*. The findings are fascinating. Researchers have found that some of the language used includes the facilitative type of speech and language models known as child-directed speech (CDS), which we discussed in chapter 2. Just as parents use CDS with their young children, so, too, do some of the children's shows on television. Studies have shown that the CDS on some television shows promotes vocabulary development and preliteracy skills, such as letter identification.

Perhaps one of the best examples of CDS on a children's program was found on *Mister Rogers' Neighborhood*. Although this show may not be shown on your local television station at this point, we encourage you to rent some of the videos sometime and watch them with your child. Fred Rogers either uses words that are familiar to his child audience or provides many examples of the meanings of words when he thinks the vocabulary may be new. He uses a slow, easy rate of speech when he talks. There is quite a bit of redundancy in the information he presents. As best he can, given the medium of television, he talks about actions and objects in the here and now. Even his sentence structure is very simple; generally, he uses sentences with one verb, much like the sentence structure of toddlers. Obviously, Rogers was not talking down to his audience. Rather, he was providing new information, much like you would with your child, in a manner that is interesting and helpful to young children.

Mister Rogers' Neighborhood didn't have the corner on being a good language model for children watching television. Other programs, such as *Sesame Street* and *Rubbadubbers,* also have similar episodes of CDS within their shows. Perhaps what's important to keep in mind here are the shows that tend not to use CDS in their dialogues or scripts. Often, these are cartoons and programs meant for adults (soap operas, sitcoms). These programs tend to have more adultlike conversations. True, when children watch these types of programs, they may get a laugh out of watching one character chase down another or a certain villainous character fall prey to frequent "accidents." However, these shows provide little help in developing a child's language skills because the language used is not developmentally appropriate for the young child. Not surprisingly, then, your job becomes one of determining how developmentally appropriate your child's television programs are.

Studies have shown that the CDS on some
television shows promotes vocabulary development
and preliteracy skills, such as letter identification.

So far, we have been discussing television in this section; however, the same principles apply to the viewing of movies, whether in a theater or on a home or car DVD player. With the advent of DVDs, children have greater access to movies and likely gain more repeated exposures to movies than ever before. We've used family movies in our own homes as a way to facilitate the establishment of positive childhood memories and appreciation for routines. For example, when Caleb was about three years old, his mom and dad took him to Disneyland. They took along the video recorder and filmed Caleb as well as some of the shows and performances. Interestingly, Caleb (at that age, anyway) wasn't interested in television shows. He was quite interested, however, in viewing the videos of himself at Disneyland or the shows that he had seen at Disneyland. We would watch those over and over again and comment about his experiences. It was a great way to facilitate his use of language to refer to the past, an important component of language development.

TELEVISION MAY ENRICH PLAYTIME

Television also may be helpful for children's development of positive imaginative play. Children often will act out characters they have grown to know from television with their friends. In fact, your child may actually use what he sees on television as a basis for playing with his friends. Studies show that children may use the topics of television in a number of ways in their play. First, they may enhance their playacting with their friends, increasing the variety and fun of their regular play adventures. Second, children may use television themes to explore what they can do and how they can play. Children may take on the role of a television character by pretending to be that character, thus possibly extending the limits of what they have done in the past and perhaps challenging themselves to try new actions or methods of play.

So far in this book, we've offered several illustrations from the lives of our children. For this point, let us offer one from our own backgrounds. One of us (we'll let the reader cleverly decipher which one . . .) spent many hours pretending to be Samantha from the 1960s television show *Bewitched*. She had some fun alone, imagining all sorts of delights that appeared with a simple twitch of her nose. Things were a lot more fun when her best friend, Leah, came to play. However, the presence of Leah did add a complication. Quite honestly, they both wanted to be Samantha. Fortunately, another television network developed a similar show, *I Dream of Jeannie*, about the same time. They negotiated, and Leah was happy to become Jeannie (probably because it was a lot easier to cross your arms and blink than it was to twitch your nose). In any case, the theme of "witch and genie" was carried through hours and hours of playtime between two childhood friends. In their world, Samantha and Jeannie were "moms who had to take care of babies," "wives who had husbands with jobs," and other scenarios that they observed in their own mothers' lives and on the television shows. All in all, these experiences with television led to rather rich "stories" that were enacted through pretend play.

Finally, a third way that television may increase play abilities is by increasing your child's socialization skills when playing with other children. When children select a theme for play based on a mutually viewed television show, they are able to develop and expand on a common ground or knowledge base. It is not unlike when you are chatting with a colleague or coworker at your job site and you discover you have mutual interests. Not only does this allow you to increase the length and breadth of your conversations, it also may lead to other means of connecting (arranging a golf date, attending an arts and crafts show together). The same can be said for children who jointly engage in play focused on a television program they have watched. The familiarity of this theme allows them to expand and elaborate in their play, possibly resulting in more detailed, complex play situations.

> *Television may increase play abilities by increasing your child's socialization skills when playing with other children.*

Taken as a whole, then, television can be a positive influence in your child's development, especially as a means for social interaction with his peers during play. Play is an important skill, which is intricately connected to language development. Play is often a means for children to further develop high-level language skills, such as using and understanding more complex sentences or using groups of sentences related to one topic. Through cooperative and imaginative play, children learn to use language to negotiate with and manipulate others toward a common goal, as illustrated in our example of the two childhood friends negotiating to take on different television characters. In group play situations, children also learn to use language out of the here and now. Thus, play is a special situation that often allows children to learn and practice new language skills.

TELEVISION MAY PROVIDE EXPOSURE TO DIFFERENT CULTURES AND LANGUAGES

Interestingly, television also may influence your child's attitude and behaviors toward other children from different cultural and linguistic backgrounds. For example, researchers have studied with whom preschoolers choose to play after watching shows involving children from a variety of racial/cultural backgrounds. As it turns out, at least immediately after watching these shows that depict people from different cultures, children are more apt to choose to play with children from any culture, either theirs or another. Those children who do not view such programs are less likely to choose to play with children from outside their culture.

Although studies such as this do not have any direct impact

on language development, one can argue that encouragement to play with children from different cultures leads not only to better understanding of others but also to additional exposure to other languages and dialects. Such exposure can definitely contribute positively to language development. When children hear different words or different pronunciations for the same object or event, they begin to understand how languages differ and yet are used for the same purpose: communication. With this realization, they are beginning to think about language, that metalinguistic skill we mentioned in chapter 4 that is so important for developing reading and writing skills. Thus, children benefit both socially and in language development by hearing languages and dialects other than their own.

Television has been shown to positively affect the language skills of children learning a second language.

Television has been shown to positively affect the language skills of children learning a second language. Children who watch a television program based on another language can actually learn some of that second language via this medium. Of course, no child will learn a new language completely just by watching television. However, the audio and visual support of television can help preschoolers learn some rudimentary aspects of a second language.

How Might Television and Movies Hinder Language Development?

The helpful effects of television on your child's language development may be lessened considerably depending on a number of factors, including the length of time television is watched, how much she understands about the "reality" of the programs she watches, and the type of program and its content.

Not surprisingly, researchers have discovered that the more hours children watch television, the more likely they will demonstrate lower language abilities. This is true at least for the features of language that have been studied, such as sentence length and complexity and preliteracy skills. Why is this? Most language specialists would say that excessive television viewing takes away from social interactions between children and their parents and peers. A study by the Kaiser Family Foundation found that heavy TV watchers between ages four and six spent an average of 30 minutes less per day playing outside and 8 minutes less per day reading than children who were not heavy TV watchers. It also may be that children are watching television programs that are not matched to their level of language understanding.

It is difficult to determine how much television watching is enough, but not too much, to benefit in the area of language development. One study found that children who watched as little as 15 minutes of a developmentally appropriate program per day had noticeably better language skills than children who watched "less sophisticated" programs, such as cartoons, for longer periods of time. Thus, large amounts of television watching, together with the viewing of developmentally inappropriate shows, may result in a less-than-optimal language-learning situation.

Young children may not always have a clear understanding for differentiating the television shows they watch from real life. When they are toddlers, children may not realize that what they see on television does not exist in the world. For example, they may assume that *Sesame Street* is a real neighborhood. They also are less likely to understand that characters on television cannot hear or talk to them. What this research suggests is that young children are susceptible to believing that what is on television is real.

Why the concern about reality versus fantasy? It all may center on the content of a television program. When children watch shows with a great deal of conflict or aggression, they are more likely to imitate that conflict in social interactions. This may occur because, as toddlers, children do not always understand the "bigger" picture, or plot, of the story. Instead, they focus more on isolated incidents within stories. When toddlers view stories containing examples of violence or conflict, it is likely these individual events are remembered and acted out, rather than the larger story. In the study sponsored by the Kaiser Family Foundation, almost half of the parents reported that they had seen their children imitate aggressive behaviors from TV. However, it's also important to note that a higher percentage of parents (87 percent) said that they had seen their children imitate positive behaviors from TV.

Research has shown that this attention to conflict and violence also extends to real-life depictions, such as nightly news programs. Preschoolers who watch nightly news programs may be at risk for experiencing more nightmares than children who do not watch these shows. For these children, the events that appear to be most frightening are those that involve violence by strangers or contain a great deal of visual coverage of destruction, such as natural disasters. Thus, it is important that you are aware of what your child is watching and the possible effects of that show on her. Some of the conflicts in everyday life can't be avoided. But as a knowledgeable parent, you can be aware of their effect on your child.

How do conflict and violence in the programs your child watches affect her language acquisition? In many ways, there may be no significant effect. Chances are your child will have no problem acquiring different words or linking her thoughts together within more complex sentences. However, it may be that children who view acts of conflict and then act them out restrict the amount of social interaction they have with others (who wants to play with an aggressive peer?). Given this, the benefits of that interaction for social language development are lessened or lost completely. Because we know that children learn language best in situations that involve reciprocal interactions, we want to ensure that children have every opportunity to participate in these situations.

Summary of Television and Language Development

As parents and child language professionals, we suggest you be neither complacent nor overreactive to the facts about television's effects on your child's language development. In reality, the effect of television viewing on language development is a double-edged sword. Too much viewing, and the "wrong" kind of viewing, may impact your child's language and social development in a number of different and negative ways. However, your child can actually learn new language skills and supplement those language skills already acquired by watching developmentally appropriate television shows. Your best approach to dealing with this predicament is to be an active, knowledgeable guide of your child's television viewing habits. At the end of this chapter, we will provide some additional suggestions for how to handle this dilemma of television use.

Computers and Language Development

When we wrote the first edition of this book in 2001, 69 percent of American households had a home computer, and

43 percent of American homes had access to the Internet. Today, those statistics have increased dramatically. Computers are in 77 percent of the homes of children between ages 0 and 6 years of age, and 63 percent of them have Internet access. Internet access increases for students older than 8 years of age to 84 percent, and about a third of students at this age have Internet access in their bedrooms. Twenty-six percent of children between 0 and 6 were reported to use a computer "several times a week," and these children averaged almost an hour of usage per day. One in five children younger than age three can use a mouse to point and click and play video games; an amazing 14 percent of these toddlers can use a computer by themselves. This is astounding, especially for those of us who grew up without any computers at all!

As a parent of a child growing up in the third millennium, you undoubtedly have begun to wonder about the impact of computers on your child's language development. Indeed, it is not unusual to see a commercial or advertisement for a new computer program that will increase your child's language and literacy skills. Even though computers have been in American homes far less than televisions and movies have, we still have some idea of how their use may affect language development.

How Might Computers Help Language Development?

Children can best benefit from computer use when the programs involved are developmentally appropriate to their level of language development. In this case, developmentally appropriate not only means at a level of language that the child understands, it also means that the program is designed in a way that allows the child to explore the content of the program. Not all computer programs are designed this way.

Some computer programs follow a drill-and-practice format, requiring the child to practice one specific skill repeatedly to "get it right." The praise that the child receives suggests there is only one correct answer. Throughout these programs, the computer is in control of the learning. In essence, the child is a passive learner, simply responding to the computer versus actively engaging in the learning process. Common examples include programs that work on "memory" by presenting a sequence of two or three sounds, objects, or tones and having the child select buttons on a screen corresponding to those stimuli. The format goes like this: (1) Computer presents stimulus, (2) child responds, (3) computer says "right" or "wrong." Granted, few computer programs actually say, "Wrong." They use phrases like "Try again" or "Nice try but not right yet." However, the message is the same—the child has failed to do what the computer is requiring.

Other computer programs, however, require much more active participation from your child. These developmentally appropriate programs stimulate your child's physical, emotional, social, and cognitive growth through flexibility and variety in the ways they allow your child to respond. Children using these programs can explore and make choices within situations that represent familiar, everyday events in their lives. A "talking book" is a great example of this type of program. There are many programs on the market in which familiar children's stories are presented with animation that can be interactively explored. That is, each screen presents the story text along with animation elements that can be further selected, based on the child's interest.

It is these types of developmentally appropriate computer programs, then, that can help in language development because they mirror the types of good, language-learning situations your child encounters in other aspects of her life. Just as when she is exploring a new toy, learning a new game, or interacting with others to solve a problem, she can experience similar outcomes with appropriate types of computer programs, such as learning new vocabulary, relating thoughts across sentences, and talking about future situations. Studies have shown that developmentally appropriate programs can lead to higher scores on tests of language development.

Most computer programs involve multimedia presentations, or on-screen activity that involves sights, sounds, and words. One particularly positive outcome of these multimedia presentations is that children's preliteracy and literacy skills may be enhanced. With multimedia computer programs, preschoolers have the opportunity to link the visual aspect of words with the spoken form simultaneously. The "talking books" that we mentioned earlier usually highlight the words as they are read to the child. Older children, who are developing early reading skills, can take advantage of the opportunity to click on individual printed words or even phrases and hear them read aloud again. This allows the child to begin to associate a word that she knows with the printed version.

One particularly positive outcome of these multimedia presentations is that children's preliteracy and literacy skills may be enhanced.

Given these capabilities, it may be tempting for parents to assume that a computer can take the place of the parent in book-reading activities. However, this would be a mistake. While the computer may be able to provide some experiences that help develop preliteracy skills, it will be unable to provide those experiences to the same breadth and depth that *you* can for your child. Thus, the usefulness of the computer for language learning should be viewed as a supplement, not a replacement, for your role in helping your child learn language.

The use of a computer necessarily involves several basic skills, such as the use of certain cognitive skills, visual-perceptual skills, and motor control skills. For example, children must be able to comprehend the use of symbols, so that when they see icons or images on the computer screen (e.g., an hourglass or clock to indicate that the machine is processing information), they understand their meaning. Children also must be able to recognize that the symbols or pictures on the screen stand for objects in the real world. Finally, computer use generally involves fairly sophisticated use of a mouse, requiring the child to understand how to "point and click." Fortunately, as we mentioned earlier, many children younger than three years of age demonstrate all of these cognitive, visual, and motor skills.

These skills needed to use a computer are similar to the skills needed to access other "tools" of learning, such as books. When you think about it, a child must understand the symbols, or pictures, in a book, recognize them as standing for real objects, and be able to manipulate the pages of books to best benefit from book-reading experiences. Thus, computer use is one more way to practice and develop these skills. The skills themselves, whether used for computers or for books, are not language skills. Rather, they allow the child to better experience the language that is inherently part of that experience.

How Might Computers Hinder Language Development?

One major concern with the use of computer programs is that children will devote more time to the computer and less time to non-computer situations. Half of the 8- to 18-year-olds who are heavy users of computers report that they get good grades, and 47 percent report that they get fair to poor

> *One danger with the use of computer programs is that children will devote more time to the computer and less time to non-computer situations, especially those involving peers.*

grades. In contrast, 66 percent of the light users of media report that they get good grades, and only 23 percent reported getting fair to poor grades. A decade ago, there was concern that overuse of solitary computer activities would prohibit children from experiencing and using the social language skills they will need to become good conversationalists and communicators as they mature. Social networking technology has changed this somewhat. There were no differences in heavy, moderate, and light users of computer media in their reports of having a "lot of friends." However, higher numbers of the heavy users reported being bored, getting into trouble, and being sad or unhappy. What is the moral to this story? Everything in moderation.

Drill-and-practice computer programs, as mentioned earlier, also are not conducive to helping language develop. However, even multimedia presentations—those programs that tend to be supportive of learning because of the multiple sources of information—also may cause problems in language learning if designed inappropriately. Some multimedia computer programs pride themselves on the amount of extra auditory and visual effects present in the program. Take, for example, a computer program that is designed to increase a child's ability to tell stories. It may be developmentally appropriate in the language and cues given for the child, and it may follow the expected sequence of a story plot: problem, action, solution. However, the multimedia presentation may include extra animations, sound effects, or songs that are meant to maintain a child's attention. Unfortunately, in some cases, these bells and whistles distract from or interfere with the main purpose of the language experience. In this case, then, the child may benefit less from the experience of learning about the story format because he is more focused on creating sound effects or watching an animation that does little to further the plot of the story.

Summary of Computers and Language Development

More and more, computers are exciting tools and toys that most parents and children are likely to encounter on an almost daily basis. Having prepared this book on computers, we know firsthand what a lifesaver they are! As parents, we also know they have been valuable learning tools and creative toys for our children. As with television, you will need to understand how the computer can enhance your child's language development but also take away from experiences that might be more beneficial for your child. With your growing knowledge base in language development and the influence of computers on that development, you have the power to make wise decisions about your child's use of this type of media. We will provide you with some specific suggestions for computer use later. But first, let's review the effects of video game use on language development.

Video Games and Language Development

It may seem odd that we would include this type of media in our discussion on factors that may influence language development. However, statistics show that 62 percent of all American homes have a video game player and that the average child spends up to seven hours a week playing video games. As parents, we sometimes feel we have *lived* these statistics! It is not unusual to hear the familiar *ring*s, *ding*s, *boof*s, and *gotcha*s when you step into one of our homes. Our children are older than your child at this stage, but like you, we wondered how these games might influence our children's development. Let's review, then, how video games might have a positive and not-so-positive impact on children's language development.

How Might Video Games Help Language Development?

Believe it or not, there are some positive aspects to those noisy games you hear in your den or in the car. Video games often are the first way your child becomes familiar with modern technology. Thus, the fine-motor abilities and visual–spatial skills needed to participate in the task may pave the way for use of other types of technology, such as computers. More important for language development, many video games require a certain level of problem solving and logic as well as the ability to follow directions. Thus, although video games most likely won't be the way to facilitate language development, they may be tools for your child to use to practice understanding fairly complex sets of directions.

With some video games, there is a built-in need for interaction between two players. We see this as a positive aspect of video games and one that can help in language development. Given the right game, you can set up a situation in which you and your child can jointly participate and focus on a common goal or topic. During this time, you can help your child's language to develop further by talking about the game, the directions, and how the game relates to his everyday activities and by modeling appropriate levels of language. In other words, just like you do when the two of you are talking about *any* toy, video games have the potential for enabling a good, language-rich interaction to occur.

One of the special benefits of interaction regarding video games is that it places the child in the role of "teacher" or "facilitator" and the parent in the role of "learner." This can give your child several opportunities to consider another person's perspective and provide the appropriate amount and kind of information accordingly. Both Caleb and Caitlin tried faithfully to teach their mom the ins and outs of games such as Mario Brothers. It was quite apparent in these situations that the children's visual and spatial memories, as well as their eye–hand coordination, far surpassed their mom's. It was a nice change for them to get to be the experienced ones, the ones in the conversation to be instructing, facilitating, and so on. Of course, they also got to see what it was like to have a student who wasn't always optimally attentive!

Opportunities for interaction set video games apart from other media, such as television. Television is a fairly noninteractive activity. Most people just sit and watch it. Typically, little interaction occurs between parent and child during television viewing (but see our suggestions below!). However, video games either require two players at a time or provide a great chance for the child to teach someone else how to play. These opportunities for active learning and interaction are definitely a plus!

How Might Video Games Hinder Language Development?

Just as there are video games that encourage critical thinking, problem solving, and interaction among participants, there also are games that encourage social isolation of the player from others. Children who play games that are for single players for excessive amounts of time are, by definition, decreasing the amount of time they can spend in social interactions with their peers. As we mentioned previously, this may adversely affect language development because these children are not receiving the language models and play interactions upon which further language acquisition is built.

Similarly, some games do not require any type of active involvement of the mind, other than to shoot a character on the screen or jump one more hurdle. With excessive amounts of this type of play, a child is decreasing the opportunities he has to engage in other activities that are more beneficial to language development. Language is a means for solving problems in our heads. That is, we often will talk to ourselves, either within our minds or aloud, to help figure out a solution to a problem. When little thinking is involved in a video game, then that means less opportunities to practice using language for critical thinking activities. Just like any other skill, additional practice leads to better development and performance.

Now some parents might think that there is no real harm in their child occasionally playing one-person games or games with little creative thinking required. They are probably right. However, as children become more entrenched in the playing of video games, what used to be occasional occurrences may soon become more frequent occurrences. It is at that point that parents need to be concerned whether their children are participating in situations that encourage and facilitate further language use and development or becoming socially isolated.

Finally, just as some young children have a difficult time separating fantasy from reality on television, so, too, do they have difficulty separating animated violence in video games from real violence. Studies show that children who play excessive amounts of violent video games may demonstrate more aggression in their play with others. Certainly, this type of behavior is not conducive to developing social language skills within play situations.

Summary of Video Games and Language Development

Video games are no different in many respects from television or computers. They can contribute to your child's language development, and they can diminish the usefulness of the experience. As parents, if you consider these games mostly as another toy you can use to play *with* your child, then chances are your child will reap the benefits of this type of media. You are an informed parent, so making decisions about the types of video games your child uses should become quite easy. We also provide some concrete ideas to follow to help you make some decisions about video games, computers, and television use by your child. Isn't it amazing how many issues you have to consider as a parent? At least you know, though, that the major benefactor of all of this knowledge building is your child.

Texting and Language Development

Erin and Robert had decided to give their daughter, Abby, a cell phone for her birthday. They decided to learn to use texting themselves because their friends said that it was a great way to communicate with their kids. Erin received the following message from Abby:

"Hey Mom. GTG to mall w BFFs 2 shop. No u luv that! ROFL! C U L8R."

Erin could only interpret a portion of that message. Was something good happening? Should she be happy? Worried?

Within a brief 10-year period, texting has become a major method of communicating for children, adolescents, and adults. The age at which children get their first mobile phones has dropped markedly, and most children in developed countries have their own mobile phone by the late elementary years. To make texting more efficient, a variety of acronyms, abbreviations, and other terms have become widely used, and this has resulted in some concerns expressed both in the popular press and by parent groups and educators. Will the use of the abbreviations B4, PLZ, QT, and PPL hinder the spelling and reading of *before, please, cutie,* and *people,* respectively? You may be surprised to find that the answer is "Absolutely not!"

Research regarding the relationship between texting and literacy is just becoming available. This is partly due to increased ownership of mobile phones in general, but it also is related to the relative increase in texting itself. For example, one study reports that there were 100 billion text messages sent in the United Kingdom in 2009! That was approximately 1,700 per person, or 4 per day. Texting comprises over half (63 percent) of the use of mobile phones in people between 16 and 24 years of age. Even the children between 8 and 11 years included in this study reported using their phones more often to send text messages than to make calls.

The concerns over potential negative effects of texting seem legitimate on the surface. After all, there is no need to use conventional grammar or spelling; in fact, its use is discouraged because of space limitations and the need for speed and efficiency. However, numerous studies confirm the notion that just as language and literacy skills affect the quality of conventional reading and writing, they also affect an individual's proficiency with texting. This actually makes sense. It is similar to learning a "different language," and the more you know about how words work, the better you will be at cracking this new code. For example, we talked about the importance of phonemic awareness and letter–sound knowledge in chapters 4 and 5. These skills are definitely required when the word *great* is texted as *GR8*. Most of the abbreviations (BFF, LOL, ROFL) are actually the first letters (and/or sounds) in the conventional spellings of the words they represent.

The beauty of texting is that it is a form of written language that is extremely motivating for children to learn and use. Any medium that encourages children to read and write frequently must be advantageous, right? Our own texting skills do not even approximate the skills of young people; however, we use the medium ourselves fairly frequently to communicate. Initially, we used it in order to communicate with our own kids, but now we use it to communicate with friends and colleagues. We use that medium for the same reasons that kids do—sometimes it's more convenient and efficient to text rather than call.

Your Role in Your Child's Use of Media

The research speaks loudly and clearly. All four of these types of media can be helpful to your child's language and social development if used correctly and wisely. As you think specifically about your child's use of media, there are a few key points to keep in mind for each type of media.

Your Child's Use of the Television

Your child has many television shows from which to choose. Some of these programs will be educationally and developmentally appropriate for your child and others will not. Television has a ratings system now, but we have found that the best way to determine what is right for your child is for you to either preview an episode of the show before your child watches future episodes or view the show with her. Only then will you be sure that your child's time in front of the television is useful.

> The best way to determine what is right for your child is for you to either preview an episode of the show before your child watches future episodes or view the show with her.

As you watch television with your child, keep in mind that you want to explain and discuss what your child is thinking about the programs she watches. Also, just as you do during your book-reading time, you can draw links between the "unreal" world of television and the real world of the child's everyday experiences. We find a good time for this discussion is during commercials or by pausing a video temporarily. An exchange might go something like this:

> **DAD:** "Wow. This is exciting. Tell me what you think about the show so far."
>
> **CHILD:** "That bear is a bad bear. He's mean."
>
> **DAD:** "Yes, he is. Do you think that all bears are like that?"
>
> **CHILD:** "I don't know."
>
> **DAD:** "Well, sometimes, bears can be mean, but many times they aren't. I learned from books that the best thing to do is to watch them from far away . . . or in a zoo. Do you think we have bears around here?"
>
> **CHILD:** "Yeah, just like that one on TV."
>
> **DAD:** "Well, actually, that bear isn't from around here. This is a movie from a place far away. The only bears close by us are in the zoo. Remember when we went to the zoo? We saw those bears? They were safe in a special area, where we could see them, but not be too near them."

In this exchange, the father is helping the child to learn that the program is not representative of where she lives, broadening her understanding of the topic, indirectly showing the importance of book reading, and engaging the child in thinking about what she is watching. All of these are strategies that will enhance television viewing.

As a parent of a young child, you also can begin to set up viewing habits that will develop a realistic relationship with the television. For example, you want to discourage watching television during mealtimes. If you recall from chapter 4, mealtimes are actually great times to develop preliteracy skills, as well as for engaging your child in conversations. These activities are very difficult to do if one or both of you are focused on the television screen. Also, set certain limits for television viewing. The American Academy of Pediatrics suggests no more than one to two hours per day, which is less than half of what the average American child watches. With limited television time, your child will have additional time for the experiences that can strongly influence language development, such as dialogues with you or play interactions with her peers.

Finally, when setting up daily rituals, consider leaving the last few minutes of the day, the bedtime minutes, for quality book reading and talking with you. Studies show that parents who read to their children are more likely to have children who grow up to be readers themselves. In addition, this time, which typically is a calming down time, allows your child to focus on the language of the book and the models you use to link the book to her everyday experiences. What a wonderful and fruitful way to end the day!

Your Child's Use of the Computer

As with television, you want to be fully aware of what your child does on the family computer. Many times you have control of this because you buy the computer programs that will be used. With the increase in relatively low-cost computer programs, parents have many choices when buying programs for their child. Consider the content and purpose of the computer program you might purchase. Is it geared toward educating your child or just entertaining him? Both can be enjoyable, and both can be learning experiences, so it makes sense to have both kinds of programs available to your child. Is the purpose of the program to drill and practice a specific skill, or is it to allow your child to explore and solve problems as he interacts with the program? It will be these latter programs that enhance your child's language development and make his time spent on the computer well worth it.

Talk to your child about the purpose of the program. You will find it is fascinating what your child is learning, or not learning, as the case may be. Remember, sometimes programs distract the child from the real learning experience. Take, for example, the following scenario:

> **MOTHER:** "That's a fun little story. Tell me what you learned from it."
>
> **CHILD:** "If you click the dog's tail, it wags, but if you click on its mouth, it barks really loud!"
>
> **MOTHER:** "Yes, that does happen. What about the story? What happens with the dog?"
>
> **CHILD:** "He will keep barking each time you click on his mouth."
>
> **MOTHER:** "Yes. But didn't he lose his bone? What happens when he loses his bone?"
>
> **CHILD:** "I don't remember."
>
> **MOTHER:** "Well, let's go through it together and see if we can figure it out ourselves."

This short scenario emphasizes how a well-meaning program can mislead a child about its purpose. In this case, the excitement of making the dog bark and wag its tail has overshadowed the experience of learning about the problem, the action, and the solution. Luckily, the mother is there to help the child appreciate what he can learn from the computer program.

Finally, you also want to consider setting some guidelines for computer use. If you have a computer with Internet access, monitor your child's use of it. There are many programs available to parents that allow them to block parts of the Internet that are unsuitable and inappropriate for their child. Place the computer in a location of the house where you can see what your child is doing. By doing this, you more likely will be aware of what your child is seeing and playing on the computer.

> *You want to consider setting some guidelines for computer use.*

Your Child's Use of Video Games

Like many parents, you may have gone to a Redbox station or searched online via GameFly with your child and seen the sheer volume of video games available. It is staggering! However, you have the tools to help you and your child make wise decisions about which games to choose.

First, consider video games that allow multiple players at the same time. As we said before, this likely will lead to more social interactions. Also, read the description of the game on the box. Does the game involve thinking and problem solving? If so, not only will your child's hands be working, but her mind will be, too. Games that require thinking skills also allow you to model for your child how you can use language to solve problems. This is easily done by "thinking aloud." For example:

> **PARENT:** "This is hard. It seems like I have to be smarter than the wizard. Okay, I'm thinking I should try and sneak the jewels into the castle. What do you think?"
>
> **CHILD:** "If you do that, you need something to hide them."
>
> **PARENT:** "Okay, good point. I see several things around me. I could use a box, but it is too big. I could use my pockets in my jacket, but they are too small. Hmm, I'm still thinking, are you?"
>
> **CHILD:** "Yeah! Why don't you use the bag?"
>
> **PARENT:** "Good idea. Now let's talk about our next problem."

This little dialogue not only shows how language can be used to convey how you think, but it also emphasizes another important point: Play *with* your child using this media of video games. Just as you join in on other play activities, you can engage in this play as well.

Finally, just as with the other types of media, be aware of what options you and your child have. You can limit the amount of time spent with video games so that there is plenty of time to play non–video game activities. You can keep the video game player and other media out of your child's bedroom. Remember, increased access can lead to playing to excess. You also can be knowledgeable about the content of the games. You may be aware that video games now have ratings to help parents determine appropriateness for their child's use. Often, even the picture on the front cover will help you decide this! If you follow these simple suggestions, we bet your child will obtain all the benefits of video games for language development with few or none of the drawbacks.

Your Child's Use of Texting

Based on current research as well as the experiences we've had with our own children, we offer the following comments and suggestions. First, texting has become one of the main ways that young people keep in touch with their friends and plan social activities. Consequently, allowing your child supervised access to this technology may contribute to positive relationships with her peers.

Second, make sure your child understands the financial limits on his use of texting. As with any media, texting involves a cost. Many of our friends have reported horror stories of getting their monthly phone bills with hundreds of dollars for texting that exceeded their plans. Don't wait until something like that happens with your child. Make sure he understands how many text messages he can send in any given month. This could provide a wonderful opportunity for him to see "math in action"!

Third, take advantage of this medium to communicate with your child. If you don't already text on a regular basis, this will provide an opportunity, like video games, in which your child can be the leader and you can be the learner. On the other hand, if your child is just beginning to text, offer to help her interpret some of the messages she receives. She also may need help in using the T9 system (that's more or less a word prediction system that is employed by many basic phones. Usage is beyond the purview of this book, but there are lots of resources for the system available online.)

Finally, make a determination of the extent to which you will monitor your student's texting. This is one of the many personal decisions that we have to make as parents, and it is affected by the maturity level of the individual child. Frankly, all text messages are stored on a mobile phone until space is exceeded or they are deleted. Consequently, monitoring can range from one extreme to another. You can (1) directly read all of the text conversations in which your child engages, (2) check the phone numbers that are either sending or receiving texts from your student's phone, or (3) monitor volume of usage to ensure that it falls within acceptable ranges and plan limitations. There are likely other levels of monitoring along this continuum, and once again, you as the parent are best equipped to determine which level is best for your child at a particular point in time.

Chapter Summary

The most important point to keep in mind is that you have the tools to make these media helpful and important for your child. You know how to monitor the content of these media and how important it is to talk about what your child views. You know to discuss whether the actions he sees on the screen are similar to real-life experiences or not and how possibly aggressive or violent actions are potentially dangerous and inappropriate in everyday situations.

You also know that it is important to provide alternative, non-media activities to enhance your child's language development, because these experiences will far outweigh those from media experiences. Engaging in all activities as a family shows you are committed to making the most out of all situations you encounter.

Finally, don't forget what we talked about in chapters 1 to 5. Using media is no different from using other objects in this world when it comes to helping your child develop language. If you know how language develops, and you use that knowledge in practical, meaningful, everyday situations, your child will benefit greatly.

9

LANGUAGE DEVELOPMENT AND CHILD CARE

D ID YOU KNOW?

- The educational background of a child care provider can affect a child's language development.

- Simple household items like kitchen utensils, pots, and pans may be more beneficial to children's language development than fancy toys.

- The number of children per child care provider may affect children's language development.

"*Daddy, don't leave! I want to go with youuu...Daddy, I love you...No, Daddy...Don't gooooooooooo.*"

These words were spoken...well, screamed...by Genevieve every day for the first three weeks of her first experience with out-of-the-home child care. They pretty much broke the heart of her father. She was only three. He was abandoning her. Her tears were flooding the child care center. How could he be so insensitive? In fact, this association between tears and screams and excruciating pangs of guilt continued until about halfway through the third week, when Genevieve's child care provider informed her father that as soon as he was out of sight, she immediately stopped crying and started playing with her peers.

Although the guilt somewhat diminished, her father was still bothered by the overriding question of how day care would affect his child. Most important for this book and for this particular father, what are the effects of child care on the language development of young children? The purpose of this chapter is to provide the answer to this last question. We will review the factors that make child care situations effective, and noneffective, in furthering your child's acquisition of language. In addition, we will provide you with some ideas for how you can determine whether a particular child care situation best meets your child's needs, given her age.

Like the information we presented in chapter 8 on the media, the research in the area of child care and language development spans many different types of families, families that vary in socioeconomic status, culture, and education. Studies have been conducted in child care programs based in homes as well as in public and private child care facilities. Thus, the information we provide should be relevant to almost all situations in which you might find yourself when searching for child care.

When it comes down to the bottom line, the most important factor in your child's child care situation and its effects on language development is *quality adult language stimulation.* Thus, whether your child receives it from you as a stay-home parent or from you as a working parent in collaboration with her child care provider, your child's language development will be enhanced when the adults around her know about language development and use age-appropriate strategies. So let's begin looking at this situation of child care and what seems to be most crucial for your child's development.

Research on the Effects of Child Care on Language Development

Can a child care situation positively or negatively affect language development? The answer to this question is yes in both ways. Researchers have been studying the effects of child care on children's development for quite some time, and the results are very interesting. But before we share those with you, let's take a few minutes to talk about *how* researchers look at child care situations to determine what works and what doesn't work.

The most important factor in your child's child care situation and its effects on language development is quality adult language stimulation.

Most child care situations (in-home care, public or private child care, and preschool) are evaluated in a number of ways, including (1) appropriateness of activities, (2) provider-to-child ratio (the number of children for which a provider is responsible), (3) the quality of the provider–child and child–child interactions, and (4) the physical environment of the care facility. These situations have been examined in relationship to various characteristics of the children who are enrolled in the programs, such as their language skills and play behaviors. Sometimes, child care environments are judged simply through observations. Other times, they are rated by performances on tests or by questionnaires. Some studies even try to compare child care facilities that have different philosophies.

The point we make here is that our review of child care and its effect on language development comes from a number of studies that have looked at the situation in a variety of ways. We will try to provide you with the main facts, regardless of how the researchers studied the child care situation and what type of situation it was. We have organized this information around three main aspects of child care that can positively impact language development: the providers, the environment, and the curriculum (the activities and philosophy of the provider).

We believe the main feature to look for in your child's care provider is warmth and a genuine interest in your child.

What to Look for in Child Care Providers

Speaking as parents, we believe the main feature to look for in your child's care provider is warmth and a genuine interest in your child. Nothing can lead to stifled development more than a child care provider who shows little care, affection, compassion, or positive regard for your child and his development. We know of no way to measure this other than to use your own parental feelings and intuitions. However, besides providing affection and attention to your child, you also want to ensure that the provider will help your child's language develop.

Studies have shown, perhaps not surprisingly, that one of the best features in a child care provider for helping your child acquire language is an understanding of child development. If your child care provider is strongly grounded in her knowledge of how children develop, chances are your child will score better on tests of language development than children who have providers who have little understanding of typical development in children.

The educational level of providers is strongly tied to their understanding of child development. For the most part, children who have child care providers who have higher levels of education (beyond high school) will score better on language tests than their peers. This is especially true for providers who have some type of teacher or educational certification, although this is not necessary to be an informed and knowledgeable provider.

What is it that more knowledgeable providers do that sets them apart from less educated providers? All the research suggests that educated providers are more likely to understand how to fine-tune their interactions and activities to the needs of the individual child—your child. Researchers call this taking advantage of "teachable moments," those times when it seems the child is ready and willing to learn something new. Instead of providing activities or toys that require all children to play in the same way regardless of their developmental level, educated providers are able to tailor an activity or use of a toy to best help your child develop the skills that are next to be learned. In essence, educated child care providers interact with children just as we discussed in chapters 1 to 5. They follow the child's lead in play and language, provide models of language at or just above the level of the child, and show respect and understanding for what the child says.

Of course, a provider's knowledge and education about language and child development should not be static. A provider cannot simply take one or two classes on child development and have all of the information that will ever be needed. Like other individuals involved in health and education, child care providers should be periodically updating their knowledge base. Some public and private child care facilities allow this, offering providers workshops or time off to attend conferences so they can increase their understanding of child development and current "best practices." Child care providers also have opportunities to learn new information via the Internet. The number of websites dedicated to this topic is phenomenal. Thus, it will be important that you determine whether the prospective child care site values continuing education.

To best help your child's language develop while he is in child care, then, you will want to think about several factors surrounding the provider. You will want to inquire about the educational level and certification status of the providers at the child care site and their opportunities for continuing education. You also will want to determine whether the providers have a background in child development, including, it is hoped, language development. Finally, you will need to determine how much attention and care the providers typically give the children at the site. A thorough search of the facility's website is a great place to start. It will help you know which centers to include or exclude in your list to visit. Ultimately your best ways to evaluate a prospective facility is to observe the providers at different parts of the day and talk to other parents whose children currently attend the child care center. By investigating these aspects of the child care site, you can begin to develop an opinion about the people who will be caring for your child while you are away.

What to Look for in Child Care Facilities

When we were considering different child care options for our children, one of our first criteria was that it had to be clean, light, open, and welcoming. However, we also looked for other factors that have been shown to be effective for language development. First, we looked at the materials that were available to the children in the child care site. We wanted a variety of toys and materials that could encourage the use of our child's imagination. Interestingly, one of the best ways to encourage imagination and increase a child's use and understanding of language is the presence of toys and play areas that mirror everyday situations. We also determined the number of children assigned to any one child care provider. The ratio of students to teacher may influence the quality and quantity of language models your child receives.

Play Materials and Learning Events

For some time, researchers have known that children can learn and use more language when they are engaged in games and activities for which they have some prior knowledge. Most children, even by the age of two, have developed some fairly good ideas about familiar situations, such as grocery shopping, birthday parties, trips to McDonald's, and so forth. This knowledge about familiar events is called script knowledge (recall our discussion of scripted events in chapter 3). Scripts contain all the information children have about the people and objects involved in the situation, what actions happen, and possibly the order of the actions that occur. When a child has a good understanding of how events occur and who does what, this means the child can concentrate more on the language that is used to talk about or converse within those situations.

Think about your own experiences as an adult. Most likely, the first time you tried to line dance or play chess, you struggled so much with learning the objects and actions involved, that you had a hard time talking during the activity. However, the more you continued to participate in these activities, the more the objects and actions became familiar. Pretty soon, you were probably talking about "ball changes" and "crossovers," or you were able to talk about the day's events while taking your opponent's pawn! The same is true for children. The more they know about an event, the more they can converse during the activity and use the specialized language terms involved.

Of course this doesn't mean that children should not be asked to play with toys or participate in situations with which they have little experience. If we said this, children would never learn all the wonderful things they do about this world! Rather, this means that helpful child care sites have plenty of toys and play areas that capitalize on children's knowledge of familiar events, their script knowledge, so that the children have multiple opportunities to learn about and use language without the burden of learning a new activity. Child care sites that have scripted play areas are more likely to have children who maintain topics of conversation longer, ask for more clarifications for understanding, and demonstrate more social play behaviors than do those without these play areas.

Of course, what might be a scripted play situation for one child may not be a scripted play situation for another. For example, a play area modeled after a school setting would be inappropriate for children who have not yet attended school. Children who are growing up in rural areas might benefit from areas, or "centers" (specific areas of play), that are devoted to farm life, with toys and houses that represent those found on a farm. Conversely, children in urban areas might benefit more from toys and activities that reflect their everyday lives, including large street maps, cars, buses, and trucks representing a downtown scene. Moreover, most children, by the age of four, should have some familiarity with events and situations dealing with acts of literacy (reading, writing, spelling). It is these types of play situations that also have been shown to be very beneficial to children's language development.

Child care facilities that include centers where literacy actions (pretend reading or writing) can occur using the tools of literacy (paper, pencils, crayons, books, and so on) tend to have children who score higher on tests of language and literacy. This makes a lot of sense. These child care centers, in essence, are creating what we described in chapter 4 as high-print environments. We have seen child care facilities that have centers based on the post office or grocery stores. Children play in these centers, "writing" notes, sticking them in envelopes, and mailing them. They "write" lists of needed items and then shop for the items, "reading" the items on the list and crossing them off after each item is put into the shopping cart. These types of play experiences reinforce children's understanding of the events while simultaneously providing them experience in literacy events.

The more experiences children have with literacy, the better prepared they will be as they enter formal schooling. Keep in mind children do not need formal reading or writing instruction at this stage of development. In fact, most children do not have the prerequisite skills needed for this. That is why activities focused on preliteracy skills will best help your preschooler's language and literacy skills develop.

Child care facilities that include centers where literacy actions (pretend reading or writing) can occur using the tools of literacy (paper, pencils, crayons, books, and so on) tend to have children who score higher on tests of language and literacy.

Most child care sites offer more than just literacy and play experiences. For example, there is a very good chance that the child care facility you observe will provide television, or videos, for the children in its care. A recent study found differences in the use of television between home-based and center-based child care settings. Children in center-based settings viewed less than a half hour (0.4) of television per day, whereas children in home-based day care watched 2.4 hours per day. That is quite a difference! You know from chapter 8 that television in and of itself is not a negative contributor to language development. Rather, it is what is watched, and for how long, that can affect language development. Thus, it will be highly important for you to know whether the television is used as just one means for helping your child develop or as a time filler so that adults do not need to interact with the children.

Finally, you will want to determine whether the providers consider child care to go beyond just their facility. Quality child care providers recognize the importance and impact of the family on developing children, so they attempt to include parents and siblings as much as possible. Involving parents and other family members, either by encouraging volunteerism at the site or by providing means for the family to be better informed of what the child does while at the site, may increase the quality and quantity of rich, language-learning experiences. For example, one group of researchers examined the effect of parents' knowledge of their child's daily activities on language use. On alternating days, children left the child care facility with materials that were either "child-focused" (art projects completed by the child, souvenirs from field trips) or just their personal items (coats, lunch bag). The researchers then audio-recorded the parent–child conversations held in the car on the way home. They found that when the parent and child had the child-focused materials to discuss, the language used by the child was more mature. The children maintained the conversational topic longer, and the parents were able to question and comment more. Thus, in very simple ways, child care providers and parents can extend the benefits of child care beyond the four walls of the facility.

As you tour a prospective child care facility, ask yourself about these key elements. Does the facility include centers or play areas that contain toys and materials representative of the familiar events in your child's life? Will your child have at least some knowledge of the types of toys available? Does the facility provide opportunities for toddlers and preschoolers to play with materials that are used for the literacy acts of reading, writing, and spelling? Does the facility limit the amount of television watched and have appropriate guidelines for the type of programs provided? Are parents encouraged to be active in their child's child care experiences? If you are answering yes to most or all of these questions, then chances are you have found a child care site whose environment is conducive to your child's further language development.

Provider-to-Child Ratios

Considerable research is available examining provider-to-child ratios. Ratios of 1 to 7 or less are considered desirable for toddlers and preschoolers. The ratio is considerably less for younger children. Infants should have a ratio of 1 to 1 or 1 to 2. Babies may have a ratio of 1 to 3 or 1 to 4. Results from several studies suggest that smaller provider-to-child ratios lead to better overall language development for the children involved. In addition to adult-to-child ratios, you should also consider the overall number of children in attendance. Even if a facility offers a provider-to-child ratio of one adult to six children, three adults with a group of eighteen children would be considered large and not beneficial to language development. The larger the group, the lower the scores on tests of language development. In fact, children who are cared for in large groups may use fewer words per sentence, use fewer different words, and talk at a different rate than children in smaller groups.

What is it about larger provider-to-child ratios and large groups that hinder language development? The answer can be summarized easily: There is a lack of quality interaction between the adult and the children. When an adult is responsible for many children, there is little time to meet the needs of individual children. The adult is no longer able to easily follow a child's lead in a conversation, determine the focus of a child's attention and talk about it, or provide meaningful models of language that are just above the level that each particular child is capable of producing. The research shows that most adults who find themselves trying to interact with a large group of young children spend a great deal of time organizing and managing the group, rather than in quality interactions with the children.

What to Look for in the Child Care Curriculum

The curriculum of a child care facility primarily refers to the activities provided. Some child care facilities emphasize a direct-instruction curriculum, where children are presented information in a traditional teacher–student mode and maybe even tested on the material. Other sites provide a more open-atmosphere curriculum, in which children are expected to learn when they are ready to learn. In this type of curriculum, the provider supports the child in whatever she wants to do or learn but gives little actual direction. Finally, other child care facilities may follow a type of hybrid curriculum that views learning as an interaction between directed instruction from the adult and activities chosen by the child. In these situations, the adult sets up activities specific to certain types of learning and then guides, as opposed to teaching, the child to learn new information and expand on known information.

Perhaps the differences among these three styles can best be exemplified using a book-reading activity. In a direct instruction situation, a provider would have a goal of teaching reading. She may use drill cards to teach certain words or letters, or she may read a book and then require the children to answer questions to check for understanding or comprehension. The focus would be similar to traditional school classrooms, where the provider teaches, asks a question, then judges the answer.

In an open-atmosphere curriculum, a provider would read books to the children but not necessarily ask questions about the book or check for comprehension. If a child asked about something in the book, however, the provider would respond with the needed information. In this case, the child determines what will be gained from the book reading. It may even be that the child does not want to listen to the book reading, choosing to engage in some other activity instead.

Finally, in the hybrid curriculum, a provider would read a book, knowing the level of the children and what they might need to learn new language or literacy skills. For example, if she thought the children were ready to start using their knowledge of story plots to predict what happens in stories, she might first model and then ask the students to predict upcoming events in a story. If she felt the students were ready to learn more about letter sounds, she might make comments about how certain words start with the same sounds, either as she read the book or after she had completed reading the book and was reviewing it. In all cases, she would guide the students, through her models of language and thought-provoking, leading statements, to higher levels of understanding of language and literacy.

The research shows that for young children, up through the preschool years, the direct-instruction curriculum is least effective in helping them learn. The other two types of curricula can both be helpful, most likely at different times or in different situations. For example, it may be that the open-atmosphere curriculum is most helpful when children are first exploring new situations and new toys, where their focus will naturally be on learning how the particular activity or object works. This approach appears to allow more child-to-child interactions, which have been shown to encourage longer sentences. Conversely, the hybrid curriculum is likely best for when children are engaged in activities that are somewhat familiar and ready to learn more about those situations. In these situations, there will be more adult-to-child interactions, which have been shown to increase children's conversational turn taking and use of complex language skills, reduce the number of gaps between conversational turns, and lead to greater use of language to solve problems.

As you can probably guess, these last two types of curricula best meet what we feel are appropriate types of language-learning situations. They reflect what we said in chapters 1 to 5. Just as we suggested that you follow your child's lead in conversations, model appropriate types of language, and so on, so, too, should the providers for your child.

The curriculum of a child care facility is crucial. No matter how educated a provider is, if she must provide for too many children at one time and has little flexibility in meeting the needs of the children, she will not be helpful in further developing your child's language. Thus, as you observe different child care facilities, observe the size groups they provide and the number of adults per children in those groups. Ask about the facility's philosophy of care and education, and determine how well you think it matches what is known to be beneficial to acquiring language. By becoming an informed and knowledgeable parent about the providers, the child care site, and the curriculum, you will be ready to make appropriate and important decisions about your child's care.

What Child Care Is Best for My Child?

As you might guess, if we could provide the definitive truth in answer to this question, we would be touring the world doing seminars devoted solely to this topic! Instead, the best answer will need to come from you. As you contemplate this answer, we encourage you to think about the information we have provided, and combine that information with what you learned in chapters 1 to 5. Undoubtedly, just as we discovered, you will find your answer will vary somewhat with your family's specific needs as well as with the age of your child. In the last few pages of this chapter, we will provide some suggestions regarding what to look for in a child care situation and what to ask depending on the age of your child. We start off each developmental stage with a scenario of a child care facility. Read that scenario and then determine whether you think it is appropriate before reading our answer. Let's see how much you have learned!

No matter how educated a provider is, if she must provide for too many children at one time and has little flexibility in meeting the needs of the children, she will not be helpful in further developing your child's language.

What Type of Child Care Is Best for My Infant?

Mr. and Mrs. Bardzecki are looking for a child care facility for their six-month-old daughter, Anna. As they enter one site, they notice that it is bright and clean and has a wonderful, homelike atmosphere to it. There are several rooms to the child care facility, one that is specific to infants. Observing the room, they see that there are several adults, up to three, in the room at any given time. Each of the 12 cribs appears clean and well kept. There are bright posters on the wall and cute little mobiles hanging over each crib and over the changing tables as well. There are several rocking chairs and some blankets on the floor for the infants to lie on and play with toys. As the Bardzeckis talk with some of the providers, they learn that each woman seems very warm and friendly and that each has been providing care for more than 10 years. The director of the child care emphasizes that the infant providers are all women who have had their own children and are experienced in child care.

What do you think? Is this an appropriate setting for little Anna? Are there any concerns or questions you have? The facility seems clean and the providers well intentioned.

There appear to be visual stimuli for the children to look at and toys for the children to manipulate. However, looking at the information provided, we definitely have some questions and concerns.

First, we worry about the provider-to-infant ratio. If all the cribs were filled, the ratio, at best, would be one provider to every four infants. This would be quite high. In addition, the size of the group, 12 infants, suggests that individualized attention would be scarce. Remember, infants are fascinated with the human face and voice and can learn a great deal about language by interacting with an adult. With such a large group and large provider-to-infant ratio, we wonder how likely it will be that the providers can encourage joint attention with the infants, engage them in playful babbling back and forth, and follow their interests and visual gaze and make it the topic of a conversation.

We also wonder and would require more information about the providers' level of education and understanding of development. As you know from reading chapter 1, the first year of life involves an incredible amount of learning. Experience can provide a lot of knowledge regarding child development. However, we wonder how much the providers are aware of the special skills that infants have and develop during the first year of life, such as their preference for differences in shapes, contours, and shadowing; their developing ability to babble in more mature ways; and their use of gestures and vocalizations to comment and question, to name a few.

The point here is not to put down this particular child care facility. Chances are the providers are well meaning and really care about the infants in their charge. However, as a parent, you want to consider all the facts before deciding where your child will spend a large portion of her day. So, as you look for child care for your infant, make sure that there is an adequate provider-to-infant ratio, a small group, and an educated and caring set of providers.

What Type of Child Care Is Best for My Baby?

Mrs. Dodds has a neighbor, Virginia, who provides child care in her home. She has known Virginia for some time and considers her bright (she went to community college for two years) and thoughtful. When she first started offering child care, Virginia mentioned that she had joined an Internet group for in-home child care providers so that she could stay up on current practices in child care. Virginia takes care of her own 19-month-old son and a 23-month-old niece. She has turned her den into her child care room. There are plenty of windows to allow in light and plenty of toys, including large-size dolls, cars, a house and furniture, a play kitchen with kitchen materials, and a large shelf of children's books. She lets the children watch Sesame Street once every morning and afternoon. Virginia prides herself on cleanliness and ensures that she constantly washes her hands after helping each child with his or her food and toileting needs.

Mrs. Dodds is trying to decide whether she should let Virginia care for her 22-month-old son. What do you think?

Though we might ask a few more questions, like you, we are feeling very confident about this situation and its helpful influence on language development. In this case, the provider, Virginia, appears to be eager to educate herself on what the children might need for learning. She has stocked her play areas with toys that should be familiar to the children, allowing scripted play to occur. The ratio of provider to baby is relatively small and the entire group is small. The environment seems conducive to learning.

Given this, we still would like to observe Virginia to determine how she interacts with the children. Does she spend all her time with them, following their leads, letting them explore new toys and play together with familiar toys? Will she be adding any extra children? What is her policy on allowing Mrs. Dodds to pop in to play with the children, and will she keep Mrs. Dodds aware of what her son does on a daily basis? Depending on the answers to these questions, this particular child care situation seems like a good choice.

While you may not place your child in an in-home child care setting, the same qualities evident in Virginia's home are important for any site. Your child care provider needs to be aware of the new language skills your baby is acquiring. During this time, your baby will be using one-word sentences, so his care provider needs to know how important it is to repeat and expand on what he says, to help him bridge to the next level of language development, which is multiword sentences. The provider should be setting good speech models for your child, not expecting him to say all the speech sounds in the words he uses correctly but saying the word back to your child with the correct pronunciation. With this knowledge of language development and the appropriate environment, your baby should benefit from the interactions he encounters in his child care setting.

What Type of Child Care Is Best for My Toddler?

Lillie Grace is three and a half years old. She has stayed home with her mother up until now, but her mother, Joanne, has decided to return to working outside the home, so Joanne and Lillie Grace's dad, Fred, are shopping around for an appropriate child care placement. On this particular day, they visit the child care associated with Fred's corporation. They have heard excellent feedback about it from other parents whose children attend this facility, which maintains a *provider-to-child ratio of 1 to 6. The information they hear about the program seems to make it an ideal choice. It is known for its attention to detail, both in meeting the standards of health and safety and in meeting the individual needs of the children involved.*

As they look around the room, they see areas devoted to centers: a grocery market center, a computer area, a library with many different children's books, and an art center. There is also a large area devoted to free play, including blocks, houses and dolls, pretend household items, small balls, and so on. They notice on one bulletin board that there is a certain schedule to the day, involving free playtime, circle time for sharing, center time, lunchtime, book-reading time, and nap time. As they come into the room, they read the parents' board, which indicates, among other things, that some of the providers will be attending an upcoming workshop at the local community college on new findings in child development. The director of the program, who escorts them around, appears friendly and open. As they listen to the providers interacting with the children, they hear frequent examples of the children talking and the providers expanding on the children's sentences. They also see instances of the providers encouraging the children to interact with one another. Finally, Lillie Grace's mother notices that one little boy is difficult to understand because his speech is "mushy." The provider interacting with him always tries to acknowledge what he says, repeating what he says using a correct speech model but never asking him to repeat her.

What should Lillie Grace's parents do? Well, if you are like us, you would suggest that they sign Lillie Grace up now! This particular setting, given the information provided, appears ideal. There appear to be knowledgeable and caring providers, who are interested in continuing their understanding of child development. The amount of attention the providers can offer to the children seems appropriate, given the number of providers and children. There seem to be opportunities for both child-initiated and adult-guided learning. The providers are expanding on the children's sentences, which should help the children increase their length of sentences and the topics they can discuss. In essence, this seems to be the total package in child care. What else could a parent want?!

What Type of Child Care Is Best for My Preschooler?

Lee is a single father raising four-and-a-half-year-old twin boys. His job allows him to work out of his home, enabling him to be with his sons every day. However, lately he has felt his sons need more interaction with other children and, perhaps, other adults, so he begins investigating local child care situations. At one local facility, he is initially impressed. The literature for the program states that all teachers have a minimum of a college degree, and all have some specialization in child development. The program boasts of its academic program, reporting that most of the students graduate from the program and go into a prestigious local private elementary school that is notoriously selective. As he looks around the classroom for the four-year-olds, he sees respectful children sitting in chairs around small tables. They are filling in papers dealing with their ABCs. At one point, he hears a teacher call on one child, who recites the alphabet and then counts to 100!

Further observation of the school reveals a large section devoted to books. Children check out these books, along with CDs, and listen to them via headphones. A chart documents all the books each child has completed. A schedule of events on the bulletin board reveals that a typical day involves circle time, focusing on weather and calendar study, math time, reading time, exercise, lunch, nap, and then free choice (math, reading, or writing). All providers in the program are very well groomed and polite.

How would you advise Lee about this facility? We would advise Lee to turn around and walk away! This program, though well meaning, has several significant characteristics that do not match what we know about language development and child care. First, although the "teachers" are well educated, it appears their intent is to provide care against what we know to be best practices for preschool children. Remember, as we said earlier, preschoolers are active learners and explorers who should be guided, not directed, in their learning. These providers are not following the children's lead; rather, they are dictating what the children should do. In addition, they are assuming reading and other academic areas should be taught at this age. As you know, children can learn a great deal about literacy at this stage of development, but that learning should be accomplished through natural, engaging, and entertaining everyday activities. Asking children to sit down and memorize certain concepts does not help them acquire skills any faster than other children. Plus, it may lead to a stifling of development, because the children resent not being able to explore and learn on their own. Finally, even though the program encourages literacy through books, it relies on CDs to do the "teaching." Thus, even though the children are hearing books being read, there are no opportunities for them to interact with others about the books' content or to learn the functions of books, words, or print.

In essence, it seems that this program has lost sight of the fact that these children are preschoolers, not high school students! Lee's sons can do much better at a different site that follows what you know about language development and best practices in child care.

Chapter Summary

Finding a child care situation for your child is not an easy task, as you might imagine. However, we have found that the more informed parents are as they begin choosing a place for their child, the more successful the outcome.

The four scenarios we presented represent real child care situations. The experiences these parents had in their pursuit of an appropriate child care program are not unique. What perhaps *may* be unique is that all of these parents did the right thing: They investigated each program. They observed and they asked questions. This approach to finding a child care placement for your child is crucial. By observing and asking questions, you have a better chance of finding the right place. And, after all, isn't that the objective of all parents who find it necessary to use child care? We want our children to be safe, happy, learning, and developing. We know you have the tools to be knowledgeable judges of child care. Good luck on this important decision. May the best child care win!

FADS, SCAMS, AND MYTHS: KNOWING WHAT TO LOOK FOR

DID **Y**OU **K**NOW?

• Promoters of products make claims that are not always true; you need to determine the truth value of claims yourself.

• Some myths go on and on even when science refutes them.

• Some products are not bad for your child; however, it is likely you can do the same activity with your child for a lot less expense.

Theresa and Russ were so enthralled with their little Robin. She was a lively, energetic, and talkative two-year-old. One evening, after putting Robin to bed, they were watching television when a commercial came on that advertised a program that purported to help young children, children as young as Robin, read. The video clips shown were amazing. Such young children reading so many words! It seemed almost too good to be true. But what parents wouldn't want their child to have an upper hand on reading before she goes to school? Both Theresa and Russ were aware that children now had to pass reading (and writing) tests to progress in school. Why not give Robin a head start?

It really is difficult to watch television, listen to the radio, or even peruse the Internet without being bombarded with advertisements about how you can help your baby, preschooler, or young student excel in his spoken and/or written language skills. Frankly, we believe these types of advertisements for specific products have increased since *our* children were young. This may be due to greater access to media, but it also is possible that manufacturers play on parents' guilt for not being around their children as much because both parents work outside the home. Some products suggest parents can boost their child's spoken language skills by engaging in specific activities they provide (for a cost!). Others suggest they can prepare your child for school by turning him into a reader before he enters kindergarten (or even preschool!). And there are those myths about why certain children have difficulties in acquiring language and/or social skills or how certain treatments can cure reading difficulties. What is a parent to do?

We believe the best way to intelligently examine the claims and types of products that you see advertised on television or hear others discuss by word of mouth is to be well educated. Part of that education is knowing how and when spoken and written language skills develop. After reading the first five chapters, along with the others about specific factors that may influence language development, you have acquired this knowledge. Congratulations! But we believe you also need to be knowledgeable about the kinds of questions to ask when "experts" suggest you need a certain product or type of treatment to help your child talk, read, or write.

In this chapter, we will first provide some examples of fads, scams, and myths that relate to language (including literacy) development. As you will note, we do not use the actual names of the products. This is not out of a fear of a lawsuit, as all we discuss is public domain knowledge. Rather, we do not label these programs or products because the principles behind the discussion are the same regardless of the product. The products and programs we discuss, as well as the myths we review, will go away. But others will soon take their place. What is important for you is to have the knowledge and ask informed questions to best educate yourself on what might be beneficial and what might not be to you as a parent and your child. After we discuss these different fads, scams, and myths, we then provide you with a list of questions to ask whenever you are confronted with a new product or new story about the "next best thing." Let's get started!

How Early Can My Baby Read?

There is a popular program being advertised that provides materials and guidebooks for parents to help teach their babies, as young as 12 months, to read. With the flashcards provided, babies, toddlers, and preschoolers are taught to recognize the words on a series of cards through a high degree of repetition and drill, a crucial component of the program. On television or on the Internet, parents can see short video clips of children who are quite young responding as parents flip through flashcards, calling out the word or performing an action in response to the word. Written and video testimonials from parents attest to the fact that their child can *read* at an age when most children are still learning to talk in simple sentences. The developer of the program suggests that waiting to teach children to read at the typical age, as they enter school, is too late. His company reports that children who learn to read earlier will perform better in school, and in life, than those who start later, presumably at the start of school.

This is the company that provided the commercial that Theresa and Russ viewed. As a means to help you think through how you discern if a program is right for you or not, we take some of the claims and points about this particular product made by its developer and/or company and work you through the evaluation steps that can be applied to other programs as well. We start with some of their specific claims.

Claim 1: We Can and Should Start Teaching Children to Read at 12 Months

The company that purports to teach your child to read suggests starting their program as early as 12 months of age. The basic premise is that your baby's brain is undergoing a high level of growth and participating in the program will take advantage of that brain growth, leading to increased reading abilities. The impression is that the sooner you get started, the better. Children trained using this program will have an advantage over other "late starters" and the trained children will continue to stand out above their peers throughout their academic life.

The easiest way to address this program is to say there is no scientific evidence for these claims about babies or toddlers reading this early. We will return to that claim in a bit. But you don't even need to know there are no scientific data. Having read the first five chapters of this book, you know that the notion that babies and toddlers can read is completely at odds with what we know about typical language development.

Babies at 12 months are just saying their first words. During their second year of life, they are expanding on their vocabulary and, toward the end of that second year, starting to put two words together. We know you recognize that to be able to read, which as you learned in chapters 4 and 5, means you must be able to *think* about language. Given that toddlers are just learning language, it seems a rather large leap to suggest they can think about this new skill they are learning, doesn't it? As you recall, it is not until preschoolers have developed a large portion of their spoken language skills that they begin to develop the ability to think about language. Thus, the notion that babies can read seems absurd.

This notion also is absurd when you consider how we have defined reading in this book. We defined reading as the ability to sound out or recognize written words and to derive meaning from words and groups of words (phrases or sentences). The type of "reading" one sees babies doing in the videos is quite different. In essence, through drill and repetition, the babies and toddlers have been taught to recognize the word shapes on the cards and to say a word (or perform an action) associated with that word image.

Interestingly, this notion of simply connecting a word shape with the concept it represents is not necessarily absurd. Indeed, there is plenty of scientific evidence (and evidence from our own family adventures) that demonstrate that toddlers and preschoolers recognize words associated with specific signs or symbols. When we would drive past the "golden arches," our preschoolers would point to the word underneath those arches and say, "McDonald's!" Of course, we really wanted to call our parents and brag about how their grandchild was reading at the age of three. However, common sense stopped us. Our children, like those in the videos, had learned to associate the word image with a shape. We knew that we could go deface the sign in the middle of the night, changing the letters *D-o-n* to *P-i-g*, and our child would still exclaim at first sight, "Look! McDonald's!" and not "McPigald's."

The point here is that associating a word image with a concept is not reading. It is word calling at best. There is no evidence that suggests this type of word calling relates to or predicts later true reading. True reading occurs when one can read words by sounding out them out and then relating that information not only to the object, person, or action they represent but also to other words in a sentence. In other words, reading is more than word calling; it is comprehending.

Claim 2: Repetition Is Important!

The program we have been discussing involves heavy use of repetition and drill. The children are repeatedly exposed to the words on the flashcards and trained to say or perform an act when they see them. We agree with the basic premise that repetition is needed to learn language. Indeed, even though very young children (babies and toddlers) can hear a word spoken one to four times and actually develop a rudimentary notion of the word, that concept is not fully developed. They need multiple exposures to the word to develop a full meaning. However, the difference between receiving multiple exposures to a word or concept and the constant drill and repetition notion of the program we are discussing is in the *what* and *how*s of the repetition.

As we mentioned in chapter 2, parents (and others) use a lot of repetition in their speech to babies and toddlers. It's not unusual to hear parents repeat words three or four times in one conversational turn: "Oh, look at the cute puppy. What a sweet puppy. Give the puppy a kiss." As you can see, though, this type of repetition is vastly different from holding up a card and asking the child to repeat a word or action. Natural repetitions provide meaning and context to the word that is being repeated. They demonstrate the part of speech it is (in this case, *puppy* is always in a noun position) and show how the other words uttered around the focused word relate to it (ways to describe the puppy, how to act on the puppy, etc.). The richness in information to be gleaned from simple repetitions parents use with their children in naturally occurring situations is lost in the "drill and kill" mode.

There is another aspect to consider about any program that requires substantial segments of drill and repetition in situations in which little context is available, especially when it is promoted for children under the age of five. First, the parent risks the chance that the child will become so turned off by the situation that she may not wish to have anything to do with like situations (such as actually reading books). Further, the activity takes away valuable time that could be spent in real-world events that truly help the child acquire language (see our examples in the first three chapters of the wonderful learning opportunities that occur in everyday situations such as bath time, mealtimes, car rides, etc.). When parents use a drill-and-kill approach to "teaching" language, in this case written language, the may be robbing their children of much more valuable learning opportunities.

The program we have been discussing, like some others that are promoted and advertised in the media, has a heavy emphasis on the use of the computer to administer the program. At first glance, this might seem appropriate, especially given we are so attached to and connected with our computers and other technology (smart phones, tablets, etc.). But remember that television is not recommended by the American Academy of Pediatricians for children under the age of two. Television, even the great programs for children, still cannot capture the give-and-take of language that occurs between two people. It especially cannot mirror the kind of child-specific modeling that occurs when a tuned-in adult interacts with a child. Children cannot act on the objects about which they are learning when watching television. In the first few years of life, nothing beats hands-on learning while receiving high-quality, child-focused language models!

Our purpose for talking about this program was to use it as an example of the type of programs that are out there that suggest they can turn your baby, toddler, or preschooler into a super reader. But you already know a lot about typical spoken and written language, and you can draw on this knowledge to help you discern what is useful or not when interacting with your child. Later in this chapter, we will provide a series of questions you can ask yourself to help determine whether a product is a fad or scam. But for now, let's turn to another, similar kind of program that is more aimed at improving spoken language skills.

My Baby Can Be as Smart as Who?

The criticisms and critiques we presented in the section above relate equally well to those products that purport to turn your little baby into a genius akin to Einstein! We all have seen advertisements in magazines or commercials on television that promote a product that will boost your child's spoken language skills. For a decent amount of money, parents can buy books, computer programs, and other activities that enable them to interact with and relate to their child.

We will be the first to acknowledge that reading with your child is an important activity (and we devoted our first five chapters to it!). Reading with your child allows you to model different types of language (vocabulary, sentences, etc.), show children how to manipulate books (turn pages, read from left to right), and demonstrate the power of language itself (the book dictates the topic of conversation, for the most part). But those important concepts can be achieved with *any* book. It is just as easy to read books you bought at the local flea market or garage sale that cost you 50 cents as it is to read books that are part of a baby scientist product that costs you $7 to $10! And the CDs and DVDs or computer games are subject to the same criticisms we expressed above about the other computer program; they may take away from the naturally occurring interactions that truly help your child understand what language is and how to use it.

Promotions for products that purport to develop mini-Einsteins sometimes recognize these products are just tools for parents. That's a good thing. If nothing else, you've learned from us that *what* we use when we interact and encourage language growth with our children is somewhat immaterial. Whether it is a book from a library, the rubber ducky in the bathtub, the milk carton at the breakfast table, or the car pushed under the tunnel made of blocks, all toys and other materials are simply tools that parents use as they interact and model the language their children are in the midst of learning. So why do we bring up products, such as this last one, that only suggest they are tools? It is because parents can easily fall into thinking of these products as lessons. When the materials are seen as lessons to administer, then the same criticisms we had for computer programs come into play. Early in development, children learn language best when they are involved interactively with others and, much of the time, when the language used with and around them is about the here and now, what they are looking at and what they are playing with in this particular moment. It is difficult to simulate this spontaneous and child-focused type of language modeling when administering prescribed lessons.

One last, related comment about programs that advertise how they provide specific ways for parents to interact with their children: Remember, you do not need to schedule time to interact with your child. Scheduling time sounds too much like scheduling a lesson. You now know that *any* situation or context can be used to model the type of language that helps your child learn how to communicate. Yes, reading books is a great learning opportunity. But so are the conversations in the car, at the grocery store, at the kitchen table, and during bath time. You may be working hard and long hours and only have a few hours per day with your child. However, as long as you are engaging him in the activities you are doing when he is with you, and talking about what is going on and what he is doing, you are helping him grow in his language skills. You have become knowledgeable about how language develops. You can use this knowledge to optimize any situation!

Is It All in the Eyes?

We now turn to advertised and word-of-mouth programs that focus on helping children with identified language delays. In particular, we want to discuss one type of intervention that often is promoted for students who are struggling to learn to read. In some areas of the country, vision therapy· is a heavily publicized approach to treating reading disorders such as dyslexia. The basic premise is that because most children use their eyes to read, reading problems likely are caused by, at least partially, eye movement disorders. Popular Internet sites that discuss vision therapy suggest it is used to correct visual–motor and/or perceptual/cognitive deficiencies. Vision therapy often consists of eye exercises and the use of tinted glasses or filtered lenses to help "retrain" the eyes. The intent is to help children learn to focus better on print, thus leading to better reading. Some individuals who promote vision therapy suggest that visual–motor or perceptual problems occur in 20 percent of the general population and in up to 70 percent of children with reading difficulties!

Frankly, after hearing facts like those last two, what parent of a child who was struggling to read would *not* sign up for vision therapy? Again, however, you have the knowledge and background now to question these facts and this approach. First, you know that reading (and writing) is a language skill. The interpretation of these black lines (the print) on the page you are reading takes place in the language portions of the brain. We must use our knowledge of sounds, letters, and meaning to interpret these black lines. Thus, the eyes are just the means for getting the black line information to our brains, where we then can interpret them and make sense of what is on the page.

Now you might argue that maybe the eyes are not good at getting the black lines to the brain, and that is causing the problems in reading. Let's talk about that argument. First, knowing that reading is a language skill, if a child had problems focusing on the black lines, the print, and getting that information to the brain, then one would need to acknowledge that the issue is a general focusing problem, not a reading problem. However, if the child had a general problem with visual focusing, then you would expect to see that problem occur in tasks other than reading, too. For example, you would expect to see that the child had difficulty during activities that required fine-motor skills, such as constructing a toy out of blocks or sticks. If the child had a visual-focusing problem, then the child likely would have problems doing fine-grained activities that require specific visual focus to complete them. We don't usually see these issues.

All of these arguments aside, the real answer to whether vision therapy might be appropriate for children who struggle to read comes directly from the eye experts themselves, the American Academy of Optometry (AAO), the American Optometric Association (AOA), and the American Academy of Pediatricians (AAP). All three have weighed in on this controversial therapy. As the AAO and AOA state, there is no evidence that vision therapy techniques help improve reading. Vision therapy may, in the very rare cases of children with visual–motor, perceptual–cognitive deficits, help improve eye movements and focusing, but there is no evidence that it helps improve reading or that poor eye movements are linked to reading problems. Any studies that have reported positive outcomes of vision therapy for improving reading abilities have not been able to be replicated. Indeed, the AAP states that there is no scientific evidence that supports the idea that vision therapy helps alter how one's brain interprets and analyzes language from print.

One last caveat: We want to be sure that it is clear we are talking about *vision therapy designed to help students who can otherwise see normally* become better readers. We have raised several questions about this type of treatment; however, it is very important for parents to ensure that their child's visual acuity is being screened regularly in case she needs any type of correction, such as glasses. Difficulty with general vision can certainly cause problems with reading, headaches, frustration, and so forth. Pediatricians include visual checkups as part of their yearly examinations, and many schools offer screenings as well. You should make sure that your child's vision (and hearing, too, for that matter!) is being checked at least every year.

In some ways, this news might be somewhat disappointing to parents of children who are struggling to learn to read and write. It would seem to be so much easier and "tangible" to be able to use special lenses or eye exercises to remediate the problem. We understand that. Although our children did not have problems learning spoken and written language, they have had their share of difficulties in other areas across the years. It was as natural for us as it would be for parents with children with language problems to want a "quick fix." However, as you undoubtedly are realizing from this book, we believe the best approach is to be knowledgeable of the issue you are addressing. With a good understanding of the issue, in this case, language learning, parents can make much more informative and educated decisions about how best to help their children.

Speaking of being informed parents, we want to address one more area in which parents need to be informed. That is the case of what might cause a child to struggle to learn language. When parents have a child diagnosed with a spoken or written language-learning delay, they need to feel confident that they can separate truths from myths when it comes to the popular media's view of causes for delay.

A Myth That Won't Go Away

In recent years, autism, or autism spectrum disorder, has received a tremendous amount of attention in the media not only because of popular movies (*Rain Man*, *What's Eating Gilbert Grape?*, *Temple Grandin*) and reports of rising incidence numbers but also because of other reports about causes of the syndrome. One such reported cause that has received great attention, perhaps primarily because of heavy promotion by certain celebrities, is that autism is caused by a routine childhood vaccine. The media seemed to latch on to this notion and thousands of parents have forgone certain vaccines for their children because of a fear of causing their child to be autistic. Interestingly, this myth had its roots in "science."

In 1998, a group of researchers published a small study that suggested a possible connection between autism spectrum disorder and the mumps-measles-rubella vaccine that is typically administered to young children. The results attracted worldwide attention. What gained less attention was the fact that in subsequent years other researchers could not replicate the original group's findings. Further, as time went on, more information came out about one of the research group's members and his "dishonesty and irresponsibility" in conducting the research and publishing the findings. Unfortunately, this information did not create as much media attention as did the celebrities who promoted the idea of a connection between autism and vaccines. In fact, some individuals decided to ignore the condemnations of the original research by key experts. Despite the emergence of evidence repudiating the original claims, parents continued to be afraid of vaccines. Thus, a myth lived on (and, to some extent, still does).

How do you as a parent deal with myths like this? On the one hand, parents could argue that, at least initially, there was "scientific evidence" to support the claim. And we would agree and say three cheers for thinking about scientific evidence. However, everyone, including parents, must be open to and continue to seek further for additional evidence or, as in this case, refuting evidence. It can be highly attractive to believe celebrities we have grown to know and love, but we must remember that our ultimate guide should be authoritative sources, such as our child's doctor, a leading expert in the area, or unbiased professional documentation available in libraries or on the Internet.

Being an Informed Consumer of Information

As your child's first and strongest advocate, you will need to be fully educated and aware of all information so you can make informed decisions regarding products, programs, interventions, and even health care that potentially affect your child's spoken and written language development. In this last section, we will provide some questions for you to ask yourself or others as you try to determine what is a fad or scam, what might be a myth, and what is the real deal.

Show Me the Data!

One point you may have noted as you read about the fads, scams, and myths we discussed above is that they all share one common theme: statements made without much or any scientific evidence. Sometimes it may *seem* as if a product or procedure has scientific evidence, given how the product or procedure has been marketed. However, just like you do for anything else in your child's life, such as new medicines or new approaches to treating certain illnesses, you'll want to make sure there is some evidence or data to suggest the product or procedure actually leads to the outcomes you desire. In this section, we talk a bit about what it means to have evidence, what it means when a product or procedure does not have evidence, and how you can be an informed, knowledgeable consumer of the products and procedures that are marketed to parents. We are not expecting you to start reading scholarly journals to determine whether there is scientific evidence for certain products or procedures. However, by thinking about these points we present, you hopefully will be able to separate potentially helpful products and procedures from fads, scams, and myths.

What Is Evidence?

Evidence comes in many forms. We are researchers as well as parents, so when we think about evidence, we think about the results of well-designed, well-implemented scientific investigations that have been published in peer-reviewed scholarly journals. We hold high the notion that when the outcomes of a study are published in a journal after being reviewed by other scientists, it demonstrates that the data are important and worthy of distribution. Although not infallible, most of the time the evidence that comes from well-respected scientific journals represents the type of information in which professionals *and* parents can have trust.

The tricky point about relying on scientific evidence is that individuals who promote certain products or procedures may report they have published evidence to back up their statements. They may even attach copies of scientific papers that support their claims on their websites. The catch is that *sometimes* these papers are not actually journal articles from peer-reviewed journals; instead, they are papers (sometimes called white papers) published by the promoters themselves. They have *not* undergone any type of peer review at all. In fact, they have never been published at all, other than by those promoters on their own website. These types of white papers can be misleading, often because they look very authentic, impressive, and scientific.

So how does a parent decide whether the paper is truly

from a scientific journal or self-published? One quick solution is relatively simple. Look at the first page of the paper. Does it list the name of a journal, a volume number, and the page numbers? If yes, then it likely is a publication from a journal. One quick way to confirm that is to simply put the name of the journal into your Internet search engine and view the outcome. For example, say you read about a new instructional procedure to help improve children's literacy skills, which seems to make sense. The professionals discussing the procedure provide a list of references to back up their statements, and one of the articles discussed is in the journal called *Language, Speech, and Hearing Services in Schools.* If you type that title into your search engine, and you will find that the first link to come up is http://lshss.asha.org/. Further, you would find under the "About LSHSS" section that this is peer-reviewed journal. Voilà! You now have more confidence that the evidence the professionals discuss for this procedure is backed by science and is likely trustworthy.

We have found that certain promoters of products or procedures will cite as evidence presentations they have given at conferences. We would be wary about evidence that is based solely on presentations for two reasons. First, not all presentations are equal. Some individuals will note presentations that they have given in support of their product or procedure, but the conferences at which they presented were not scientific conferences. Indeed, sometimes they are conferences developed by the same promoter of the product. In other words, the presentation was designed to promote the product rather than to talk about the evidence or science behind the product or procedure. Second, although scientists can and *do* present their data at scientific conferences, this usually happens right after they have obtained the evidence. Publications typically follow these presentations. When we see someone citing a presentation for evidence of the legitimacy of their claims, but no publication has resulted, it makes us wonder whether the evidence did not stand up to peer review. This is not always the case, but as an advocate for your child, it helps for you to question the legitimacy of claims made.

In an ideal world, there would be solid, scientific evidence for everything that all professionals do. We would know exactly what the best procedures were for any kind of ailment or disability, and we would know exactly which products were the best at helping your child develop. In reality, though, we don't live in that world. Although most professionals are well meaning and interested in helping you help your child in the best way possible, there simply is not complete evidence for everything that is promoted or produced. The bottom line, then, is that you need to be inquisitive and ask questions so you'll understand the level of evidence that exists for what is being promoted and whether the product or procedure is worth the investment. Several years ago, Kenn and a colleague, Dr. Julie Wolter, came up with an acronym for a strategy parents can use to be critical consumers of products and procedures. It is called the MART strategy. This strategy will help you ask the right questions.

1. M IS FOR MOTIVATION. Whenever we hear an individual making a presentation about a new product or procedure, or we read about it on a website, we ask ourselves, what is the individual's motivation? Is this person attempting to share new research results that point to the use of that particular product or procedure, or is he trying to sell the product solely for personal gain? We aren't saying that individuals who are knowledgeable of the research evidence that supports the use of certain products or procedures should not talk about them or be part of the process of promoting them; we are saying one should question if selling the product or process is the primary and sole objective. If it is the latter, it makes us pause and wonder whether we are buying into a fad or scam.

2. *A IS FOR ACTIVITY LEVEL.* When we listen to or read about professionals promoting certain products or procedures, we ask ourselves, is this person a researcher herself or part of a research team? And is her research in the same area as this product or procedure? If there is little published literature, is this person at least attempting to collect data to support her claims? These questions help us to make decisions about the product or procedure by determining whether there is a scientific process occurring. For example, with the early reading program we discussed in the beginning of the chapter, the main promoter of the product is a person with research experience; however, the research was not really connected to the product being promoted. This makes us question that person's ability to objectively and knowledgeably consider whether the product "works" and why it works.

3. *R IS FOR REPUTABLE RESOURCES.* This aspect of the questioning strategy relates to the type of evidence to support claims and where this evidence is contained. When we hear or read about a product, we ask ourselves, does the person making the claims provide specific sources of information to back up those claims, such as articles in peer-reviewed journals? Or, put a different way, is the promoter of the product or procedure pretty much just claiming, "It works! Believe me!" Sometimes individuals make claims and back up those claims via testimonials. We know we don't need to remind you that such testimonials are highly at risk of being biased and, frankly, bought. At the very least, they would not be considered reliable or reputable resources.

4. *T IS FOR THEORY.* We ask one more final question. This one may be a bit more difficult for you to discern an answer to, but we believe it still is important to consider. When we hear or read about a highly touted product or procedure, we ask ourselves, does this product or procedure match how we know children learn language or literacy? We have tried to provide you with the essentials about how language and literacy develop, based on current scientific evidence. With that knowledge, at the very least, you can begin to question products or procedures that seem to counter what we know about development.

We hope this "MART Strategy," with its accompanying list of questions, provides you with some concrete examples of how you can ask specific, informed questions, which will allow you to be a critical consumer when attempting to separate valid products and procedures from fads, scams, and myths. You can put your newfound knowledge to work as you navigate the many different products or procedures focused on you and your child that will arise.

Can I Just Do This Myself (and for a Lot Less Money)?

Some products or procedures will be inexpensive (e.g., certain applications for smartphones or tablets); others will be quite pricey. We would encourage you to consider whether you need to pay for something that you can do on your own, regardless of price. Sometimes individuals who promote certain products or procedures may play into parents' worries: If I don't buy this product, will my child miss out on the jump start she needs to succeed? If I don't buy this product, will it look like I value price over my child's development? We hope you have learned enough from this book to know that spoken language development occurs primarily in the first five years of life, and it does not require anything fancy. Children learn by acting on their environment and having attentive adults around them talking about and commenting on what they are doing. Similarly, for written language development, parents can be great facilitators of development by modeling and engaging in reading and writing. The materials used to help encourage this development are readily available; they are right there in your home, in your car, and in the places you visit. Learning is cheap, and as long as an adult helps facilitate it, it's also effective!

We come now to our final point. Not all products and procedures you will read about or see advertised on television are bad. We believe many of them can be useful. The key for you (and for professionals working with your child) is to recognize that they only are tools. As you know, a tool is just a means to an end. When we use a hammer to build something, the hammer is not the focus. The end product, the item being constructed, is the focus. The same is true for products or procedures that purport to improve language or literacy skills. They should be means to an end, not the end or goal itself. As long as you keep that in mind, you will go a long way in determining how or when (or not) to use a product or a procedure. We believe you are well educated about how language and literacy develop and how you help this development occur. Relax and enjoy your child and his progress through this amazing set of skills he is acquiring. We believe it is a fascinating process and one you undoubtedly will enjoy!

WHEN YOU SUSPECT A LANGUAGE DELAY: GETTING HELP

- Hearing loss can be temporary or permanent.
- Children with intellectual disabilities often make significant advances in their speech and language development.
- Parents concerned about their child's speech and language skills should seek the help of a certified speech-language pathologist.

A few years ago, we had the opportunity to collaborate on a case involving a four-year-old boy. We had recently begun working in a university training program when one of the supervisors approached us about Joe. "I don't know what to do about Joe. I have tried everything I can think of and he is still almost unintelligible. His parents, Barbara and David, are concerned about his lack of progress in speech therapy, and now his pediatrician is suggesting that they go elsewhere for services."

Well, we reacted positively to several things the supervisor told us. First, Joe's parents obviously placed a high priority on speech and wanted the very best services for their son. Second, Joe's pediatrician was not content to simply hope for the best, to see if he would "grow out of this problem." These factors indicated strong outside support for Joe and his communication skills. Third, we were excited about the challenge. We wondered whether there might be something particularly unique about Joe's speech development. As it turns out, there was! Joe said *tan* for *can* yet pronounced other *k* or *g* sounds correctly, like *coke* and *goose*. Joe also said *ko* for *toe* yet pronounced *tea* correctly! This confusion between the *k* and *t* sounds appeared at first to be random. However, when we looked closer, we found that it was not random at all.

Joe's choice of sounds was dependent on the vowel that followed them. The *o* and *u* sounds are made in the back of the mouth and so is the *k*, so Joe could say those together. On the other hand, the *ee* and *a* sounds are made in the front of the mouth and so is the *t*, so Joe would say those together. It was mixing the vowels in the back of the mouth with consonants in the front of the mouth (or vice versa) that was tricky for Joe. Once we discovered this, we set up our treatment activities to help Joe pronounce words like *cat*, *keep*, and *get* as well as words like *tooth*, *do*, and *dough*. He soon made great progress in treatment.

When You Have Questions

After reading the first ten chapters of this book, we hope you have a good working knowledge of how your child is acquiring her speech and language skills and the factors that influence her development. We have written this book so you can be filled with the same joy and awe we have experienced with our children and grandchildren and that we continue to experience as we learn and teach about this fascinating subject. However, because of our work as language specialists and because we're parents, too, we know that parents may have concerns about their child's language skills and desire specific, professional advice.

In this chapter, we will provide some information on possible causes for language problems in children. Within each section, we provide a brief overview of the problem and suggestions for what to do about your concerns. As you will see, the professional most likely to be involved is the speech-language pathologist. Speech-language pathologists, who sometimes are referred to as SLPs, speech therapists, or speech and language clinicians, have specific knowledge about all aspects of language and literacy development and the procedures used to determine whether a language delay exists and what should be done if a problem is found. To become a certified speech-language pathologist, an individual must complete a graduate degree. During the graduate program, our students log hundreds of hours of supervised experiences working with a variety of individuals with communication disorders and differences. As a result, you can be confident that consulting with a certified speech-language pathologist is a good place to begin should you have concerns about your child's language development.

Speech-language pathologists have specific knowledge about all aspects of language and literacy development and the procedures used to determine whether a language delay exists and what should be done if a problem is found.

Depending on the setting to which parents take their concerns, they may see other professionals in addition to speech-language pathologists. If the parents are seeking help in a medical setting, there is a good chance that the insurance company will require them to first see their child's pediatrician. If the parents are seeking help through the local school system, their child's classroom teacher will be involved as well as other professionals such as the school psychologist. Regardless of the situation, though, the speech-language pathologist is the professional most qualified to determine whether a language problem exists.

Chances are you won't need the information contained in this chapter. However, statistically, we know that approximately 5 to 10 percent of all children struggle to some extent in learning language and/or literacy. We encourage you to read the following information carefully, and if some of the information seems to characterize your child's language skills, consult a speech-language pathologist. If the diagnosis confirms your concerns, keep in mind what we said in the introduction: Early intervention can make a world of positive difference to your child.

Possible Causes of Language Delay

We see many children—infants, babies, toddlers, preschoolers, and even school-age children—who are struggling with one or more areas of language development. Some of these children are having a difficult time in the area of phonology, showing signs of problems learning to produce speech sounds. These are children who continue to be difficult to understand beyond the age you would expect. Other children may have problems in the areas of semantics or morphology. These children are slow to develop new words; word endings (e.g., *-ing*, or *-ed*); smaller "functional" words (e.g., *is*, *am*, or *was*); or complex, multiword sentences. Other children may be struggling with how to *use* their language to get their needs met. For example, some children may not know how to ask for objects or actions they want. Some children experience problems in more than one of these areas. Finally, some children appear to develop their oral language skills just fine; however, they struggle when beginning to read and spell.

What is causing these problems in development? As we

often say to parents who ask us this question, if we could provide a definitive answer to this question every time it is asked, we would both be millionaires! Unfortunately, at this point we often do not know why many children with language-learning problems struggle in their development. For some children, the cause is a bit more obvious. They may have other conditions that lead to language problems, such as hearing loss, intellectual disabilities, autism, and so on. We will begin our discussion about these conditions first. However, for many children with language delays, the cause of the problem is unknown. Thus, we conclude this section on possible language delays with information on "specific language impairment."

Hearing Loss

Missy and Ron were worried about their two-year-old son Michael because he wasn't using any meaningful words and didn't always respond when Missy or Ron spoke to him. Although most states mandate hearing screenings for newborns, unfortunately, Michael was born in a state in which hearing screenings were not mandated; thus, the hospital did not provide this service. Consequently, Michael's parents talked to his pediatrician and decided to take him to a speech, language, and hearing clinic for an evaluation. Michael babbled some, gestured some, and screamed to let his parents know when he wanted something or was unhappy. During the evaluation involving a number of professionals, the speech-language pathologist noticed that Michael looked her in the eye, smiled consistently, and used gestures and pointing to indicate that he wanted toys in the room. When his hearing was tested by an audiologist (the professional trained to assess hearing), the team of professionals discovered he had a significant hearing loss.

Although Missy and Ron were frightened and worried at first, they worked with the professionals to develop a plan of *treatment that the parents and team felt best met Michael's needs. He was immediately fitted with hearing aids by the audiologist. Over time, Michael responded well to a speech and language treatment involving sign and spoken language. Through the help of the team members, Missy and Ron became quite proficient in sign language and the strategies they could use at home to encourage Michael's speech and language development.*

Michael's hearing loss was preventing him from learning spoken language. In fact, there are two different types of hearing loss, one of which is more severe than the other. A conductive hearing loss is one in which sound is having a difficult time reaching the inner ear, that part of the hearing system that sends the message to the brain. Typically, a conductive loss means that there is either something blocking the sound from getting to the eardrum (e.g., a heavy buildup of wax or some "foreign" object) or something causing the middle ear bones not to move (in most cases, this may be fluid buildup from ear infections). Sometimes simply removing the obstruction or decreasing the fluid in the middle ear can fix this kind of hearing loss. Thus, conductive hearing losses can be temporary. It is important to note, however, that conductive losses can continue to occur and, depending on the severity and frequency, have lasting effects, such a weak or damaged eardrums.

A second type of hearing loss is called a sensorineural hearing loss. This is the type of hearing loss Michael had. With this type, there is a problem either with the inner ear itself or with the transfer of messages from the inner ear to the brain. This is more difficult to remedy because it is a permanent hearing loss. Children with sensorineural loss are usually helped with one or more compensatory measures. These measures include, for example, the use of hearing aids to amplify the sounds the children hear, the

The more severe the hearing loss and the longer before it is addressed, the greater the chance that spoken language will be delayed.

surgical implantation of a cochlear device to take the place of the part of the inner ear that is not working, or the use of another communication system, such as sign language.

As you probably already know, hearing loss can affect spoken language development. However, the manner and extent to which language development will be affected varies from child to child. Much of this effect depends on the *type* of loss it is (conductive, sensorineural, or a mix of both types), how *severe* the hearing loss is, and *when* the hearing loss begins.

The severity of a hearing loss can range from a mild loss that may minimally affect what the child hears and learns, to a severe loss, meaning the child is able to hear little if any of the spoken language around her. Thus, the more severe the hearing loss, the greater the chance that spoken language will be delayed.

The effects of a hearing loss also depend somewhat on when the loss begins. In general, the earlier the hearing loss begins and the longer the time period before it is addressed, the greater the effects will be on spoken language development. If a child has acquired some language and then loses a significant amount of her hearing, she will have already developed some knowledge of how language works. Helen Keller is a good example of this phenomenon. However, if a child is born with a significant hearing loss and the loss is not diagnosed early, such as through a newborn hearing screening, there is a good chance that she will miss out on the language models she needs early in life to develop spoken language in a typical manner.

We are not suggesting that children who are born with significant, sensorineural hearing loss cannot acquire *language.* In fact, studies show that children who are born with significant hearing loss but have early and consistent access to sound through hearing aids and/or cochlear implants can develop good spoken language skills. Additionally, children with significant hearing loss whose parents immediately begin communicating with them using a means other than spoken language, such as sign language, can acquire language skills. Unfortunately, even with newborn hearing screening readily available, many children fall through the cracks and valuable time is lost. Early identification and treatment is the key to better speech and language outcomes.

As mentioned earlier, most states require that hearing be screened in newborn babies, so instances where children are identified later should continue to decrease (see www .infanthearing.org/index.html). The most important point is to ensure that treatment begins as soon as a hearing loss is identified so that the child can quickly receive consistent and constant language models.

WHAT SHOULD PARENTS DO IF THEY SUSPECT A HEARING LOSS?

So what are parents to do if they think that their child cannot hear or does not hear well? Most likely the first step is to consult their pediatrician with their concerns. Parents should be ready to provide specific examples of behaviors that suggest to them that their child is not responding, or responding well, to sounds. For example, it may be that the parents have noted that their child does not turn to the sound of his parents' voices or does not startle when pots are dropped on the floor. The more descriptive the parents are in their concerns, the clearer the picture for the pediatrician.

A wise pediatrician will take the parents' concerns seriously and likely do one or more tests. It may be that the pediatrician will first rule out that the child does not have a conductive hearing loss by examining the child's ear canal and eardrum and performing a test called tympanometry. This test will allow the physician to determine whether your child's middle ear area is working well or not, perhaps because of a buildup of fluid. The doctor next will likely order an assessment of the child's hearing.

As we mentioned earlier, the professionals who are highly qualified to test individuals' hearing are called audiologists. An audiologist determines how well an individual responds to sounds of varying types and loudness levels. This kind of testing, called audiometric testing, can provide a good picture of a child's hearing capabilities. The audiologist also may be the professional who conducts the tympanometry testing.

If a child's hearing is not within typical limits, then the family and the professionals involved will need to jointly decide the course of action. Decisions may need to be made about the use of other communication systems, such as sign language, and the use of assistive amplification devices, such as hearing aids or cochlear implants. There are many materials and resources that parents can obtain to help them in those decisions, and we've listed some of these at the end of this chapter. Additionally, if your child is under the age of three, you should be introduced to the early intervention program in your state. Most states have active Early Hearing Detection and Intervention (EHDI) programs and services to help guide parents through the many decisions that they will need to make after their child is diagnosed with hearing loss. The EHDI program will help link the family to services that best meet their specific needs and choices (See www.infanthearing.org/status/cnhs.html). In the meantime, it is important to keep in mind what we said earlier in this section. *The child needs to have consistent language models provided to him as soon as possible!* This will help the child to learn language in a more timely and efficient manner.

Intellectual Disabilities

It seems that this is the diagnosis parents consider most frequently when their children are not learning language at the typical rate. Children with intellectual disabilities, often referred to as children with cognitive or developmental disabilities, experience problems with routine, daily activities. One of these activities is communication, or using and understanding language. Other activities include dressing oneself, caring for oneself, using gross and fine-motor movements to play or conduct daily actions, and so on. Children with intellectual disabilities may be slower to develop in one or more of these areas.

Common types of intellectual disabilities include Down syndrome and Fragile X syndrome, although there are many other types of intellectual disabilities as well. Both of these syndromes involve abnormalities in the child's chromosomes. Even though these two types of intellectual disabilities can be traced back to the child's genetic makeup, the cause for these occurrences, and of other types of intellectual disabilities, is often not known. We have worked with parents who feel *they have caused* their child's intellectual disability. Except in cases involving physical child abuse by the parent, the chance that a parent actually caused the intellectual disability is extremely low.

We have worked with parents who feel *they have caused* their child's intellectual disability. The chance that a parent actually caused the intellectual disability is extremely low.

Children can vary in the extent of their intellectual disabilities. Some children are mildly affected; others are affected to a much more significant degree. As a general rule, the more severe the intellectual disability, the greater the effect on language development. It is important, though, not to assume that a child with an intellectual disability has just a "fixed" amount of capabilities to learn language. Unfortunately, some individuals, including some professionals, assume that a child is able to develop language only to a certain extent when she has the label of an intellectual disability. They feel that children learn language to a level that is commensurate with their IQ. However, scientific studies do not support this assumption. Researchers have shown that children who have scored low on tests of intelligence are able to make gains in language development that would not have been predicted given their supposed IQ. Thus, one should never assume that a child with an intellectual disability will be limited in her capabilities based on some preconceived stereotype. It is important that all children with intellectual disabilities receive services to allow them to communicate to the fullest extent of their capabilities. The best way to determine a child's capabilities is, in reality, by providing specific and individualized intervention and monitoring her progress in language development.

WHAT SHOULD PARENTS DO IF THEY SUSPECT AN INTELLECTUAL DISABILITY?

For the most part, parents of children with Down syndrome will know their child has this form of intellectual disability almost immediately. The facial characteristics are typically visible at birth or shortly thereafter. This was true for the Carters, a couple who had three children. When their third daughter, April, was born, they were told she had Down syndrome. However, if it is not until later that some parents suspect their child might have a form of intellectual disability, they should seek professional advice by going to their pediatrician or their local school. It is likely that the pediatrician or special-education professional for their school district will consult a number of different professionals, including a developmental or educational psychologist and a speech-language pathologist. An audiologist will probably be involved, because children with Down syndrome or other forms of intellectual disabilities often have frequent ear infections as well. In the case of the Carter family, April often had ear infections, resulting in conductive, or temporary, significant hearing loss. April received antibiotics for the infections and special attention was given to making communication clearer when the adults around her knew she was not hearing as well.

To determine whether a child has an intellectual disability, and to what extent it exists, testing will involve descriptions and observations of the child's basic skills. The testing will be conducted to determine the child's language, cognitive, social, motor, and other common, functional skills. Parents should be ready to provide descriptions of what their child can do on her own and what she can do with some help or guidance from her parents. This type of information is crucial to determining the child's capabilities and is often not available when children are formally tested outside of their everyday life experiences. Whenever parents are reporting what their child can do, it is important (though sometimes difficult) to be as descriptive and objective as possible. It will not be helpful to the professional or the child to overestimate or underestimate the child's skills.

When a child is diagnosed with an intellectual disability, it may be that the professionals and family will determine that an additional communication system, such as sign language, a computer-based device, and/or picture boards, should be used to supplement the learning of spoken language. These alternative means of communicating have been shown to be a type of bridge or guide to helping children with intellectual disabilities to learn spoken language. Parents must keep in mind what we said earlier: It is difficult to determine a child's potential in language development by just knowing that she has an intellectual disability. Parents should advocate for their child if some professionals take the stance that children with intellectual disabilities are automatically limited to a prescribed degree. On the other hand, they should also be open to options that professionals offer that focus on increasing their child's capabilities.

April's speech-language pathologist used sign language as part of the language development treatment plan she implemented, and she helped April's parents learn sign language, too. In April's case, sign language seemed to help her begin to use spoken language. Soon April was using spoken words more than signs. When this happened, the sign language use was phased out and April was encouraged to build up and refine the speech and language skills she was developing.

Autism

Parents may have some specific ideas about what autism is. Because of popular movies such as *Rain Man*, there is a media view of autism that is somewhat narrow. Many people assume that individuals with autism are somewhat antisocial yet have excellent memory skills for what seems to be unimportant information. Children with autism, or more specifically and accurately, autism spectrum disorder, demonstrate a wide range of abilities and behaviors that fall under this very general heading. Autism spectrum disorder is characterized by one or more of the following: delayed language development; unusual speech rhythms; high levels of exact imitations of others' language; decreased social interactions; lack of emotional contact with others and poor friendship building; sensitivity, or lack of sensitivity, to touch; repetitiveness in language and actions; preoccupation with certain actions or objects; and a desire for "sameness" in surroundings. The degrees to which these characteristics are demonstrated and the number that are present vary considerably among children with autism spectrum disorder.

As the name suggests, autism spectrum disorder represents a whole spectrum, or continuum, of disabilities. For example, one condition that currently falls within the autism spectrum disorder is called Asperger's syndrome. This particular syndrome may not be as obvious as other forms of autism spectrum disorder in that the child with Asperger's syndrome has a much milder form of language impairment and may not demonstrate some of the more common characteristics of autism. The term *pervasive developmental disorder* also is associated with autism spectrum disorder. This term is used at times as a diagnostic label for young children who have problems in many different developmental areas, with characteristics similar to those of autism.

The cause of autism spectrum disorder is unknown. Unfortunately, many years ago when autism spectrum disorder was first discussed, some researchers erroneously thought that the disability was due to "cold mothers." In other words, they thought that the children were reacting to nonnurturing mothers. Today we know this to be untrue. Causes have been speculated, ranging from chemical imbalances in the brain to toxins in the environment to disturbances in diets. In reality, the exact cause is unknown at this point. What is known is that autism spectrum disorder has its onset early in development, within the first three years of life. Parents often report that their child appeared to be developing appropriately, but then "something happened." The child suddenly stopped talking or started developing some of the characteristics mentioned. Should this occur, parents are urged to consult a professional, such as a speech-language pathologist, or a team of professionals to determine the cause of this disruption in language development and the appropriate means of intervention.

What Should Parents Do if They Suspect Autism?

Judy and Steve were concerned about their four-year-old son. He could spend hours lining up his cars into different rows. He rarely said anything, and when he did, it was a rather high-pitched squeal. Family members suggested that perhaps Judy and Steve were talking too much for their son. However, Judy had other thoughts. When she was a teenager, she had volunteered at a neighbor's house, working with a young boy with autism. Both Judy and Steve were quite worried but had no idea who to ask for help.

Because some of the hallmark characteristics of autism spectrum disorder are a lack of language development and an underdeveloped intent to communicate, it may not be until the child is two or three that parents become sufficiently concerned to seek professional consultation. Again, depending on the setting they choose, they may consult their pediatrician or the local school district. In either case, the professional in charge will likely assemble a team of experts, including a speech-language pathologist, a physician, a developmental psychologist, and possibly a special-education teacher with expertise in autism spectrum disorder. Much of the testing will involve descriptions of the child's skills that come from observations and parent reports. Just as we have mentioned in earlier sections, parents' reports will be crucial to developing a complete and accurate picture of the child's capabilities.

Once a child has been diagnosed with autism spectrum disorder, the family and the professionals involved will need to make some specific decisions as to how to help the child develop his language and social skills. Some decisions will include whether an additional communication system should be used (sign language, computer systems that

> *Professionals should use strategies that help children communicate in a meaningful way with those in their environment.*

represent language through computer-generated speech or pictures) and what type of intervention or teaching the child should receive. Some professionals may advocate for instructional programs that have a strict behavioral modification approach underlying them. In these programs, children are taught language by strict imitation and stimulus-response techniques. Other professionals may suggest programs that emphasize creating a need for the child to communicate, with active and consistent modeling by the adults. Some programs may fall somewhere in the middle of these. Parents of children with autism spectrum disorder will need to educate themselves on the rationale for these different types of programs, the research that supports their use, and how children's language skills have changed based on these programs.

Regarding this last point, it is particularly important that parents determine how the professionals measure language and whether they look at how children communicate in real-life, everyday situations. Although improvement on specific tests might seem impressive, the important issue is whether the treatment is resulting in an increase in the way that the child communicates with those around him in daily, natural situations. Once again, the important point is that professionals should use strategies that help children communicate in a meaningful way with those in their environment. Likewise, parents should make every attempt to ensure that true communication is the ultimate goal and that the professionals are working with them, as well as their child, on the development of the best strategies for communication.

In the case of Judy and Steve, they received help from their local school district. A team of professionals helped evaluate their son and decide on a treatment plan. He indeed had autism, and the team developed a system of communication that emphasized ways the young boy could communicate using signs and pictures. As the months progressed, Judy and Steve began to see some progress in their son's communication development. Though they knew it would be a lifelong process, they felt relieved that they were able to participate in helping their son develop to his fullest potential.

Specific Speech or Language Impairment: Delay of Unknown Origin

Heather and James brought their daughter, Joy, to a university-based speech, language, and hearing clinic when she was three years old. Both were faculty members at the university. Joy was speaking in one- and two-word sentences. Because Joy's older sister, Renee, had begun talking early and quickly progressed in her language skills, they wondered whether they were expecting too much from Joy. They wanted to allow Joy to develop at her own pace but also were worried that they should be doing more to help Joy develop her language skills faster. The speech, language, and hearing evaluation confirmed that Joy's language skills were below what was expected for her age.

Based on typical language development, the speech-language pathologist established specific goals for Joy. For example, she needed to use a greater variety of two-word sentences and increase the frequency of certain types of three-word sentences. At the same time, Heather and James were guided in how to model these specific language skills at home. Both parents had inadvertently decreased their own communication with Joy because of her lack of responsiveness. In subsequent sessions with the speech-language pathologist,

Heather and James happily reported that they were using the new strategies at home, even when it seemed Joy did not respond the way they expected. Joy made wonderful progress in treatment, and by the time she started school, her spoken language was similar to the other children's. The speech-language pathologist then provided Heather and James with specific suggestions for increasing Joy's opportunities to learn about written language through language play and reading experiences.

Children with a history of language or learning delays in their family are prone to language problems, but that does not necessarily mean that those children will have a language delay.

For many children like Joy, the cause of a speech or language impairment remains a mystery. They may not be learning the speech sounds correctly, so their speech is highly difficult to understand. They may be experiencing difficulties linking words and word endings together, such that their sentences appear immature for their age. No matter the type of language problem, it seems unrelated to their ability to hear, their mental capabilities, or any autistic-like tendencies. In cases like this, children are labeled as having a specific language impairment.

Researchers have tried to determine whether common childhood illnesses, such as recurring ear infections, may be the culprits in specific language impairments. At this point, there is nothing to suggest that constant ear infections always lead to language problems. While infections and fluid in a child's ear do not help the child hear his parents' language models well, it often is only a temporary, conductive hearing loss. Thus, this cannot be a "pat answer" to why a child is not learning language in the typical manner.

Other researchers, and many parents, have wondered

The child begins with an idea to communicate, which her system must translate into the appropriate speech sounds, words, and type of sentence structure to use.

whether language problems are related to language delays that parents or other close relatives have experienced. This is definitely a possibility. Research has shown that at least for some children with language problems, there *is* a genetic component to the delay. Children whose parents struggled learning to talk or to read and write are more apt to have a language problem. Note how we have written this, though. Children with a history of language or learning delays in their family are prone to language problems, but that does not necessarily mean that those children *will* have a language delay. Again, it is difficult to determine just who will have a language delay.

Ultimately, for children with language delays of unknown origins, or children with specific language impairment, we typically explain to parents that the "wiring" in their child's brain that is used to learn language is not helping the child to the extent it needs to. We know this for sure: Language is in the brain. That is where we understand language and make the commands to produce it. Just as some of us are born with wiring that is less than efficient in helping us learn to do certain athletic moves, sing, or calculate difficult math problems, some children are born with wiring that is less efficient for helping them learn language. As our medical technology becomes more sophisticated, there will likely come a day when we can be more specific about what seems to be going awry.

In the meantime, it is important for parents not to panic when they hear discussions about language in the brain and wiring that isn't helping their child learn language in a timely manner. When a child is language-delayed, it means that she will require special input and models to help that wiring accomplish the task that needs to be done: to learn language.

WHAT SHOULD PARENTS DO IF THEY SUSPECT A SPECIFIC LANGUAGE IMPAIRMENT?

When parents notice that their child is not developing language as outlined in chapters 1 to 5 of this book, they should take their concerns to a local speech-language pathologist. Again, it may be that they must do this via their pediatrician or local school district because of insurance or local school district mandates. Specific examples of their child's speech, vocabulary, sentence structure, social language abilities, and other developing language skills will prove to be invaluable in helping the speech-language pathologist determine whether the child has a specific language impairment. The speech-language pathologist will likely take this information and, together with information obtained from observations of the child and test results, determine a diagnosis. If the diagnosis is for specific language impairment, then suggestions for intervention to improve the child's language skills will be provided.

Speech-language pathologists use many of the principles that we discussed in the first few chapters to facilitate language acquisition in children with specific language impairment. The speech-language pathologist will set goals for specific language skills based on what is known about the sequence of typical language development. Situations in which the specific language skills naturally occur will be used in treatment. The speech-language pathologist will follow the child's interests and model the language skills frequently. She also will give the child many opportunities to use the new skills in a meaningful way that fits the communication demands of the situation.

There are other specific causes for language delay that are beyond the scope of this book. The resources we provide at the end of this chapter should help you learn more about other causes. It is important to know, though, that for many children with language problems, the exact cause will always remain uncertain.

Other Problems Associated with Language Delays

Children who are struggling to learn language, as well as children who are learning language in a typical fashion, sometimes have accompanying problems that may or may not be related to language development abilities. Two such problems are stuttering and attention deficit disorder.

Stuttering

As children are learning to talk, they invariably experience moments when their speech is anything but fluent. It is not uncommon to hear a young child of three repeat the first word of a sentence over and over again. When Nick was age three and a half, he decided to announce to his parents, his grandparents, and a whole slew of relatives his recent accomplishment. It sounded something like this:

"My-my-my-my-my-my-my-my-my-my-my car won!"

Of course, all of Nick's relatives turned to his father with a look that said something like "Well, what are you going to do about *that*?" Fortunately, being a student of child language development, Nick's father knew that this type of repetition was completely typical and even somewhat expected for children Nick's age.

When children are developing language, they have an incredible number of different tasks to perform simultaneously. The child begins with an idea to communicate, which her system must translate into the appropriate speech sounds, words, and type of sentence structure to use. Not only are the sounds, words, and sentence types new and challenging for the child, but she usually chooses to communicate while also engaged in a very exciting, playful activity. It is no wonder that children sometimes end up overloading the system, resulting in nonfluent speech. These "nonfluencies" often are characterized by repetitions of whole words and phrases or even parts of words (*dog-dog-dog-doghouse*). Typically developing children may do this as much as one out of every ten words. When these symptoms occur, parents should consider them to be typical aspects of language development.

However, there are times when children begin to show nonfluent speech that is different from the typical examples found in language development. In these cases, a child may begin to repeat just the sounds of a word (*b-b-b-b-boy*) or perhaps prolong one sound over a period of time (*sssssssssister*). The child also might show some kind of facial tension or grimace. Finally, it may be that the child produces any type of repetition or prolongation quite often (i.e., on more than 1 out of every 10 words). These types of "dysfluencies" are considered to be out of the typical realm and *may* indicate a stuttering condition. If these occur over a period of a month, the parents should have the child evaluated by a speech-language pathologist.

Whether the child is producing typical nonfluencies or nontypical dysfluencies, one of the best approaches for parents to take is to allow the child to finish his communication. It is so easy for a parent to want to finish the child's sentence for him. However, that will not help the child produce more fluent speech. In addition, parents also can model easy, slower, less complex speech for their children. This does not mean parents should talk so slowly that the typical person falls asleep! It means that parents can break their normally complex sentences ("We need to stop by the grocery store because we have the party that is for your grandmother who is turning 65 coming up") into smaller, less complex sentences with pauses at appropriate places ("We need to stop at the grocery store. [pause] Remember, we're having a party for Grandma. [pause] She's going to be 65 years old."). By modifying their speech rate and showing patience for their child's speech rate and fluency, parents can provide the help their child might need to become more fluent.

Attention Deficit Hyperactive Disorder With or Without Hyperactivity

In the last decade, perhaps no other disabilities have received so much attention and been so highly diagnosed as attention deficit disorder, with or without hyperactivity (ADD/ADHD). Children with ADD/ADHD are said to suffer from an inability or poor ability to attend to or concentrate on the topic at hand. They are characterized as distractible and impulsive. Up to two-thirds of children with ADD/ADHD also have a language delay.

Adding to the controversy is that many, if not most, children with ADD/ADHD are prescribed medications that have not been examined for their long-term effects on humans.

ADD/ADHD is a controversial diagnosis. Specific, definable, and consistent criteria for this diagnosis, which discriminate this disorder from others, are not used. That is, the criteria used by one professional to diagnose a child with ADD/ADHD may not be the same collection of behaviors used by another professional to diagnose another child. There is concern that some of the behaviors attributed to ADD/ADHD may be just typical behaviors in young children. Additionally, many children with the ADD/ADHD label are able to maintain attention and concentrate in some situations (playing games) even though they cannot in other situations (structured activities requiring specific language skills, such as reading). Adding to the controversy is that many, if not most, children with ADD/ADHD are prescribed medications that have not been examined for their long-term effects on humans.

When parents suspect their child has ADD/ADHD, or a professional suggests this to the parents, they would be well advised to educate themselves on all aspects of this disorder, including what research supports the label, any new research about the long-term effects of medication on children, and nonmedicinal interventions that can be used. We also urge parents to consider having their child's language abilities evaluated in depth to determine whether other possible factors, such as language delay, may be leading to the symptoms identified as ADD/ADHD. Even when parents and professionals determine that a medicinal course of action is warranted, services to help the child learn how to best use his abilities to attend, listen, and so forth should be considered.

Implications of Language Delay for Later Learning

It is important to know that children who experience difficulties learning to use language in the first five years of life are at risk for having difficulties in learning to read and write. As we discussed in chapter 5, reading and writing are language skills. Like talking and listening, they are ways to communicate with others. Reading and writing tap into the areas of semantics, phonology, morphology, syntax, and pragmatics, just as talking and listening do. However, unlike talking and listening, reading and writing require children to *actively think* about the language system. Children who have had a difficult time learning the rules of language may have an additional struggle when they then have to think about the rules of language to read and write, sometimes referred to as learning disabilities in school systems.

This does not mean all children who are delayed in spoken language will be delayed in written language. It does mean, however, that parents of children with delayed language development should be encouraging their child's early literacy skills and observant of their children's reading and writing abilities as they enter formal schooling. In chapters 4 and 5, we provided some examples of what parents could do at home to encourage their child's written language abilities. Parents could use these activities to be proactive in developing their children's literacy skills. We also would suggest that parents of children with language problems notify the child's teachers to be aware of any special help the child might need as she learns to read and write.

The bottom line for concerned parents is to be persistent in seeking help for their child and to be the child's best advocate. If any professional with whom a parent consults does not seem to discuss language development in the manner in which it has been discussed in this book, consider consulting with another professional. In our experiences, children whose parents have learned as much as they can about language development and have been actively involved in the evaluation and intervention processes are the children who have made some of the best progress in their language skills.

Where Do Parents Find Help?

No matter the cause of the language problem, parents must seek help from the appropriate professional. As we have stated, the speech-language pathologist is typically involved directly as the main professional conducting an evaluation or as part of a professional team. Some speech-language pathologists work with a pediatrician or school system and thus can be contacted via either professional source. Others work in private practices and can be contacted directly through a local directory.

Parents will, of course, want to seek services from a

qualified professional. They should look for specific credentials when selecting a speech-language pathologist. Optimally, the speech-language pathologist should be certified by the American Speech-Language-Hearing Association (ASHA). This is the national association for more than 145,000 speech-language pathologists and audiologists. This organization, which has been in existence for more than 85 years, is dedicated to helping speech-language pathologists and audiologists help children and adults and their families with communication disorders and differences. ASHA certification in speech-language pathology is indicated by the letters "CCC-SLP" after the professional's name (e.g., Kenn Apel, Ph.D., CCC-SLP). This means the professional has a master's or clinical doctoral degree, has clinical training, has passed a national exam, and participates in continuing education. Parents can find a certified speech-language pathologist by going to www.asha.org/findpro/. In fact, ASHA's website (www.asha.org/public) contains a wealth of information about communication development and disorders across the life span, so check it out!

Professional credentials are also administered at the state level. Many states require that speech-language pathologists be licensed to practice. Finally, school districts usually require that speech-language pathologists be certified. The educational requirements for ASHA certification, state licensure, and school certification often are similar. Most require a graduate degree and appropriate clinical training.

When an evaluation is conducted, the speech-language pathologist and the other professionals involved will determine whether a language delay exists, possible causes for the delay, what skills the child uses on her own and with the aid of helping adults, what skills she needs to learn, and what strategies might best work with her. The prognosis for improvement, or the likelihood for further developing her language skills, also will be discussed. Should the speech-language pathologist and other members of a team decide that the child requires intervention to improve her language skills, then a direct plan or set of goals will be established for how to best accomplish this task. You will be part of the team that makes these decisions for your child.

Just as in other professional areas, there are slight differences in how specific professionals intervene. For young children, we generally advocate for intervention that promotes language development in situations or activities where real communication is occurring rather than asking a child to imitate language for imitation's sake. In this latter situation, the adult is not helping the child understand *why* he is saying what he is saying.

We also believe in early intervention. That is, as soon as a child is diagnosed as having a language delay, no matter the cause, we suggest he receive language intervention. In some settings, this may not be possible. For example, in many school districts, federal or state laws mandate that school-based professionals can see only children who have disabilities that interfere with their education. If, for some reason, a child does not qualify for school-based services, or if parents want services provided by another professional, in addition to or instead of school services, this generally is possible.

In some communities, there may be a university that has a speech-language-hearing clinic associated with a graduate program in speech-language pathology. Some speech-language pathologists work out of local hospitals, developmental centers, specialized clinics, and Head Start programs. Most pediatricians and local school districts should be aware of options for services in the area. In addition to local sources, parents also may seek advice and information at the state level by visiting their state's Speech-Language-Hearing Association (e.g., Missouri Speech-Language-Hearing Association). Access numbers and websites can be obtained from the ASHA website (www.asha.org).

Perhaps you are wondering about Joe, the young boy we discussed at the beginning of the chapter. Several years later, we saw Joe at a grocery store. He was a tall middle school student, whose speech was quite good. In fact, had we not known Joe's history, we probably would not have guessed that he had struggled with speech so much as a preschool child.

Book Summary

We have provided you with information about how children develop both spoken and written language as well as the factors that may influence language development. We also have reviewed what might be some possible causes of language problems in children and what parents should do if they are concerned about their child's language skills. We hope this book has been both informative and interesting to you. Our real hope, though, is that you have come to understand as we do how language development is one of life's true miracles. Throughout the first five years of life, your child is acquiring a skill that serves as a foundation for almost every action and purpose he will undertake in life. We hope you have learned how important you are in this process and how completely enjoyable the process can be. We wish you well as you engage in this fascinating area of child development. Enjoy it and have fun.

BIBLIOGRAPHY

Academy of Orton-Gillingham Practitioners and Educators. Accessed July 28, 2011. http://www.ortonacademy.org/.

Ackerman-Ross, S., and P. Khanna. "The Relationship of High Quality Day Care to Middle-Class 3-Year-Olds' Language Performance." *Early Childhood Research Quarterly* 4 (1989): 97–116.

Aoyama, K., A. N. Peters, and K. S. Winchester. "Phonological Changes During the Transition from One-Word to Productive Word Combination." *Journal of Child Language* 37 (2010): 145–57.

Apel, K., and L. Apel. "Identifying Intra-individual Differences in Students' Written Language Abilities. *Topics in Language Disorders* 31 (2011): 54–72.

Apel, K., J. J. Masterson, and E. B. Wilson-Fowler. "Developing Word-Level Literacy Skills in Children with and without Typical Communication Skills." In *Insight and Impact: Applied Linguistics and the Primary School*, edited by S. Ellis, E. McCartney, and J. Bourne, 229–41. Cambridge: Cambridge University Press.

August, D., and K. Hakuta. *Improving Schooling for Language-Minority Children: A Research Agenda*. Washington, DC: National Academy Press, 1997.

Babrow, A. S., B. J. O'Keefe, D. L. Swanson, R. A. Meyers, and M. A. Murphy. "Person Perception and Children's Impressions of Television and Real Peers." *Communication Research* 15, no. 6 (1998): 680–98.

Barton, M. E., and R. Strosberg. "Conversational Patterns of Two-Year-Old Twins in Mother–Twin–Twin Triads." *Journal of Child Language* 24 (1997): 257–69.

Bilingual Therapies. Accessed September 22, 2000. http://www .bilingualtherapies.com.

Bishop, D. V. M. "Pre- and Perinatal Hazards and Family Background in Children with Specific Language Impairments: A Study of Twins." *Brain and Language* 56, no. 1 (1997): 1–26.

Bishop, D. V. M., and S. J. Bishop. "'Twin Language': A Risk Factor for Language Impairment?" *Journal of Speech, Language, and Hearing Research* 41, no. 1 (1998): 150–60.

Bock, R. (n.d.). "Why Children Succeed or Fail at Reading." Rockville, MD: U.S. Department of Health and Human Services, National Institutes of Health, National Institute of Child Health and Human Development. Accessed May 14, 2001. http://www.nichd.nih.gov/publications/pubs/readbro.htm.

Burchinal, M. R., J. E. Roberts, L. A. Nabors, and D. M. Bryant. "Quality of Center Child Care and Infant Cognitive and Language Development." *Child Psychology* 67 (1996): 606–20.

Cantor, J., and A. I. Nathanson. "Children's Fright Reactions to Television News." *Journal of Communication* 46, no. 4 (1996): 139–52.

Cervantes, C. A., and M. A. Callanan. "Labels and Explanations in Mother–Child Emotion Talk: Age and Gender Differentiation." *Developmental Psychology* 34, no. 1 (1998): 88–89.

Christakis, D., and M. Garrison. "Preschool-Aged Children's Television Viewing in Child Care Settings." *Pediatrics* 124, no. 6 (2009): 1627–32.

Cochran, P. S., and L. K. Nelson. "Technology Applications in Intervention for Preschool-Age Children with Language Disorders." *Seminars in Speech and Language* 20, no. 3 (1999): 203–18.

Coe, J., and J. Oakhill. " 'txtN is ez f u no h2 rd': The Relation Between Reading Ability and Text-Messaging Behavior." *Journal of Computer Assisted Learning* 27 (2011): 4–17.

Conti-Ramsden, G., G. D. Hutcheson, and J. Grove. "Contingency and Breakdown: Children with SLI and Their Conversations with Mothers and Fathers." *Journal of Speech and Hearing Research* 38 (1995): 1290–1302.

Craig, H. K., C. M. Connor, and J. A. Washington. "Early Positive Predictors of Later Reading Comprehension for African American Students: A Preliminary Investigation." *Language, Speech, and Hearing Services in Schools* 34 (2003): 31–43.

Craig, H. K., and J. A. Washington. "Grade-Related Changes in the Production of African American English." *Journal of Speech, Language, and Hearing Research* 47 (2004): 450–63.

DeHouwer, A. "Two or More Languages in Early Childhood: Some General Points and Practical Recommendations." ERIC Clearinghouse on Languages and Linguistics Digest. July 1999. Accessed May 14, 2001. http://www.cal.org/ericcll/digest/earlychild.html.

Dodd, B., and S. McEvoy. "Twin Language or Phonological Disorder?" *Journal of Child Language* 21 (1994): 273–89.

Dunn, L., S. A. Beach, and S. Kontos. "Quality of the Literacy Environment in Day Care and Children's Development." *Journal of Research in Childhood Education* 9 (1994): 24–34.

Fenson, L., V. A. Marchman, D. Thal, P. S. Dale, J. S. Reznick, and E. Bates. *MacArthur-Bates Communicative Development Inventories: User's Guide and Technical Manual.* 2nd ed. Baltimore: Paul H. Brookes, 2007.

Fitch, M., A. Huston, S. Piemyat, R. Truglio, and J. Wright. "Occupational Portrayals on Television: Career Aspirations and Perceptions of Reality." *Child Development* 66 (1995): 1706–18.

Flavell, J. H., E. R. Flavell, F. L. Green, and J. E. Korfmacher. "Do Young Children Think of Television Images as Pictures or Real Objects?" *Journal of Broadcasting and Electronic Media* 34, no. 4 (1990): 399–419.

Fowler, W., K. Ogston, G. Roberts-Fiati, and A. Swenson. "The Effects of Enriching Language in Infancy on Early and Later Development of Competence." *Early Childhood Development and Care* 135 (1997): 41–77.

Frassica, M. "For eBook Devotees, Reading Is a Whole New Experience. *USA Today*, July 3, 2011.

Frede, E. C. "The Role of Program Quality in Producing Early Childhood Program Benefits." *The Future of Children* 5, no. 3 (1995): 115–32. Accessed May 14, 2001. http://www.princeton .edu/futureofchildren/publications/journals/article/index .xml?journalid=58&articleid=352&sectionid=2365&submit.

Gleason, J. B. *The Development of Language.* 5th ed. Needham Heights, MA: Allyn and Bacon, 2000.

Goldberg, M. E., and G. J. Gorn. "Television's Impact on Preferences for Non-white Playmates: Canadian *Sesame Street* Inserts." *Journal of Broadcasting* 23, no. 1 (1979): 27–32.

Goodson, M. S., R. A. Hough, and J. R. Nurss. "Prereading/ Language Development in Two Day Care Centers." *Journal of Reading Behavior* 13 (1981): 23–31.

Hanen Centre. Accessed July 28, 2011. http://www.hanen.org/ Home.aspx.

Hayes, D., S. Kelly, and M. Mandel. "Media Differences in Children's Story Synopses: Radio and Television Contrasted." *Journal of Educational Psychology* 78 (1986): 341–46.

Hoff-Ginsberg, E. "Older Siblings as Conversational Partners." *Merril-Palmer Quarterly* 37, no. 3 (1991): 465–82.

Hoff-Ginsberg, E. "The Relation of Birth Order and Socioeconomic Status to Children's Language Experience and Language Development." *Applied Psycholinguistics* 19, no. 4 (1998): 603–29.

Hoffner, C., J. Cantor, and E. Thorson. "Children's Understanding of a Televised Narrative." *Communication Research* 15, no. 3 (1988): 227–45.

Holloway, S. D., and M. Reichhart-Erickson. "The Relationship of Day Care Quality to Children's Free-Play Behavior and Social Problem-Solving Skills." *Early Childhood Research Quarterly* 3 (1988): 39–53.

Hopman-Rock, M., F. M. Gerritsen, and P. Talsma. "Socioeconomic Status and Gender Differences in Language Development of Children Aged 3 to 6 Years." *Pedagogische Studieen* 65, no. 11 (1988): 437–50.

Hughes, M., and D. Searle. *The Violent* E *and Other Tricky Sounds: Learning to Spell from Kindergarten Through Grade 6.* York, ME: Stenhouse, 1997.

I Am Your Child. Accessed September 22, 2000. http://www.iamyourchild.org/qualitycare/index.html.

James, N. C., and T. A. McCain. "Television Games Preschool Children Play: Patterns, Themes, and Uses." *Journal of Broadcasting* 26, no. 4 (1982): 783–800.

Justice, L. M., J. N. Kaderavek, X. Fan, A. Sofka, and A. Hunt. "Accelerating Preschoolers' Early Literacy Development Through Classroom-Based Teacher–Child Storybook Reading and Explicit Print Referencing." *Language, Speech, and Hearing Services in Schools* 40 (2009): 67–85.

Kamhi, A., J. Masterson, and K. Apel (Eds). *Clinical Decision Making in Developmental Language Disorders.* Baltimore: Paul H. Brookes, 2007.

Kayser, H. G. *Assessment and Intervention Resource for Hispanic Children.* San Diego: Singular, 1998.

Kayser, H. G. *Bilingual Speech-Language Pathology: A Hispanic Focus.* San Diego: Singular, 1995.

Kemph, N. "Mobile Technology and Literacy: Effects Across Cultures, Abilities and the Lifespan." *Journal of Computer Assisted Learning* 27 (2011): 1–3.

Key, A. P. F., W. Stone, and S. M. Williams. "What Do Infants See in Faces? ERP Evidence of Different Roles of Eyes and Mouth for Face Perception in 9-Month-Old Infants." *Infant and Child Development* 18 (2009): 149–62.

Kontos, S. J. "Child Care Quality, Family Background, and Children's Development." *Early Childhood Research Quarterly* 6 (1991): 242–62.

Koutsouvanou, E. "Television and Child Language Development." *International Journal of Early Childhood* 25 (1993): 27–32.

Krafft, K. C., and L. E. Berk. "Private Speech in Two Preschools: Significance of Open-Ended Activities and Make-Believe Play for Verbal Self-Regulation." *Early Childhood Research Quarterly* 13, no. 4 (1998): 637–58.

Kunkel, D. "Children and Host-Selling Television Commercials." *Communication Research* 15, no. 1 (1988): 71–92.

Lahey, M. *Language Disorders and Language Development*. Needham, MA: Macmillan, 1988.

Lawton, J. T., and N. Fowell. "A Description of Teacher and Child Language in Two Preschool Programs." *Early Childhood Research Quarterly* 4 (1989): 407–32.

Lee, Y. A., J. S. Lee, and J. W. Lee. "The Role of the Play Environment in Young Children's Language Development." *Early Childhood Development and Care* 139 (1997): 49–71.

Levy, B. A., Z. Gong, S. Hessels, M. A. Evans, and D. Jared. "Understanding Print: Early Reading Development and the Contributions of Home Literacy Experiences." *Journal of Experimental Child Psychology* 93 (2006): 63–93.

Marcon, R. A. "Differential Effects of Three Preschool Models on Inner-City 4-Year-Olds." *Early Childhood Research Quarterly* 7 (1992): 517–30.

Marvin, C. A., and A. J. Privratsky. "After-school Talk: The Effects of Materials Sent Home from Preschool." *American Journal of Speech-Language Pathology* 8 (1999): 231–40.

Masterson, J., and K. Apel. "Spelling and Word-Level Reading: A Multilinguistic Approach." In *Clinical Decision Making in Developmental Language Disorders*, edited by A. Kamhi, J. Masterson, and K. Apel, 249–66. Baltimore: Paul H. Brookes, 2007.

McCabe, A. E. "Differential Language Learning Styles in Young Children: The Importance of Context." *Developmental Review* 9, no. 1 (1989): 1–20.

McCartney, K. "Effect of Quality Day Care Environment on Children's Language Development." *Developmental Psychology* 20 (1984): 244–59.

McKenna, W. M., and P. E. Ossoff. "Age Differences in Children's Comprehension of a Popular Television Program." *Child Study Journal* 28, no. 1 (1998): 53–68.

McLaughlin, S. *Introduction to Language Development.* San Diego: Singular, 1998.

McMahon, S., and B. Dodd. "A Comparison of the Expressive Communication Skills of Triplet, Twin and Singleton Children." *European Journal of Disorders of Communication* 32, no. 3 (1997): 328–45.

Medcalf-Davenport, N. A. "A Comparative Study of the General World Knowledge and Language Development of Pre-kindergarten Children from Either Day Care or In-Home Care." *Early Childhood Development and Care* 93 (1993): 1–14.

Morra Pellegrino, M. L., and A. Scopesi. "Structure and Function of Baby Talk in a Day-Care Centre." *Journal of Child Language* 17 (1990): 101–14.

Morrow, L. M. "Young Children's Responses to One-to-One Story Readings in School Settings." *Reading Research Quarterly* 23, no. 1 (1988): 89–107.

National Early Literacy Panel. Accessed July 28, 2011. http://lincs.ed.gov/earlychildhood/NELP/NELPreport.html.

National Reading Panel. Accessed July 28, 2011. http://www.nationalreadingpanel.org.

Nelson, L. K., and J. J. Masterson. "Computer Technology: Creative Interfaces in Service Delivery." *Topics in Language Disorders* 19, no. 3 (1999): 68–86.

Nelson, N. W. *Childhood Language Disorders in Context: Infancy Through Adolescence.* New York: Macmillan, 1993.

Nikken, P., and A. L. Peeters. "Children's Perceptions of Television Reality." *Journal of Broadcasting and Electronic Media* 32, no. 4 (1988): 441–52.

O'Neill, M., K. A. Bard, M. Linnell, and M. Fluck. "Maternal Gestures with 20-Month-Old Infants in Two Contexts." *Developmental Science* 8 (2005): 352–59.

Oshima-Takane, Y., E. Goodz, and J. L. Derevensky. "Birth Order Effects on Early Language Development: Do Second-born Children Learn from Overheard Speech?" *Child Development* 67 (1996): 621–34.

Owens, R. E., Jr. *Language Development: An Introduction.* 4th ed. Needham Heights, MA: Allyn and Bacon, 1996.

Paul, R. *Language Disorders from Infancy Through Adolescence: Assessment and Intervention.* St. Louis: Mosby, 1995.

Pham, L. "Infant Dual Language Acquisition Revisited." *Journal of Educational Issues of Language Minority* 14 (1994): 185–210. Accessed September 27, 2001. http://www.ncbe.gwu.edu/miscpubs/jeilms/vol14/pham.htm.

Pine, J. M. "Variation in Vocabulary Development as a Function of Birth Order." *Child Development* 66 (1995): 272–281.

Polyzoi, E. "Quality of Young Children's Talk with Adult Caregivers and Peers During Play Interactions in the Day Care Setting." *Canadian Journal of Research in Early Childhood Education* 6 (1985): 21–30.

Rickard, C., and K. Younce. "Language Development." Accessed May 14, 2001. http://www.colorado.edu/slhs/SLHS 4560.

Rideout, V., U. Foehr, and D. Roberts. "Generation M^2: Media in the Lives of 8- to 18-Year-Olds." Menlo Park, CA: Henry J. Kaiser Family Foundation,

Rideout, V., E. Vandewater, and E. Wartella. "Zero to Six: Electronic Media in the Lives of Infants, Toddlers, and Preschoolers." Menlo Park, CA: Henry J. Kaiser Family Foundation, 2003.

Rodriguez, J. L., R. M. Diaz, D. Duran, and L. Espinosa. "The Impact of Bilingual Preschool Education on the Language Development of Spanish-Speaking Children." *Early Childhood Research Quarterly* 10 (1995): 475–90.

Schober-Peterson, D., and C. J. Johnson. "Non-dialogue Speech During Preschool Interactions." *Journal of Child Language* 18 (1991): 153–70.

Segal, N. L., and T. D. Topoloski. "A Twin Research Perspective on Reading and Spelling Disabilities." *Reading and Writing Quarterly: Overcoming Learning Difficulties* 11, no. 2 (1995): 209–27.

Seinow, G. W., and E. P. Bettinghaus. "Television Exposure and Language Development." *Journal of Broadcasting* 26, no. 1 (1982): 470–79.

Senechal, M. "The Differential Effect of Storybook Reading on Preschoolers' Acquisition of Expressive and Receptive Vocabulary." *Journal of Child Language* 24 (1997): 123–38.

Short-Meyerson, K. J., and L. J. Abbeduto. "Preschoolers' Communication During Scripted Interactions." *Journal of Child Language* 24 (1997): 469–93.

Silverman, I. T., and J. N. Sprafkin. "The Effects of *Sesame Street*'s Prosocial Spots on Cooperative Play Between Young Children." *Journal of Broadcasting* 24, no. 2 (1980): 135–47.

Slobin, D. I., J. Gerhardt, A. Kyratzis, and J. Guo. *Social Interaction, Social Context, and Language: Essays in Honor of Susan Ervin-Tripp.* Mahwah, NJ: Lawrence Erlbaum, 1996.

Taylor, O. L., and L. B. Leonard. *Language Acquisition Across North America: Cross-Cultural and Cross-Linguistic Perspectives.* San Diego: Singular, 1999.

Television and Health. Accessed July 28, 2011. http://www.csun.edu/science/health/docs/tv&health.html.

Thiessen, E. D., E. A. Hill, and J. R. Saffran. "Infant-Directed Speech Facilitates Word Segmentation." *Infancy* 7 (2005): 53–71.

Thompson, R. B., and K. Moore. "Collaborative Speech in Dyadic Problem Solving: Evidence for Preschool Gender Differences in Early Pragmatic Development." *Journal of Language and Social Psychology* 19, no. 2 (2000): 248–55.

Tomblin, J. B. "The Effect of Birth Order on the Occurrence of Developmental Language Impairment." *British Journal of Disorders of Communication* 25 (1990): 77–84.

University of Massachusetts, Amherst. NIH Working Groups on AAE. Accessed May 14, 2001. http://www.umass.edu/aae/.

Walker, K., and L. Armstrong. "Do Mothers and Fathers Interact Differently with Their Child or Is It the Situation Which Matters?" *Child: Care, Health and Development* 21, no. 3 (1995): 161–81.

Walma van der Molen, J. H., and T. H. A. van der Voort. "Children's Recall of Television and Print News: A Media Comparison Study." *Journal of Educational Psychology* 89 (1997): 82–91.

Washington, J. A., and H. K. Craig. "Socioeconomic Status and Gender Influences on Children's Dialectical Variations." *Journal of Speech, Language, and Hearing Research* 41, no. 3 (1998): 618–26.

Wasowicz, J., K. Apel, J. Masterson, and A. Whitney. *Spell Links to Reading and Writing*. Evanston, IL: Learning by Design, 2004.

Westby, C. E., and R. Roman. "Finding the Balance: Learning to Live in Two Worlds." *Topics in Language Disorders* 15, no. 4 (1995): 68–88.

Winsler, A., R. M. Diaz, L. Espinosa, and J. L. Rodriguez. "When Learning a Second Language Does Not Mean Losing the First: Bilingual Language Development in Low-Income, Spanish-Speaking Children Attending Bilingual Preschool." *Child Development* 70, no. 2 (1999): 349–62.

Yamamoto, M. "Birth Order, Gender Differences, and Language Development in Modern Japanese Pre-school Children." *Psychologia: An International Journal of Psychology in the Orient* 33, no. 3 (1990): 185–90.

INDEX

A

Academic "stories," 116–117
Age, language development
   by. *See* Baby development;
   Infant development;
   Preschooler development;
   Student development;
   Toddler development
Alphabet. *See* Letters
American Speech-Language-
   Hearing Association
   (ASHA), xiii, 260, 261
Asperger's syndrome, 248
Attention deficit disorder (ADD/
   ADHD), 257–258
Audiologists
   ASHA certification, 260
   finding, xiii
   minimum qualifications,
     xiii
   symptoms indicating help
     from, xii
   tests administered, 243
Autism spectrum disorder
   cause of, 248
   characteristics of, 247–248
   range of, 248
   suspecting/responding to,
     249–251
   vaccine link myth, 227–228

B

Babbling, 26–27, 35, 38–39
Baby development, 33–52
   about: overview/summary of,
     33–34, 52

best child care for, 209–210
CDS and. *See* Child-directed
   speech (CDS)
claims of babies reading,
   217–222
definition of "word" and,
   34–35
environment and, 36–37
first word, 34, 35–36
helping baby learn to use
   words, 47–51
how early babies can read,
   217–222
one-word stage, 34, 37, 41–45,
   210
overview of this book and, 8
playtime and, 50–51
reading time and, 47–49
social language skills, 42–45
styles of learning language,
   40–42. *See also* Expressive
   (noun-leaver) style;
   Referential (noun-lover)
   style
usefulness of words and,
   39–40
word selection and, 36–40
word types and, 37
Bath time, 31
Bilingual development
   dialect variations and, 152–158
   growing up with multiple
     languages, 142–152
   parent roles, 150–152
   sequential, 146–150
   simultaneous, 143–146

Birth order, language
    development and. *See
    also* Gender, language
    development and; Siblings
  about: overview/summary of,
    122–124, 138–139
  age gap and, 134
  attention, parent interactions
    and, 133–134
  causes of differences, 133–136
  conversation skills and,
    134–136
  first-born vs. later-born,
    131–133
Book overview, 5–10
  how to use book, 6–10
  purpose of book, 6–7
  style of book, 7–9
Books, reading. *See* Reading time;
    Written language (reading
    and spelling)
Boys, girls compared to.
    See Gender, language
    development and

C

Cautious calculator style, 40
Changing time, 30–31
Child care, language development
    and, 193–214
  about: overview/summary of,
    193–194, 214
  for babies, 209–210
  choosing best care, 206–213
  curriculum considerations,
    204–206
  direct-instruction curriculum,
    204, 205
  evaluating providers, 195,
    196–198
  facility options to seek out,
    198–204
  family involvement and,
    201–202
  hybrid curriculum and,
    205–206

for infants, 207–208
  literacy activities and, 200–201
  open-atmosphere curriculum
    and, 204–205, 206
  play materials, learning events
    and, 198–202
  playtime and, 199–200
  for preschoolers, 212–213
  provider-to-child ratios and,
    203–204
  research on, 194–195
  television and, 201
  for toddlers, 210–212
Child-directed speech (CDS)
  babies and, 45–47
  characteristics of, 45–46
  effects of, 46–47
  gender and, 126–127
  siblings and, 133–134
  on television, 165–166
  toddlers using, 65
Chore time, learning with, 99
Colors, toddlers learning, 72–73
Computers, language
    development and, 173–179
  about: overview/summary of,
    161–163, 179
  basic computer skills and, 177
  benefits, 174–177
  grades at school and, 177–178
  hindrances, 177–179
  hours of computer use per day
    and, 174, 177–178
  parent roles and, 176–177,
    187–188
  program design and, 174–176,
    178–179
Conductive hearing loss, 240, 243
Consonants
  infant/baby babbling and, 22,
    26, 35, 38
  preschooler development
    and, 79
  toddler development and, 62
Conversation skills. *See also*
    Social language skills

birth order and, 132–133,
134–136
child care and, 202, 203–204,
205–206
cultural variations, 159
eye contact and, 63
gender and, 127
infant sounds and, 22–23
multilingual children and,
146–147
multiple-person conversations,
135–136
preschoolers, 80–86
toddlers, 63, 64–65
Culture, language and, 140–160
about: overview/summary of,
140–141, 158–160
attitudes toward children
speaking and, 158–159
conversation skills and, 159
cultural variations, 158–160
dialect misconceptions,
153–155
dialect variations, 152–158
growing up with multiple
languages, 142–152
parent roles, 150–152,
156–158
sequential bilingual
development, 146–150
simultaneous bilingual
development, 143–146
storytelling and, 159
television and, 169–170
variations in language
acquisition, 142–152
Curriculum, of child care,
204–206

D

Deixis, 66
Delays. *See* Language delays
Development stages
hearing and understanding,
viii–ix
talking, ix–xi

Dialectal variations, 152–158
biases toward, 155–156
misconceptions about, 153–155
parent roles, 156–158
Diapers, changing time, 30–31
Direct-instruction curriculum,
204
Down syndrome, 244, 245–246

E

Ears, hearing loss and, 239–243.
See also Audiologists
Einstein-referenced products,
222–224
Ellipsis, 67–68
Environment, word use and,
36–37
Expressive (noun-leaver) style
birth order and, 132
both parent and baby with, 41
characteristics of, 40, 50, 124
gender and, 125, 126
referential style compared
to, 41
Eyes, vision therapy, 224–226

F

Fads, scams, and myths,
215–234
about: overview of, 215–217
autism/vaccine link myth,
227–228
claims of babies reading,
217–222
common theme of, 228
data, evidence and, 228–233
Einstein-referenced products,
222–224
MART strategy for dealing
with, 231–233
protecting yourself from,
228–233
self-reliance instead of,
233–234
vision therapy, 224–226
Fragile X syndrome, 244

G

Games. *See also* Playtime; Video
    games
  child care and, 199
  encouraging, 3
  for preschoolers, 95, 98,
    99–100
  for sound awareness, 104–105
  for students, 104–105
  traveling and, 99–100
  for various learning styles, 124
  for word parts/vocabulary,
    109–110
Gender, language development
    and, 124–130. *See also* Birth
    order, language development
    and
  about: overview/summary of,
    123–125, 129–130, 139
  causes of gender effects,
    126–129
  differences between girls and
    boys, 125–126
  playtime and, 127–129
Gender, this book and, 8
Girls, boys compared to.
    See Gender, language
    development and
Grammar. *See* Morphology
    (grammar)

H

Hearing aids, 240–241, 242, 243
Hearing loss, 239–243. *See also*
    Audiologists
  conductive, 240, 243
  onset and effects of, 241–242
  sensorineural, 240–242
  severity of, 241
  suspecting/responding to,
    242–243
  types of, 240–241
High-print environments,
    88–89, 90
Hinting, by preschoolers, 81
Hybrid curriculum, 205–206

I

Imitation. *See also* Modeling
    language
  child-initiated, 49
  commercial programs/
    products and, 250
  cultural variations, 159
  requiring, setting example vs.,
    2–3, 49, 159, 191
  of TV behaviors, 172
  twin talk and, 138
  using/elaborating, 49
  violence, conflict and, 172
Infant development, 11–32
  about: overview/summary of,
    11–12, 32
  bath time and, 31
  best child care for, 207–208
  changing time and, 30–31
  first six months, 19–25
  helping create language, 29–32
  interaction skills, 23–25, 28–29
  language systems and, 12–19
  listening skills, 20–21
  mealtime and, 31–32
  overview of this book and, 8
  second six months, 25–29
  vocal skills, 21–23, 26–27
Intellectual disabilities, 244–247
Interaction skills. *See also*
    Conversation skills; Joint
    attention skills
  infants, 23–25, 28–29
  preferences for parents' voices/
    faces and, 24–25
  smiling, 24

J

Joint attention skills, 25, 29,
    31–32, 137, 208

L

Language. *See also* Modeling
    language
  components/factors of, 1
  defined, 12–19

developing vs. teaching, 3
importance of, 4–5
primary role models, 1
six systems of, 12–19
Language delays, 235–262. *See also* Audiologists; Speech-language pathologists
about: overview of, 235–236
ADD/ADHD and, 257–258
brain wiring and, 253–254
causes of, 238–255
childhood illnesses and, 252
finding help for, 259–262
genetic component, 253
hearing loss and, 239–243
implications for later learning, 258–259
intellectual disabilities and, 244–247
intervention goals, 260–261
parent responses to, 242–243, 245–247, 249–251, 254–255, 259–262
professionals to help with, 237–238
specific speech/language impairments, 251–255
stuttering, 255–257
symptoms, 238
when questions arise, 236–238
Language development
by age. *See* Baby development; Infant development; Preschooler development; Student development; Toddler development
chart of stages, viii–xi
delays in. *See* Language delays
getting started, 4–6
helping child with, summary of steps, xii–xiii
how children develop, 1–3
importance of understanding, 6–7, 9–10
similarity between children, 3–4

stages of, 8–9
styles of. *See* Expressive (noun-leaver) style; Referential (noun-lover) style
this book and, 5–10
variability between children, 3–4
Letters. *See also* Literacy; Sounds; Words (vocabulary); Written language (reading and spelling)
learning, 73, 89–90
patterns of, learning, 105–109
Letter system (orthography), 17–18
Listening skills
development stages summary, viii–ix
helping child with, summary of steps, xii–xiii
infants, 19–25
Literacy. *See also* Reading time; Words (vocabulary); Written language (reading and spelling)
child care and, 200–201
foundational skills, 86–87, 103–111
helping preschoolers learn about, 95–101
importance for language development, 3

M

MART strategy, 231–233
Mealtime
infant development and, 31–32
preschooler development and, 97–98
Meaning system. *See* Semantics
Media, language development and, 161–192. *See also* Computers; Television; Video games
about: overview/summary of, 161–163, 191–192

Media, language development
    and (*cont.*)
    hours of media use per day, 162
    parent roles and, 185–191
    research on, 163–164
    texting, 183–185, 190–191
Mental pictures, of words,
    110–111
Metalinguistics, 86–87, 92
Mister Rogers' Neighborhood,
    165–166
Modeling language
    about: overview of, 2–3
    for babies. *See* Baby
        development; Infant
        development
    CDS and. *See* Child-directed
        speech (CDS)
    child care and, 198, 203–204,
        205–206, 210
    commercial programs/
        products and, 221–222,
        223–224
    cultural variations, 159
    helping baby learn to use
        words, 47–51
    natural vs. contrived situations,
        44–45
    optimizing effectiveness, 42
    for preschoolers. *See*
        Preschooler development
    protests, 44
    for school-aged kids. *See*
        Student development
    sibling differences and,
        133–136
    on television, 165–167
    for toddlers. *See* Toddler
        development
    video games and, 181, 189–190
Morphology (grammar)
    about syntax and, 16–17
    early development, 57–58
    language delay and, 258
    sentence structure and, 78–79
Multilingual children. *See*

Bilingual development;
    Culture, language and
Multiple births, 136–138
Myths. *See* Fads, scams, and
    myths

N

Narrative (story) framework,
    112–115
Negative forms, 59
Noun-leaver style. *See* Expressive
    (noun-leaver) style
Noun-lover style. *See* Referential
    (noun-lover) style

O

Open-atmosphere curriculum,
    204–205, 206
Opposites, 72, 100
Opposites, toddlers learning, 72
Orthography, 17–18
Outing times
    with preschoolers, 99–101
    shopping/learning ideas,
        100–101
    with toddlers, 74
    travel/learning ideas, 99–100

P

Phonology. *See also* Sounds
    about, 13–15
    language delay and, 258
Playtime
    with babies, 50–51
    child care and, 199–200
    gender differences and,
        127–129
    television enriching, 167–169
    with toddlers, 71–74
Pragmatics. *See* Social language
    skills
Preferences
    baby, for certain sounds/
        syllables, 38
    infant, for parents' faces/
        voices, 24–25

Preschooler development,
76–101
about: overview/summary of,
76–78, 101
best child care for, 212–213
chore time and, 99
foundational literacy skills,
86–87
helping learn about literacy,
95–101
helping refine spoken language
skills, 85–94
high-print environments and,
88–89, 90
household experiences for,
95–99
knowledge about print, 87–90
knowledge about sounds
(phonological awareness),
92–94
knowledge about words,
90–92
learning written vs. spoken
language, 86
letter knowledge, 89–90
mealtime and, 97–98
overview of this book and, 9
reading time and, 88, 96–97
rhyming, 77, 92–93, 96, 98, 99
sentence structure and
grammar, 78–79
shopping experiences for,
100–101
social language skills, 80–85
speech sounds, 79
storytelling skills, 83–85
travel experiences for, 99–100
vocabulary, 79–80
Pretend words, 27, 35
Printed word. See Reading
time; Words (vocabulary);
Written language (reading
and spelling)

Q
Questions, by toddlers, 58–59

R
Reading skills. See Letters;
Reading time; Words
(vocabulary); Written
language (reading and
spelling)
Reading time
with babies, 47–49
with preschoolers, 88,
96–97
with toddlers, 69–71
Referential (noun-lover) style
birth order and, 132
both parent and baby
with, 41
characteristics of, 40–41, 50,
124
expressive style compared
to, 41
gender and, 126
Repetition, importance claim,
220–222
Rhyming, 77, 92–93, 96, 98, 99,
109

S
Scams. See Fads, scams, and
myths
Scheduling time, 223
Scripts
at child care play areas,
199–200
knowledge about, 199
toddlers using, 63–64
Semantics
about, 15
babies and, 37, 39
language delay and, 258
preschoolers and, 80
Sensorineural hearing loss,
240–242
Sentences
complexity of, 59–60
deixis and, 66
ellipsis and, 67–68
kinds toddlers use, 56–60

Sentences (*cont.*)
structure of, grammar and, 78–79. *See also* Morphology (grammar)
using groups of, 60
word combinations and, 56–57
word order, 58–59
Shopping, learning with, 100–101
Siblings. *See also* Birth order, language development and; Gender, language development and
age gap, 134
causes of language differences, 133–136
multiple births, 136–138
reaction to birth of, 130–131
Sign language
autism and, 247, 249–250
hearing loss and, 240, 241, 242, 243
infants and, 14
intellectual disabilities and, 246
Social language skills. *See also* Conversation skills
about: pragmatics, 18–19
babies, 42–45
language delay and, 258
preschoolers, 80–85
toddlers, 62–68
Sounds. *See also* Speech; Words (vocabulary)
awareness of, 104–105
development of, 14–15
infant vocal skills and, 21–23, 26–27
learning subconsciously, 14–15
letters vs., 14
preschooler knowledge about (phonological awareness), 92–94
sign language and, 14
speech, 13–15, 61, 79
system of (phonology), 13–15

Spanish. *See also* Bilingual development
English sounds vs., 13
word order and grammar differences, 16
Speech. *See also* Sounds; Words (vocabulary)
babies and. *See* Baby development; Infant development
CDS and. *See* Child-directed speech (CDS)
delays in. *See* Language delays
development stages summary, ix–xi
helping child with, summary of steps, xii–xiii
models from TV, 165–167
preschoolers and. *See* Preschooler development
sounds, 13–15, 61, 79
toddlers and. *See* Toddler development
Speech-language pathologists
ASHA certification and qualifications, xiii, 260
finding, xiii, 261
minimum qualifications, xiii
symptoms indicating help from, xii
training and credentials, 237
Spelling, foundations of, 103–111. *See also* Letters; Written language (reading and spelling)
Story (narrative) framework, 112–115
Storytelling skills
cultural variations, 159
preschoolers, 83–85
reading time and, 96–97
Student development, 102–121
about: overview/summary of, 102–103, 119–120

academic "stories" and, 116–117

awareness of sounds, 104–105

foundations for reading/ spelling, 103–111

frameworks for organizing text, 112–117

letter patterns, 105–109

mental pictures and, 110–111

overview of this book and, 9

stories (narratives) and, 112–115

textbooks and, 115–116

vocabulary and word parts, 109–110

writing, 117–119, 121

Stuttering, 255–257

Styles of language learning. *See* Expressive (noun-leaver) style; Referential (noun-lover) style

Syntax

about morphology and, 16–17

syntax and, 258

T

Television, language development and, 164–173

about: overview/summary of, 161–163, 173

benefits, 165–170

child care and, 201

conflict, violence and, 172–173

culture/language exposure and, 169–170

hindrances, 170–173

hours of exposure per day and, 164, 171

parent roles and, 185–187

perception of reality/fantasy and, 171–172

playtime enrichment and, 167–169

speech, language models and, 165–167

Textbooks, 115–116

Texting, language development and, 183–185, 190–191

Toddler development, 53–75. *See also* Child care, language development and

about: overview/summary of, 53–54, 75

adapting to conversational partners, 64–65

best child care for, 210–212

clarifying language, 65–66

complexity of sentences, 59–60

deixis and, 66

ellipsis and, 67–68

grammar use, 57–58

helping build language, 68–74

outing times and, 74

overview of this book and, 8–9

past/future language references, 63

playtime and, 71–74

reading time and, 69–71

restating things, 65–66

scripted events and, 63–64

sentence types and, 56–60

social language skills, 62–68

speech development, 61

typical speech "errors," 61–62

using groups of sentences, 60

word combinations and, 56–57

word order in sentences, 58–59

word types and, 55–56

Travel experiences, 99–100

Twins, 136–138

Twin talk, 138

V

Video games, language development and, 179–183

about: overview/summary of, 161–163, 179–180, 182–183

benefits, 180–181

hindrances, 181–182

hours of media use per day and, 162

interactive play and, 180–181

Video games, language
    development and (*cont.*)
    parent roles and, 189–190
    passive involvement and,
        181–182
Vision therapy, 224–226
Vocabulary. *See* Words
    (vocabulary)
Vocal skills. *See also* Sounds;
    Speech; Words (vocabulary)
    first six months, 21–23
    second six months, 26–27
Vowels
    infant/baby babbling and, 22,
        26, 35
    long and short, 18, 108
    students identifying, 108

W

Word calling, 219–220
Words (vocabulary). *See also*
    Speech; Written language
    (reading and spelling)
    combinations of, 56–57
    defined, 34–35
    environment and, 36–37
    factors affecting type used, 36–40
    first spoken, 34, 35–36
    mental pictures of, 110–111
    one-word stage, 34, 37, 41–45,
        210
    ongoing development, 79–80
    opposites, 72
    order and grammar, 16–17
    parts of, vocabulary and,
        109–110
    preschoolers and, 79–80, 90–92
    pretend, 27, 35
    sounds giving rise to. *See*
        Sounds
    sounds in, 37–39
    students developing
        vocabulary, 109–110
    toddlers using. *See* Toddler
        development
    usefulness of, 39–40

Writing, 117–119, 121
Written language (reading and
    spelling). *See also* Literacy;
    Reading time; Words
    (vocabulary)
    academic "stories" and,
        116–117
    awareness of sounds, 104–105.
        See also Sounds
    building blocks, 103–111
    delays in. *See* Language delays
    foundational literacy skills,
        86–87
    frameworks for organizing
        text, 112–117
    how early babies can read,
        217–222
    knowledge about print, 87–90
    learning, compared to spoken
        language, 86
    letter patterns, 105–109
    mental pictures and, 110–111
    repetition and, 220–222
    requiring active attention to
        learn, 86
    spelling skills and strategies,
        91, 92, 94, 103, 104–109,
        110, 111
    story (narrative) framework,
        112–115
    textbooks and, 115–116
    word calling vs. reading,
        219–220

Y

Year-by-year development
    1st year. *See* Infant
        development
    2nd year. *See* Baby
        development
    3rd & 4th years. *See* Toddler
        development
    5th & 6th years. *See*
        Preschooler development
    7th+ years. *See* Student
        development

ABOUT THE AUTHORS

KENN APEL is professor and chair of the Department of Communication Sciences and Disorders at the University of South Carolina, Columbia. He teaches in the area of school-age language development and disorders with a special emphasis on literacy skills. Dr. Apel currently is the president of the Council of Academic Programs in Communication Sciences and Disorders (2012–2013) and the former editor in chief of *Language, Speech, and Hearing Services in Schools* (2007–2009), a scientific journal. Dr. Apel has more than twenty-five years of experience working with children, adolescents, and adults with language problems and language-based learning deficits and conducting research in the areas of spoken and written language, with publications in speech-language pathology, reading, and psycholinguistic journals. Currently, his research focuses on the underlying linguistic components that support the development of word-level reading and spelling. Dr. Apel is a fellow and certified member of the American Speech-Language-Hearing Association (ASHA). He lives in Columbia, South Carolina, with his wife, Lynda. When they can't be there for visits, he enjoys Skyping with his children Nick and Genevieve and his grandson Gage.

JULIE MASTERSON is professor of Communication Sciences and Disorders at Missouri State University, where she teaches courses in language-learning disabilities, phonology, and research design. Dr. Masterson served as vice president for Research and Technology for ASHA and president of the Council of Academic Programs in Communication Sciences and Disorders. She has more than 150 presentations and publications in the areas of language and literacy. Dr. Masterson is co-author of *Spelling Performance Evaluation for Language and Literacy-2* (Learning by Design) and *Clinical Decision Making in Developmental Language Disorders* (Brookes). She has been an associate editor for the *American Journal of Speech-Language Pathology* and has served as a guest associate editor for *Journal of Speech, Language, and Hearing Research; Language, Speech, and Hearing Services in Schools; Topics in Language Disorders,* and *Seminars in Speech and Language.* Dr. Masterson is a fellow and certified member of the American Speech-Language-Hearing Association. She holds degrees in both speech-language pathology and elementary education and has worked as a classroom teacher. She lives in Springfield, Missouri, with her husband, Jerry, and welcomes visits from her son, Caleb, and his family (wife, Erin, and son, Reid) and her daughter, Caitlin.